AI-Driven Decision-Making in Finance

This book explores the deep impact of AI and digital transformation on finance, its practices and decision intelligence processes. The book and its practical, analytical chapters present further insights regarding ways to effectively utilize AI, potentially even beyond the existing theoretical and practical knowledge. Regulatory, ethical, security, and moral challenges and concerns associated with the use of AI in finance are thoroughly analyzed.

Readers will take away a conceptual and practical understanding of AI and digitalization as well as real-world practical case studies, so that they can be applied appropriately in a workplace setting. It aims to differentiate itself by focusing more specifically on the practical realities of AI and digital transformation in decision-making processes within finance, offering actionable guidance and real-world case study or implications, which are less emphasized in most other competitors.

The book is appropriate for experts and professionals interested in deployment of AI, digitalization and their implementation in finance. No doubt, academics, professionals, students, and finance experts will find this book an informative practice resource. The book would suit anyone interested in AI and its broader applications in finance or its uses in decision-making processes.

Dr. Bilal Bagis is a seasoned economist, instructor, strategist, columnist, and consultant. In addition to his academic career, his extensive credentials include private sector experiences at various international and domestic companies and institutions. He has taught graduate and undergraduate-level economics, math and finance courses at prominent universities including UC Berkeley and top universities in Türkiye. His analyses and papers are published by various prominent institutions. Dr. Bagis specializes in and has a deep expertise in macro and financial stability and efficacy of policies at the discretion of policymakers. He currently works at and chairs the Department of Economics at FSM Vakif Univesity.

Security, Audit and Leadership Series

Series Editor: Dan Swanson, Dan Swanson and Associates, Ltd., Winnipeg, Manitoba, Canada.

About the Book Series

The scope and mandate for cybersecurity and internal audit continue to evolve each year, as does the complexity of the business environment and speed of the changing risk landscape in which it must operate. The fundamental goal of this exciting series is to produce leading-edge books on critical subjects facing security and audit executives and practitioners. Key topics addressed include Leadership, Cybersecurity, Security Leadership, Privacy, Strategic Risk Management, Auditing IT and Technology, and Audit Management and Leadership.

If you're interested in submitting a proposal for a book to be included in the series, please email the series editor, Dan Swanson: dswanson_2008@yahoo.ca

Dark Faces in Cyber Places: Shattering Stereotypes and Leading with Legacy in Cybersecurity
By Devon Bryan

Logic Before Language: Rethinking AI in the Age of Illusion, Bertrand Russell and the Future of Real AI
By Martin Milani

Relevant Impact: A Field Guide to Integrated Assurance
By Patrick M. Hayes

Cybersecurity and the Art of Cyberwar
By Dan Shoemaker, Tamara Shoemaker, and Amir Jabri

Trust Hacked: What Firewalls, Failures, and the Frontlines Taught Me About Trust
By Nia Luckey

Organizational Resilience & Artificial Intelligence: A Practical Framework for Crisis Leadership, Adaptability & Sustainable Performance
By Arnab Mukherjee and Sachin Kumar

Mission-Critical Governance: Focusing on What Matters Most
By Tim J. Leech

Governing AI Risk –The RIVER Charter: An Enterprise Resilience Standard
By Alex Golbin

Cloud Compliance Essentials: How to Build and Maintain Market Access in the B2B CSP Ecosystem
By Forrest R. Foster

AI-Driven Decision-Making in Finance
Edited by Dr. Bilal Bagis

https://www.routledge.com/Security-Audit-and-Leadership-Series/book-series/CRCINTAUDITA

AI-Driven Decision-Making in Finance

Edited by
Dr. Bilal Bagis

CRC Press
Taylor & Francis Group
Boca Raton London New York

CRC Press is an imprint of the
Taylor & Francis Group, an **informa** business

Designed cover image: Shutterstock ID: 1530386471

First edition published 2027
by CRC Press
2385 NW Executive Center Drive, Suite 320, Boca Raton FL 33431

and by CRC Press
4 Park Square, Milton Park, Abingdon, Oxon, OX14 4RN

CRC Press is an imprint of Taylor & Francis Group, LLC

ISBN: 978-1-041-10710-1 (hbk)
ISBN: 978-1-041-10711-8 (pbk)
ISBN: 978-1-003-65646-3 (ebk)

DOI: 10.1201/9781003656463

Typeset in Sabon
by KnowledgeWorks Global Ltd.

To Vera

Contents

About the editor

Dr. Bilal Bagis is a seasoned economist, instructor, strategist, columnist and consultant, based in Istanbul/Türkiye.

He has a merit-based scholarship-funded multidisciplinary B.Sc. (combining engineering with a business degree) from ITU (2006), a fully funded and theoretically focused M.A. in Economics from Sabanci University (2009) and a fully funded Ph.D. degree in economics from the University of California (2014). Dr. Bagis is grateful to the Turkish Government for education abroad fellowship, the Turkish TUBITAK, UC Regents, Fulbright, TEV, ITU and Sabanci University for all the awards, scholarships and financial support they have provided throughout his education.

Dr. Bagis is an experienced economist and author with a strong background in policymaking, financial systems, and technology policy. His recent works, including reports for SETA and SAM on financial innovation and technological transformation, position him well to author a book on AI-driven decision-making in economics, finance or energy. He currently works at and chairs the Department of Economics at FSM Vakif Univesity.

Since his undergraduate years, he has consistently focused on Türkiye's macro instabilities and financial crises. His research interests lie in AI applications in economics and finance as well as international finance, macroeconomics, public policy and political economy. He has recently been interested in theoretical and practical implications of AI and digitalization.

Dr. Bagis specializes in bridging the gap between theory and practice. He focuses on and has a deep expertise in macro and financial stability and efficacy of policies at the discretion of policymakers. His analysis and working papers are published by various prominent institutions including the SETA Foundation and the Turkish Ministry of Foreign Affairs' SAM. He is well-known for his extensive writing schedule, and coverage of Türkiye's economic and financial development.

Dr. Bagis's publications are already listed on some of the most prominent university library catalogs, including those at Princeton University, Columbia University and UC Berkeley. His books and academic publications may be accessed via domestic as well as some international publishing houses and academic platforms.

He has so far had short-term and long-term teaching experiences in the US, France, Poland, Türkiye, etc. He has taught various graduate- and undergraduate-level courses at prominent institutions in the US and in Türkiye, including at UC Berkeley in California, US and Sabanci University in Istanbul, Türkiye. He has so far taught various economics, math, finance, statistics and eCommerce classes. Prior to his academic instructor experience, he has worked as teaching assistant for various economics, finance and math classes both in Istanbul, Türkiye and in California.

Dr. Bagis has had numerous domestic and international presentations and publications on various venues. He has, so far, made academic presentations, given talks by invitation and attended conferences in around 20 different countries, including those in the US, Russia, Canada, Germany, France, Italy and Spain. He has had various national and international talks over economics, central banking, monetary policy, international trade & finance, public policy and political economy.

In addition to his academic career, his extensive credentials include private sector experiences at various international and domestic companies and institutions, including Akbank, Sabanci Group, the Turkish Central Bank, Yapı Kredi Bank, THY, Enquire, Monarch and family companies. He has, overall, had an extensive experience as an academic, economist, strategist, columnist and consultant at various universities and companies in Türkiye and the USA.

Preface

The intersection of AI and finance is a rapidly evolving and increasingly important area of focus. A book that focuses on this intersection, and bridges the gap between theory and practical applications, as this proposal aims to do, would be a highly valuable resource for a wide audience. The authors' qualifications and contributions from other experts suggest a high likelihood of production of a compelling and insightful work.

The book gives new insights into AI and its implications for finance and its decision-making processes. It follows a broad-based discussion opportunity on the overarching theme of AI and digitalization in finance and economics, and more specifically on AI-driven decision-making in finance. Potential risks, regulatory, ethical, security concerns and ethics associated with AI are key priorities.

Meanwhile, most books on finance or AI focus on broad applications, pure theoretical or conventional technical issues only. They mostly neglect practical case studies, cutting-edge developments, new applications and innovations in the field. Yet, the information and associated technologies continue advancement toward diversely distributed configuration environments to encode, process, store, and retrieve data.

This book explores the deep impact of AI and digital transformation on finance, its practices and decision intelligence processes. The book and its practical, analytical chapters present further insights regarding ways to effectively utilize AI, potentially even beyond the existing theoretical and practical knowledge. Regulatory, ethical, security and moral challenges and concerns associated with the use of AI in finance are thoroughly analyzed.

The book connects theory and practice. Readers will take away a conceptual and practical understanding of AI, digitalization and real-world practical case studies, so that they can be applied appropriately in a workplace setting. After finishing the book, the reader will be able to better understand the future of finance and the business world; gain informed decision-making abilities.

The book demonstrates a strong grasp of both AI methodologies and their applications in finance, referencing relevant tools, techniques, and industry challenges. Its structured approach, use of practical and theoretical applications, and awareness of ethical and regulatory considerations suggest a solid academic or professional background in the field.

The book benefits from sections on AI ethics, security, regulation and bias mitigation, as algorithms can also unintentionally reinforce biases in areas like lending and fraud detection. This could help further promote responsible and fair AI in finance and could potentially enhance the quality and coverage of the book.

It aims to differentiate itself by focusing more specifically on the practical realities of AI and digital transformation in decision-making processes within finance, offering actionable guidance and real-world case study or implications, which are less emphasized in most other competitors.

The book is appropriate for employees, investors, experts and professionals interested in ensuring or verifying the design and deployment of AI, digitalization and their implementation in finance. No doubt, academics, professionals, students and finance experts will all find this book an informative practice resource.

Academics, professionals, post-graduate students, aspiring managers, leaders and experienced executives can all benefit from the guidance and discussions in the book. Meanwhile, it would also be suitable for people aspiring to be in these roles. The book would also suit anyone interested in AI and its broader applications in finance or its uses in decision-making processes within finance.

AI IN FINANCE WORKSHOP 2025

The "AI-Driven Decision-Making in Finance" book chapters were primarily collected as part of the "AI in Finance" workshop 2025. The 2025 edition of our "AI in Finance" workshop was successfully completed on June 11th, 2025. The workshop aimed to provide an environment to discuss recent trends in digitalization, AI and machine learning, contemporary business practices and technological developments in finance and economics.

It provided a new platform to discuss, exchange ideas and learn about the latest developments related to AI, blockchain and cryptocurrencies as well as their intersection, broader digital and AI transformation. Challenges, risks and opportunities were also discussed in detail.

Given significance of intersection of AI and finance, a workshop that bridges the gap between theory and practical application, as this workshop aims to do, is highly valuable. After all, digital transformation and artificial intelligence (AI) are already revolutionizing the field of finance, reshaping how markets run, businesses operate and how decisions are made. At the core of this transformation is the integration of advanced technologies into traditional processes, allowing for greater efficiency and enhanced data analysis.

Financial institutions too leverage AI algorithms to process vast amounts of data in real-time, enabling them to make informed decisions, manage risks better, and optimize operations. These technological advancements not only improve transaction speeds but also enhance customer experiences through personalized services, predictive analytics, and automation of routine tasks.

In finance, AI-powered models are increasingly used to predict market trends and consumer behavior, offering insights that help policymakers and businesses navigate complex economic landscapes. The digitalization trend itself mostly depends on AI too. And, as these technologies continue to evolve, they are likely to play an even more critical role in shaping financial systems and fostering innovation across various sectors.

The 2025 workshop provided a unique platform, in this sense, to discuss digitalization, artificial intelligence and machine learning, as well as contemporary business practices and technological developments in the fields of economics and finance. Experts, academics and professionals in their fields shared current trends and innovative approaches with the participants.

This valuable meeting has overall shed light (as was hoped) on the world of finance that is transforming with together with the contemporary high-tech and the ongoing AI revolution!

AI-DRIVEN DECISION-MAKING IN FINANCE

The 'AI-Driven Decision-Making in Finance' book ought to be a good resource for investors and finance experts in understanding the challenges faced and the required support needed in modern decision-making processes. The interdisciplinary focus (in particular) will also enable this resource to serve a wide range of experts from academia to policy institutions and even private sector experts to industry leaders.

It would serve to help professionals, academics and executives (and even econ or finance students) understand the reality of AI, its use in decision-making processes and the digital transformation in today's fast-evolving financial world. In one modest-sized volume, the book would offer numerous valuable sets of knowledge. It provides the best practice guidance on decision intelligence tasks a manager, expert or academic may be involved in.

This is (indeed) a well-structured book that clearly articulates all related concepts, the target audience, and the value proposition, etc. The book's strong relevance, well-defined objectives, and potential industry impacts make it a worthy publication. Future editions might benefit from a slight expansion, and deeper consideration of ethical implications, real-world partnerships, and limitations related to model transparency and regulation, too.

The book does not require hardcore technical knowledge nor extreme experience, as the concepts should be understood by any professional, academic or even students working in the field. The reader will take away enough practical experience and wide-ranging guidance to emerge as a highly skilled and adept expert.

Bilal Bagis, PhD

List of contributors

Nidhi Arora
Advicon Solutions Pvt. Ltd., Ahmedabad, India

Poonam Arora
SKIPS School of Business, SKIPS University, Ahmedabad, India

Kübra Aykaş
Istinye University, İstanbul, Türkiye

Nadi Serhan Aydın
Istinye University, İstanbul, Türkiye

Bilal Bagis
FSM Vakıf University, Istanbul, Türkiye

Sezer Bozkus Kahyaoglu
Izmir Bakircay University, Izmir, Türkiye
University of South Africa (UNISA), Pretoria, South Africa

Bharath Kalappa
CHRIST (Deemed to be University), Bengaluru, Karnataka, India

Hasan Murat Ertuğrul
Anadolu University, Eskişehir, Türkiye

Cafer Deniz
Newcastle University Business School, Newcastle, England
Royal College of Surgeons in Ireland, Dublin, Ireland
The University of Uşak, Uşak, Türkiye

Ahmet Faruk Aysan
Hamad Bin Khalifa University, Doha, Qatar
University College London (UCL), London, England

Nayif Sultan M A Al-Maadeed
Hamad Bin Khalifa University, Doha, Qatar

Martha Iyambo
MK Legal Consultancy (Pty) Ltd, Johannesburg, South Africa

Swati Mehta
Raritan Valley Community College, New Jersey, USA

Fanney Msimuko
MK Legal Consultancy (Pty) Ltd, Johannesburg, South Africa

Lethiwe Nzama-Sithole
University of Johannesburg, Johannesburg, South Africa

Onur Polat
Hacettepe University, Ankara, Türkiye

Venkatesh Ankarla Sri Ramuloo
University of the Cumberlands, Kentucky, USA

Burçhan Sakarya
Başkent University, Ankara, Türkiye

Pascal Stiefenhofer
Newcastle University Business School, Newcastle, England

Ihlas Sovbetov
Istanbul Aydin University, İstanbul, Türkiye

Muhammad Syauqi Bin-Armia
Hamad Bin Khalifa University, Doha, Qatar

Deepika Upadhyay
CHRIST (Deemed to be University), Bengaluru, Karnataka, India

Ananda S Upadhyay
College of Banking and Financial Studies, Muscat, Oman

Ibrahim Musa Unal
Qatar Financial Markets Authority, Doha, Qatar

About the contributors

Nayif Al-Maadeed is a financial audit professional currently serving at the State Audit Bureau in Qatar, where he specializes in auditing government financial fraud. He combines his practical regulatory experience with advanced academic research as a PhD candidate in Islamic Finance. With a keen interest in the intersection of ethics, finance, and technology, he also serves as a Quality & Compliance Manager in the IT startup sector. His work focuses on enhancing financial integrity and governance through modern methodologies.

Nidhi Arora is a technophile and a fervent scholar with deep expertise in information technology. She has been a dedicated enthusiast in exploring fundamentals of high-end technologies and has written many research papers in National and International journals.

Poonam Arora has rich and vivid experience of over two decades in the field of quantitative and research analysis. She has been awarded with "Best Researcher Award" in 2019 for her contribution to research in management. Her areas of expertise include Research Methodology, Quantitative Techniques and Human Resource Management. She is a research enthusiast and a number cruncher who is associated as a reviewer in various esteemed national and international peer-reviewed journals.

Nadi Serhan Aydın is an associate professor at the Department of Industrial Engineering at Istinye University. He is a former affiliate of the Financial Signal Processing Lab at Imperial College London and a former visiting researcher at Heidelberg and Ulm Universities. During 2011–2016, he worked as a senior economist in an intergovernmental organization and was involved in multi-stakeholder development projects in collaboration with the World Bank and United Nations agencies. Prior to joining İstinye University, he served as an adjunct professor at the Department of Industrial Engineering at TED University. He holds the Financial Risk Manager (FRM) certification by the Global Association of Risk Professionals (GARP) and acts as academic editor/reviewer in various journals. His research interests include sequential decision making, mathematical optimization, financial engineering, predictive analytics, and machine learning.

Kübra Aykaş is a graduate of the Industrial Engineering Department at Istinye University and conducts research in the field of technology and innovation, with a particular focus on artificial intelligence applications. Throughout her professional career, she has gained multidisciplinary project, internship, and workplace experience across various departments within entrepreneurship- and engineering-oriented initiatives, providing a theoretical, analytical, and applied foundation. Building on these experiences, she continues to develop artificial intelligence and data-driven decision systems for financial applications targeting SMEs and start-ups. Her research interests include financial AI applications, data analytics, and sustainable finance.

Ahmet Faruk Aysan is a professor and associate dean for Research at Hamad Bin Khalifa University and a full member of the Turkish Academy of Sciences (TUBA). He has served on the Central Bank of Türkiye's board and consulted for institutions like the World Bank and Oxford Analytica. He has numerous publications and awards, including the 2023 Arab Fintech Forum's Fintech Researcher of the Year and the 2024 HBKU Research Excellence Award. He is also affiliated with UCL CBT and the ME Council.

Bilal Bagis is an associate professor in and Chair of the Department of Economics, FSMVU, Istanbul, Türkiye. He is also a seasoned economist, instructor, strategist, columnist and consultant. In addition to his academic career, his extensive credentials include private sector experiences at various international and domestic companies and institutions. He has taught graduate- and undergraduate-level economics, math and finance courses at prominent universities including UC Berkeley and top universities in Türkiye. His analysis and papers are published by various prominent institutions. Dr. Bagis specializes in bridging the gap between theory and practice. He focuses on and has a deep expertise in macro and financial stability and efficacy of policies at the discretion of policymakers.

Muhammad Syauqi Bin-Armia is a doctoral researcher in Islamic Finance and Economy at Hamad Bin Khalifa University, receiving a full Qatar Foundation scholarship. He is an esteemed scholar in Islamic banking and finance, with a notable academic background that includes a First Class Honors Bachelor from Islamic University in Saudi Arabia and a distinction MBA from Bangor University in the UK with best student in banking award. His expertise is further highlighted by his certification as a Shariah Advisor and Auditor from AAOIFI. His publications are wide-ranging and include quantitative analysis, applied econometrics in research, case studies, banking, fintech, AI in Finance and CBDC.

Cafer Deniz is an Associate Lecturer at Newcastle University and a Research Supervisor at the Royal College of Surgeons in Ireland (RCSI), supervising healthcare management research projects. He holds an MSc in Economics from the University of Warwick and previously worked as an analyst at the Istanbul Stock Exchange. His research interests include the ethics of artificial intelligence (AI), public finance, and political finance. He has taught across business, mathematics, medicine, and politics, receiving multiple consecutive nominations for outstanding teaching at Newcastle and being shortlisted for "University Worker of the Year." He is a Fellow of Advance HE (FHEA).

Hasan Murat Ertuğrul is a Professor at the Department of Economics, Anadolu University. He previously worked as Economic Counsellor at the Turkish Embassy in Rome and as a senior assistant at the Turkish Ministry of Treasury and Finance. He was a visiting researcher at the European University Institute. Dr Ertuğrul's work has been published in journals such as *Applied Energy, Resources Policy, Energy & Environment, International Journal of Finance & Economics, Housing Studies, European Journal of Health Economics, Defense and Peace Economics, Renewable and Sustainable Energy Reviews.* He also serves as a referee for SSCI-indexed journals and is a member of the editorial board of economics at PLOS One and Chief Editor at Anadolu University FEAS Journal.

Martha Iyambo is a Research Consultant at MK Legal Consultancy (Pty) Ltd in South Africa and holds a BSc, BScH, and MSc from Rhodes University. As the lead researcher in MK Legal's Research Department, she specializes in the intersection of artificial intelligence, data protection, and intellectual property in Africa. She serves as a Technical Partner for the Africa Privacy Roundup and is a member of Namibia's National AI Technical Advisory Committee. As an active contributor to regional AI working groups and co-author of multiple publications in this field, she is committed to advancing Africa's leadership in AI governance.

Sezer Bozkus Kahyaoglu graduated from Bosporus University with a degree in Management and holds a Master's degree in Money, Banking, and Finance from Sheffield University, as well as a Certification in Retail Banking from Manchester Business School. Sezer earned a Ph.D. in Econometrics from Dokuz Eylul University. Sezer serves as the editor-in-chief of the *Advances in Corporate Governance Journal*, which was established by the Good Governance Academy and Witz Business School. Additionally, she is a member of the CAPIA project, which is registered at UNISA. Her research interests include Applied Econometrics, Financial Markets and Instruments, Artificial Intelligence, Blockchain, Energy Markets, Corporate Governance, Risk Management, Fraud Accounting, Auditing, Ethics, Coaching, Mentoring, and Neuro-Linguistic Programming (NLP).

Bharath Kalappa is a PhD scholar in the Department of Commerce, School of Commerce, Finance, and Accountancy at the CHRIST (Deemed to be University), Bengaluru, Karnataka, India. He is a budding researcher in the field of commerce. In his research, he is fascinated by the components pertinent to behavioral finance and Robo-advisors.

Fanney Msimuko is a fintech lawyer and risk and compliance head consultant with extensive experience in banking and financial services laws and regulations. Her professional work spans regulatory compliance, governance, and risk management within complex financial systems across multiple jurisdictions. Her scholarly and professional interests focus on the intersection of artificial intelligence (AI) and finance, with particular emphasis on regulatory gaps, ethical governance, and systemic risk. She has researched and written on the dangers posed by unregulated or ethically unmoored AI in financial services and advocates for principled legal frameworks to guide its responsible use.

Swati Mehta is an academician and a researcher with over two decades of experience conducting research across diverse areas of computer science, including artificial intelligence, data analytics and software engineering. She has contributed to a variety of assignments in both academic and industry. With a career dedicated to advancing knowledge and fostering innovation, Ms. Mehta continues to explore emerging technologies and their applications in solving real-world challenges.

Lethiwe Nzama-Sithole is an Associate Professor at the University of South Africa, with over 20 years of experience in Auditing and Internal Controls. A recipient of the 2025 Woman of Stature Award in Education and Educator of the Year 2022, she leads with impact as former Deputy Head at the University of Johannesburg, Chair of First Year Experience, and board member of professional bodies. Her research focuses on governance and accounting Education.

Onur Polat is an Associate Professor of Public Finance at Hacettepe University and a Research Fellow at the Economic Research Forum and Global Labor Organization. He holds a Ph.D. in Economics from Hacettepe University and an M.Sc. in Financial Mathematics from Middle East Technical University. Previously a visiting scholar at Illinois State University and a postdoctoral fellow at Universitat Politècnica de València, his research integrates machine learning with financial risk and energy economics. His work has been published in leading high-impact journals, including Applied Energy, Resources Policy, Energy Economics, and Finance Research Letters. He currently serves on the editorial board of PLOS ONE.

Venkatesh Ankarla Sri Ramuloo is a Distinguished Industry Leader (Gulf Higher Education) and Software Engineer with over a decade of experience across healthcare, retail and insurance. He specializes in engineering leadership, AI, data science, cybersecurity, blockchain, IoT, and quantum computing. He has led enterprise-scale initiatives in sustainable development, software testing, CI/CD, and Agile delivery. Holding a Ph.D.

in Information Technology and an M.S. in Computer Science, he is an IEEE Senior Member and active researcher contributing to peer-reviewed journals.

Ananda S Upadhyay is the Director of the Postgraduate Studies and Research Department at the College of Banking and Financial Studies, Muscat. He has a PhD in Finance, with over twenty-eight years of expertise in management education, consulting and the financial services industry. He has also been a visiting professor at leading B-schools in Dubai, Germany and India. He has published around 50 articles in peer-reviewed journals and presented 35 research papers at national and international conferences. He has written books on Mutual Funds, Mergers & Acquisitions and Financial Systems & Commercial Banking. He is a Guest Editor, member of the Editorial Board and Reviewer for refereed International Research Journals. Finance and accounting-related topics are his research interest areas.

Burçhan Sakarya is a recognized figure in international trade and financial economics, currently serving at the International Trade and Finance Program of Başkent University in Ankara, Turkey. He previously held positions at the State Planning Organization, the Banking Regulation and Supervision Agency, and the Presidency of Strategy and Budget, focusing on financial stability, and development finance. His research and teaching cover banking, international finance, and macroeconomics. He earned his Ph.D. in Economics from Gazi University in 2011, after completing an M.Sc. in Economics at Arizona State University (1998) and a B.Sc. in Economics at Ankara University (1992).

Ihlas Sovbetov is Vice Head and faculty member in the Department of Economics and Finance at Istanbul Aydin University. He holds a Ph.D. in Economics from Istanbul University and an MBA (Finance) from Cardiff Metropolitan University, United Kingdom. His research focuses on macroeconomics, financial economics, behavioral economics and finance, and crypto economics, with particular interest in empirical and policy-relevant analysis. Dr. Sovbetov actively serves as a peer reviewer for a wide range of reputable international journals, including *Energy Systems, Nature: Scientific Reports, Economic Analysis and Policy, Journal of the Knowledge Economy, Computational Economics, Frontiers in Blockchain, Journal of Applied Economics* and *Journal of Economics and Financial Analysis.*

Pascal Stiefenhofer is Senior Lecturer in Economics at Newcastle University and an interdisciplinary researcher in AI, political economy, and decision sciences. Holding doctorates in Mathematics and Economics, his work examines how algorithmic systems reshape governance, legitimacy and decision-making under uncertainty. He is PhD Convenor and Director of Studies, supervising research on digital transformation and AI-enabled public policy, and he also advises the UK Office for Students on degree-awarding powers. His research spans AI governance and ethics, with particular interest in transparency, accountability, and fairness in automated administration—themes central to this chapter on AI in public tax decision-making.

Ibrahim Musa Unal is a Financial Researcher at the Qatar Financial Markets Authority (QFMA), specializing in risk auditing and capital market strategy. He holds a Ph.D. in Islamic Finance and Economy from Hamad Bin Khalifa University, where his research focused on Islamic Fintech. Ibrahim has significant expertise in the intersection of finance and technology, having served as a research assistant in AI and Machine Learning and contributed to Qatar's Capital Markets Cyber Security Guidelines. With over 15 published articles, he combines regulatory insight with advanced technical skills in Python and data analytics.

Deepika Upadhyay is an Associate Professor in the Department of Commerce, School of Commerce, Finance and Accountancy at the CHRIST (Deemed to be University), Bengaluru, Karnataka, India. She holds a PhD in Commerce from the Commerce faculty, Banaras Hindu University and has published articles in journals of repute. Her research interests lie in behavioral finance, studies on the Stock market, Capital structure, Sustainability and Entrepreneurship. In addition to these, she is passionate about teaching and guiding students, mentoring, and community outreach.

Chapter 1

AI and the future of finance

Global finance at a crossroads

Bilal Bagis

1.1 INTRODUCTION

The artificial intelligence (AI) revolution is fast transforming the global economy and the finance world. After all, finance is a purely information-rich world. Physical touch is relatively limited. It is, thus, probably one of the first areas to observe and embrace the AI revolution.

Accordingly, AI is likely to take over a wide range of financial roles in the financial world and many other related roles in adjacent sectors. AI sort of new innovations may even create much more complicated models and new instruments that provide a competitive edge.

AI adoption in finance is expected to enhance automation, optimization, financial forecasting, analytical perspectives, fraud detection as well as enabling informed decision-making processes. Yet the accompanying ethical, risk and security concerns, stability-related issues as well as regulatory and risk management-related challenges also need to be addressed.

New means and alternative approaches, regulatory arrangements are needed to mitigate risks related to AI adoption in finance. Risk and security concerns, transparency and accountability issues, new regulatory frameworks as well as other critical roles assumed by AI in shaping finance are all central to this AI-driven future of finance.

More peculiarly, the coronavirus (COVID-19) pandemic has particularly accelerated the digital and crypto revolutions and their macro-financial impacts. Yet, the digital and AI revolutions have indeed decades long history; see among others, Arf (1959), Boden (1996), Negnevitsky (2005), Moor (2006) and Flasiński (2016). They have together altered the way economies run, how information flows in the financial world and how business or trade relations are maintained.

The digital transformation itself is also further propagated by the AI revolution. In particular, cryptocurrencies and the technology behind them (blockchain technology) have already started to drastically transform the global financial landscape. The technology behind this digital transformation and the related decentralized finance (DeFi) trends are worthwhile to focus on.

DOI: 10.1201/9781003656463-1

For instance, Kaur et al. (2023) provide a comprehensive overview of DeFi's threat landscape – its vulnerabilities, adversary scenarios and the risk management strategies. However, it focuses on rather static modeling aspects and managerial responses, without exploring (among others) agentic AI, autonomous reactivity or self-healing systems.

In that line, for instance, agentic AI could (surely) be effectively used to secure DeFi and bring forth an innovative leap. Intelligent, autonomous agents could be embedded directly into DeFi ecosystems to preemptively detect and reply to the threats in real time.

This book, on the other hand, focuses rather on micro-foundations and practical applications of this recent technological transformation, and particularly on the AI-driven decision-making process in the post-AI era.

1.2 AI AND DIGITAL TRANSFORMATION IN FINANCE

The ongoing digital transformation and AI trends are surely revolutionizing the field of finance, altering market dynamics, the way businesses operate and how decisions are made. At the core of this transformation is the integration of advanced technologies into traditional processes, allowing for greater efficiency and enhanced data analysis.

Financial institutions leverage AI algorithms to process volumes of data in a timely manner, making it possible to make rational and well-informed decisions, manage risks better and optimize their operations. These technological advancements not only improve the transaction speeds but also enhance customer experiences through personalized services, predictive analytics and automation of routine tasks (Bagis, 2025a; Bağış, 2025; Nilsson, 2014).

The post-2010s digitalization also mostly depends on AI. Yet, the post-COVID accelerating digital and AI transformation and the future of finance surely need to be reassessed. Novel IT (information technology) infrastructures, quantum computing technologies, blockchain-based and mobile computing devices are all revolutionizing finance and helping build a new era altogether.

AI is likely to play a central role in the future of society and the economy, enabling new forms of interaction and innovation. A new language, but also a technological Renaissance. The IT infrastructure connected to AI is a crucial aspect to bear in mind. Generative AI tools such as ChatGPT have a huge potential in finance, economics, health and even education. Or consider the unprecedented rise of NVIDIA, turning into the biggest company, in just a year or so.

As is clear from the rise of likes of tech giants and the future that they represent (all turning into the only game in town), new chips and new effective uses of GPUs or programmable GPUs (graphics processing units) and new high-performance graphics processors needed for the AI revolution are all reminders of an unusual new era.

And then imagine the role AI could play in preventing potential future financial or banking crises, for instance. The new era might as well mean new opportunities to use AI to achieve price or financial stability (as in run-on-banks), maybe by flagging more noteworthy information much earlier. And, of course, in a much faster time. Social and digital credit scores, smart contracts are all outcomes of this novel AI and digital transformation.

In finance, AI-powered models are increasingly used to predict market trends and consumer behavior, offering insights that help policymakers and businesses navigate complex economic landscapes. Moreover, as AI and digital technologies continue to unfold, they are likely to assume a substantially more crucial part in shaping the financial systems and fostering innovation across various sectors.

The financial sector surely functions within a complex, more decentralized, highly regulated but sometimes even a rather deregulated landscape (Bagis, 2025a). AI, on the other hand, helps process much more information quickly, helps with price comparisons, etc. and enables faster responses. The intersection of the two could surely mean much more efficiency. AI can help ensure that even smaller firms and subtle information are not overlooked in decision-making processes.

Quantum computers and their contributions toward automation and computation in finance are leading the way forward. Robotic and quantum-based computation and consulting, instead of conventional gild the lily financial consulting is already trendy. AI-incorporated brokerage, machine learning in finance and similar other avant-garde tools are transforming the economic sciences and finance.

The security, risk and challenge aspects of AI adoption should matter even more. Understanding these aspects could provide a more grounded perspective when discussing the applications in banking, payments, crypto, investments, etc. Seeking new ways to deal with some of the key challenges related to decision intelligence, critical issues and finding potential alternative solutions are all of substantial importance.

Providing a forward-looking perspective, focusing on future trends and strategic implications, building resilient organizations should all be primary concerns. Discussing emerging trends, potential future applications in finance and the competence needed to steer this evolving landscape should all be key priorities looking forward.

1.3 THE HIGH-TECH TRANSFORMATION

The junction of digitalization and AI, and their implications in finance is a rapidly evolving and increasingly important area too. And hence the need to understand that connecting the theory and practical application would be highly valuable. On the other hand, consider the technological and industrial transformation or evolution of the past 200 years or so.

The ongoing Industry 4.0 and the digital transformation of the 2010s, as well as the post-COVID acceleration, are all evolving rapidly. The 5th Industrial Revolution comes with unmanned technologies, automation and robotization; along with more digitalization, isolation and mechanization in almost everything.

However, the 6th revolution and digitalization of even human cognition, leading to more automation and AI's potential takeover and social isolation, should probably be discussed more often nowadays. At the heart of this shift lies a defining question: "who should lead this new revolution?" Bağış (2025).

There is surely a very good chance that AI may have a much greater effect (than expected) on the business life, the finance world and even academia. Hence, as a specific subject, application of AI in finance and the related topics are more popular nowadays.

The reality of AI, its use in decision-making processes and the digital transformation in today's evolving financial world needs to be better comprehended (Bağış, 2025; Bagis, 2025a). Practical realities of AI and digital transformation in decision-making processes shall even offer practical, actionable guidance and lead to better real-world case studies.

AI and its applications in finance, particularly in decision-making processes, are likely to become increasingly important in the future. Hence, the deeper impact of AI and digital transformation on finance; its challenges, opportunities and the risks associated with its integration with finance needs to be researched thoroughly.

Meanwhile, public services and public institutions are also gradually digitized. The world economies are nowadays increasingly into digitalization of even tax collections, transfer payments, subsidy or retirement benefits and even the wage payments (Mastercard for Government, 2025).

Efficiently using AI in public sector or in public services (together with the ongoing digitalization efforts), on the other hand, might help enhance productivity, efficacy and boost the innovation culture (Türkiye Bilişim Derneği, 2024). It could even help achieve Sustainable Development Goals.

Digital transformation is fast-forward. What is more, AI and the digital revolutions (the two sides of a coin) are also propagating each other's impacts. Together, they have led to creation of automated systems, programs or machines to do the jobs that would normally require significant human resources. AI-powered automation also adopts much easily to changes in information flows.

Digitalization itself is about the efficient use of digital instruments to transform business models, utilizing digital technologies and digitalizing businesses. Digitalization mostly depends on AI too. However, they both should be done in such a way that they lead to innovation, efficiency and increased productivity.

Overall, though, the ongoing AI transformation is expected to lead to:

- Increased automation of tasks and operational efficiency.
- Improved, informed and data-driven decision-making.

- Personalization and customer experience.
- Optimization and Enhanced productivity.
- Help with and ensure advanced data analysis.
- Creating autonomous systems.
- Innovation and creativity.

1.4 DIGITALIZATION

Digitalization, or the shift toward digital business models, is commonplace nowadays, in private sector and even in public services. The new digital formats of doing business (leveraged by digital technologies) are expected to enhance accessibility, better connectivity and integration, efficiency, further innovation, better data analysis and its management, as well as customer-centricity.

In the meantime, digitalization is becoming a necessity too. The ever-evolving transformation from an ecosystem characterized by physical goods and service flows toward one based upon data and information flows. This will likely lead to using the cutting-edge technology to do what we already do, though in better ways and more efficiently. Businesses are effectively utilizing digital technologies to transform production processes, services or businesses in more effective ways.

Digitalization is all about the information and communication technologies (ICTs) and closely follows the modern internet technology (Brennen and Kreiss, 2016). Enhanced interconnectedness of businesses, individuals, organizations and machines as per developments in internet technologies, mobile technology or the blockchain transformation are the new realities to keep in mind.

The three processes of the digital transformation, on the other hand, may be listed as follows:

- Digitization of the ongoing economic activities.
- Development or creation of physical goods or services to serve digitalization.
- Creation or production of new economic activities that were not feasible prior to digitalization.

Meanwhile, as of mid-2024, an estimated two-thirds of the global population is estimated to access internet. The U.S. Bureau of Economic Analysis (2022) puts the growth rate of digitalization at 7 percent per annum in the US, between 2017 and 2022, versus the average of 2.2 percent annual growth during the same period. Meanwhile, the digital economy in the US is estimated at 7–20 percent of the GDP, depending on the broadness of the measure (Citi Research, 2024).

This book aims to contribute to a broad-based discussion on the overarching theme of AI and digitalization in finance and economics, and more specifically on AI-driven decision-making in finance. AI, automation and digitalization do make things easier, increase efficiency; yet, they also develop new industries, enriching work life and the level of well-being.

Concurrently, in cross-country comparisons, it should be noted that, while US and China are leading the way in AI transformation and the related cutting-edge research, Türkiye and Europe are on the heels of these two leading economies (Akman et al., 2022; CBDDO, 2021). However, the technological revolution itself is a process spanning over several centuries.

Since the 2010s (especially after the 2008 Global Financial Crisis), though, we are in a completely new phase of transformation. General Purpose Technologies (GPTs) are joined by new technologies such as digitalization, AI and blockchain. Yet, it is still imperative to think how AI and robots will change the nature of production and competition.

For example, the ongoing 4th Industrial Revolution (Industry 4.0) is digital. During this digital revolution of the 2010s, machines have begun to communicate with each other and with humans (Kiciński and Chaja, 2021). It may, indeed, be called a new era in which global power and economic struggle are shaped through parameters such as technological development and digital transformation.

Industry 5.0, on the other hand, represents unmanned technologies, with people working with robots or just the robotic factories. Industry 5.0 now represents the digitalization phase of humans as well. There is an ongoing process leading toward Industry 5.0, and in this process, everything will likely be digitized. For instance, transactions may not require any state or bank guarantees (Adel, 2022; Nahavandi, 2019). Yet, would this mean chaos for the state and large financial institutions?

The sixth revolution (Industry 6.0), though, is still in the testing phase and is expected to dominate in the 2030s and potentially the 2040s (Duggal et al., 2022). A new era in which AI manages digitized human knowledge and reshapes the workforce. This may be possible through global social isolation. The coronavirus was, indeed, a good test case in this regard.

China, for instance, is working on a smooth transition to Industry 6.0. The social points system in China is one of the best and most well-known applications of Industry 6.0. Likewise, AI is expected to overcome human intelligence by 2030 (so to say the 6th Industrial Revolution). In certain domains, AI has already surpassed human cognition on specific tasks. Impact of generative AI on production and employment also needs to be reassessed.

1.5 THOUGH, ANY SIDE EFFECTS?

The future of finance lies in technology, AI and digitalization. That part is crystal clear. Yet, it is still not clear how to overcome the resulting risks and better harness the opportunities. One thing is for sure; use of AI responsibly matters more nowadays. Ensuring ethical and responsible AI, the security issues, risks, regulations and challenges associated with the use of AI in

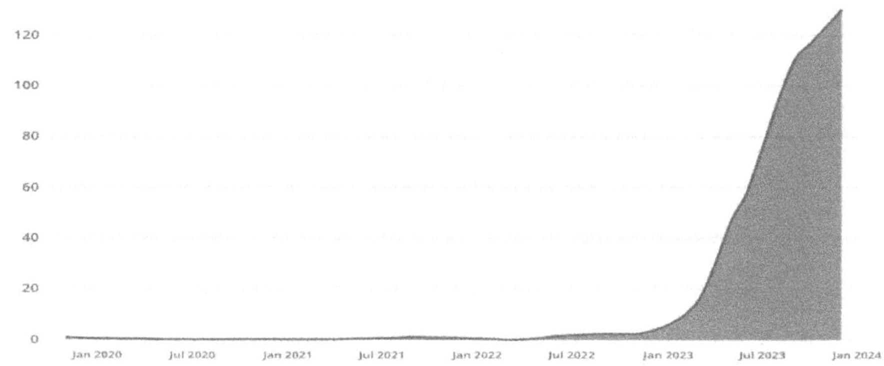

Figure 1.1 Reported incidents and hazards from the generative AI.

Source: *OECD Digital Economy Outlook 2024,* **OECD (2024)**

finance are gaining momentum (Nilsson, 2014; Rossi, 2016; Ulnicane, 2022). Figure 1.1 demonstrates one such simple example of potential side effects of AI usage.

On the other hand, blockchain sort of disruptions, digital or AI transformations are all increasing significance of a conventional phenomenon. Risk management is gaining an increasing presence in the new era's priorities. Emerging regulatory and ethical challenges (out of all these new digital or AI transformations) require an extensive governance framework and hence accountability, transparency, ethical and responsible AI as well as its fairness.

The modern business environment, finance world and even daily transactions or relations are ever more digitized today. Risk aspects are even more complicated in the digitalized world. Accordingly, risk management is more challenging. Information asymmetries, misinformation or analysis of big data matter more than ever. Cybersecurity issues and means to minimize vulnerabilities or avoid the risky practices are ever more significant today.

On the one hand, generative AI may assume a new role in bridging the digital divide while addressing challenges of inequality in access to AI technologies. On the other hand, new job categories, like AI ethicists and prompt engineers, are emerging alongside the shifts in global job markets.

Meanwhile, one also needs to keep in mind that, overall, on one hand, there is this decentralization, deregulation trend along with the blockchain technology, etc., and on the other hand, the AI revolution, which could help with maybe price and financial stability issues (as in price checks or comparisons).

AI is all about mimicking the cognitive capacity. Yet, its integration with the other transformations will matter too. AI and digital transformation interaction is the new battlefield. The new question is whether AI and blockchain type of revolutions are mitigating or propagating each other's impacts.

Moreover, together with the digitalization trend, governments and central banks are expected to record everything you do. Public or regulatory institutions will keep all the data. Digitalization and recording of all the transactions (in return) will also affect the consumer behavior. This could also affect (for instance) weaponizing the CBDC and other digital currencies (Bagis, 2022, 2025a). Such developments could force people to spend significantly more and, in other extreme cases, temporarily halt economic activity.

Financial stability concerns are as vital. As a matter of fact, as news and financial markets dynamism soars, concerns regarding how to prevent new generation banking crisis surge too. After all, markets and stock prices typically reflect the impact of news between 1 and 10 days, research shows (Cohen and Morgan, 2025). If there is more than one news, then this lag can be as high as three months.

Using AI sort of new technologies to achieve financial stability (run on banks), by flagging more noteworthy information much earlier, is hence of substantial importance. For all these reasons, AI could ensure even small companies and insignificant information to be processed and taken into account (much earlier). AI helps process much more information quickly and properly respond much earlier.

1.6 RELATED LITERATURE

AI will be a defining force in the decades ahead. This book aims to help prepare for that very future. The book will speak to the realities of digitalization and AI transformation and inquire how individuals and institutions must be prepared to face it or maybe even work with it. Furthermore, the book underscores practical case studies, numerous regulatory and policy-wise arrangements that could be used to minimize security issues, potential risks or disruptions in finance.

AI has a fast-evolving role in finance. Yet, the future might also come along with new challenges. Practical issues or even ethical concerns might need to be addressed. Challenges, opportunities and risks associated with AI's integration into finance, its roles in decision intelligence and its broader impacts on market efficacy are underlined throughout the book.

Admittedly, AI, machine learning or digital transformation in finance are relatively new areas of focus. Hence, the author is not aware of any current publications that talk to specific practical realities of AI and digital transformation in decision-making processes within finance or challenges faced in gaining acceptance and acknowledgement as well as the other challenges in ensuring the role is independent, objective and can execute certain standards.

Furthermore, this book aims to differentiate itself by focusing more specifically on the practical realities of AI and digital transformation in decision-making processes within finance, offering actionable guidance and real-world case studies, which the author argues are less emphasized in most of the cited competitors.

There are surely a few competing books currently in print, though most are either broad in scope or more theoretical than practical. Yet, compared to these existing alternatives, the proposed book stands out for its practical, case-based approach and specific focus on AI-driven decision-making processes in finance.

No other volume (to our knowledge) provides actionable, task-by-task best practice guidance on this particular aspect of AI usage in finance. Meanwhile, most AI and finance books out there are relatively old-fashioned, more general, purely academic and conceptual.

Moreover, this book differentiates subject matter through a very specific AI adoption under an adaptive system, using a control-based approach and harnessing real-world cases. Furthermore, the book underscores numerous regulatory and policy-wise arrangements that could be used to minimize potential risks or disruptions in finance.

However, a few similar books are listed as follows. Harvey et al. (2021), for instance, focus on macroeconomic impacts of DeFi without integrating the agentic AI or cybersecurity innovations, while Smith (2024) offers a broader overview without focused technical depth on agentic AI or decentralized security paradigms.

Regarding the fundamentals and the required technical infrastructure, Aldasoro et al. (2024) provide a very general introduction to changing technical foundations. Kshetri (2022), on the other hand, focuses on the rise of a parallel technological revolution, the blockchain revolution aspects only.

Moloi and Marwala (2020) have a rather more theoretical focus. Tsang's (2023) "AI for Finance" is the closest related book in that the two books (indeed) complement each other. Yet, we aim to provide a more focused and to-the-point picture of AI usage in decision intelligence. Meanwhile, just like our practical applications, Wolfram (2023) digs into the details of a practical AI cases such as ChatGPT and their broader AI implications.

1.7 AI IN FINANCE WORKSHOPS

In line with this transformation, a special inaugural digital workshop took place at Ayasofya Campus of FSM Vakif University in June 2025 (Bagis, 2025b).[1] It was, indeed, a timely and to-the-point workshop. The (AI in Finance) workshop was organized by the PERPAL lab and planned as part of the Ayasofya Digital Campus project, aiming at triple integration between theory, business and academia. And hence, connecting the theory and practice.

The AI revolution, its methodologies and their applications in finance were discussed thoroughly, all day. Challenges, risks and opportunities were analyzed in detail. Overall, it provided a broad-based discussion opportunity on the overarching theme of AI and digitalization in finance, and more specifically on AI-driven decision-making in finance.

The workshop aimed to fill in the gap between theory and practice, the missing connectivity with cutting-edge technologies, innovation, AI and the digital transformation as well as their impacts on decision intelligence processes within finance. The participants' qualifications and the potential contributions from other experts suggested a high likelihood of producing a compelling and insightful workshop.

The workshop also provided a unique platform to discuss digitalization, AI and machine learning, as well as contemporary business practices and technological developments in the fields of economics and finance. This valuable meeting shed light on the world of new-era finance that is transforming with the technology.

Participants included professionals, academics and executives. Experts, academics and professionals shared current trends and innovative approaches in their fields with the participants. The author was pleased to host and collaborate with distinguished faculty members, experts and scholars working on these topics.

Participants had a full day of enriching discussions over the AI revolution and its potential impacts over the financial world. And the organizers are hoping to see all experts and academics interested in AI and its applications in finance and economics again, during the upcoming conferences as well.

1.8 AI-DRIVEN DECISION-MAKING IN FINANCE

This book has a unique focus on recently more practical, yet often underexplored area of AI in finance. In particular, the practical cases and application-focused chapters make the book unique amongst all the other relevant options. AI applications and related ethical, security and regulatory issues in finance serve as a recurring theme throughout the book (Nilsson, 2014; Rossi, 2016; Ulnicane, 2022).

Furthermore, advances in applied AI, big data, and analytics shall deepen our understanding of complex economic and financial phenomena, improve decision-making processes, and support evidence-based policymaking. Hence, improved efficiency is at the core of the discussions in the book.

The book provides a comprehensive exploration of AI and its implications and pivotal roles in addressing modern challenges in finance. The transformative potential of AI in addressing financial challenges is underlined extensively, including its regulatory and ethical challenges as well as the broader governance issues (Rossi, 2016; Ulnicane, 2022).

In that line, the book concentrates more on issues such as

- How AI can transform fields such as economics and finance, addressing pressing challenges through innovative applications.
- And how AI can be applied to advance understanding and innovation in economics and finance.

Key themes of the book include ethics, governance, transparency, fairness and accountability in AI applications. Other primary topics include machine learning in finance, the blockchain technology, big data, digital currencies, related risks and opportunities as well as AI-incorporated brokerage, security and regulations. A dedicated section in finance applications would specifically focus on the intersection of AI and financial fraud, investigating how technology is reshaping both the prevention and perpetration of financial crimes.

Given the ever-surging need for more sector-specific applications of an extensive new technology, this book presents a clear, timely and technically sound plan for applying AI to enhance financial decision-making in areas such as risk assessment, fraud detection and portfolio management. The book's strong relevance, well-defined objectives and potential industry impacts make it a worthy publication.

The book demonstrates a strong grasp of both AI methodologies and their applications in finance, referencing relevant tools, techniques and industry challenges. Its structured approach, use of case studies, and awareness of ethical and regulatory considerations suggest a solid academic or professional background in the field (Rossi, 2016; Ulnicane, 2022).

Before diving into sector-specific applications, we have decided to add this early chapter focusing on evolution of AI in finance, AI and digital transformations in finance. This should set the historical, technological and theoretical stage, and provide a macro-level view of why AI matters. The digital transformation sections also overlap with the AI-focused content.

Regulations and risk aspects related to the cross-border impacts will (indeed) enhance the scope. Though by doing so, it not only deepens our understanding of the intersection between technology and regulation but also contributes valuable insights into the existing literature, eventually fostering a culture of responsible innovation and ethical accountability in the financial technology sector.

The book moves from foundational concepts to practical applications across key financial domains, concluding with security, risks and broader challenges. This progression effectively builds the reader's knowledge. To enhance the book's appeal, the book also includes case studies – featuring real or anonymized examples from the finance sector – that would demonstrate practical impacts.

More specifically, to improve coherence, the book sticks to the subsequent flow:

- Part I: Foundations: Intro, AI Overview and Digital Transformation.
- Part II: Applications: Banking and Finance Applications, Payments and Crypto.
- Part III: Risks and Challenges: Security, Ethics and Regulation Aspects.
- Part IV: The Road Ahead: Trends, Policy and Future Opportunities.

The sectoral chapters such as banking and payments or the application-focused chapters make this book a unique resource. The security, risks and challenges chapters give the readers a balanced view of both the benefits and limitations of AI adoption.

These issues are indeed central to AI adoption. After all, understanding these aspects could provide a more grounded perspective when discussing applications in finance in general or in its payments, crypto and other investment dimensions. The concluding chapter looks ahead to the future of digital banking, highlighting emerging trends, future AI use cases in finance and the skills needed to navigate this evolving landscape.

1.9 DECISION INTELLIGENCE FOCUS

The intersection of AI and finance is a rapidly evolving and increasingly relevant area of concentration. A book that well-connects theory and practice, discusses real-world market implications, as this book aims to do, would be a highly valuable resource for a wide range of audiences.

After all, there is surely a very good chance that AI will have a much greater impact (than expected) on all the business life, the finance world and the academia in general. Therefore, as a specific subject, application of AI to finance in depth is valuable.

This book particularly aims to dig further into regulatory or discretionary measures to limit risks related to AI adoption. The book underlines emerging ethical, regulatory and practical issues due to contemporary applications of AI in finance (Nilsson, 2014; Ulnicane, 2022). Hence, it could potentially help lead to more effective and responsible AI utilization, too.

The book emphasizes on AI-driven decision-making within finance. In addition to a broad perspective regarding practical applications of AI in finance, this first chapter explores the deep impact of AI on finance. It digs into challenges, opportunities and risks associated with AI's integration with finance.

Moreover, the impact of digital transformation also extends to regulatory compliance, security issues, fraud detection, and investment strategies. AI systems adopt to identifying patterns and anomalies that may potentially represent fraudulent activities, leading to the need for more robust security measures.

Thus, digital transformation and AI adoption have turned into a priority (and in many cases a necessity) for modern institutions and businesses alike. They both significantly affect daily interactions and the way business is conducted. This book aims to elaborate on all these recent trends in digital transformation, AI use, and AI-driven decision-making, as well as the contemporary business practices and technological developments in finance.

This book puts a stronger emphasis on the risks and security-related implications of AI-driven decision-making. Efficiency is another key issue of this process. Better use of data will also enable increased efficiency in business practices.

With AI or automated systems, new programs or machines are created to do the jobs that would normally require significant human resources. An

AI-powered automation is also dynamic and quickly adapts to changes in information flows. Digitalization, on the other hand, is about the use of digital technologies to transform business models, utilizing digital technologies and digitalizing businesses.

However, both should be implemented in ways that foster innovation, improve decision-making, increase efficiency, and enhance productivity. Accordingly, the goal is to harmonize theory and practical implications to enhance innovation, decision-making and efficiency. Hence, the real-world practical examples of the contemporary digitalization and technological transformation are in order.

Meanwhile, in an era of innovations, rising trend of uncertainties and countless efforts to build new standards, the significance of the twin transformations of AI and digitalization is a new reality. They represent a relatively dynamic environment. The drivers behind these rapid and impressive developments are also of major curiosity. This book provides a new opportunity to discuss, learn and even shape the future of digitalization and AI. It aims to bring together different opinions, forecasts, cutting-edge research in these new fields together.

Analysis in this book summarizes the drastic changes post the COVID-19 pandemic, accelerating digital and AI transformation, and the future of finance. The book provides deep discussions, latest developments related to crypto or blockchain technologies, innovative new technological solutions, AI-driven decision-making and more efficient payment and transfer systems.

Digital currencies, digitalization and AI-driven risk management, decision-making, security and automated advisory services are just a few of other examples of inter-connected discussions. The need for an enhanced AI-driven decision-making process, e-commerce and better resource management should also be underlined.

The book (hence) touches upon:

- Implications of AI on decision-making in finance.
- Post-Pandemic accelerating digital transformation and information flows.
- The digital globalization.
- Digital economies and relevant digital policies.
- New developments and business practices in the financial sector.
- Opportunities and challenges of digitalization in decision intelligence.
- Opportunities and challenges of AI adoption in decision-making.
- The ICT sector development.
- The macro-financial impacts of artificial intelligence.
- Impact of artificial intelligence on public policy and decision intelligence.
- Theoretical and practical aspects of digital currencies (Bagis, 2025a).

Meanwhile, to make sure AI is reliable and applied for the good of people and the environment, it will be essential to have a common understanding of the primary advantages and disadvantages. The pros and cons as well as security and risk challenges of new technologies and innovations such as digital currencies are also underlined (Bagis, 2022).

Concurrently, in its analysis over the contemporary business practices and technological developments in finance and economics, the book also aims to assess ways to overcome risks, security implications and better harness the opportunities of AI-driven decision-making.

Other potential key issues that could potentially influence decision intelligence may include:

- The Internet of Things (IoT).
- Transforming globalization.
- The digital economy post-COVID-19.
- Generative AI.
- Remote or hybrid work trends.

Based upon these theoretical fundamentals, book chapters touch upon:

- AI in Banking: Digitalization and AI-powered decision-making in banking sector.
- AI in Payment Systems: AI-powered decision-making, security and risk issues in payment systems.
- AI in Cryptocurrencies: AI-driven decision intelligence, security issues and decision making in digital currencies,
- AI in Investments: Machine learning and AI-driven financial modeling, decision intelligence and risk management in investments,
- Security, Risks and Challenges: Security issues, risks and challenges associated with AI adoption in finance and decision-making processes.

1.10 CHAPTER SEQUENCE

This book project brings together chapters from prominent scholars, experts and practitioners focusing on AI implications in finance and broader economics covering market trends, data-driven informed decision-making, governance and digital banking aspects, morality and ethical issues. Decision-intelligence processes in policymaking, governance or ethical dilemmas are all thoroughly analyzed, as well as what this transition means for FinTech, risk managers, investors and policymakers.

Accordingly, the first (and introductory) chapter examines decades-long evolution of AI and the implications of this transformation in finance. This should set the historical, technological, and theoretical stage, and would provide a macro-overview of why AI matters. It explores the deep impact of AI on finance and digs into challenges, opportunities and risks associated with AI's integration with finance.

This section's introduction to AI-driven decision-making and digital transformation introduces the reader to AI in finance-related contextual considerations and simple practical case studies. It presents a broadband introduction and covers many of the key concepts of digitalization, finance, AI and informed-decision subjects covered throughout the rest of the book.

Part of the discussion here is running over policymaking. For instance, Al-Maadeed, Aysan and Unal's "AI in Central Banking" chapter proposes a dual-pipeline design that allows the integration of AI with forward-looking exploratory synthetic data alongside real-world data as an empirical base. The chapter introduces a new model to guide this transition, culminating in a "high preparedness" stage characterized by hybrid models. They conclude that the strategic adoption of a hybrid real-synthetic data approach is essential for enhancing resilience and foresight of monetary policy.

Meanwhile, Ertuğrul, Sakarya and Polat's "A New AI-Based Index" is another timely and policy-relevant chapter that develops a novel, high-frequency economic confidence index (ECI) created using natural language processing (NLP) and sentiment analysis on economic news articles. Inspired by the S&P Twitter Sentiment Index, the model captures fluctuations in economic sentiment by analyzing public discourse in near real-time using great quantities of textual data scraped daily from Turkish news sites to create a web-based, AI-driven index.

No doubt, at the core of this policymaking focus lies data-driven decision-making processes. Accordingly, Nzama-Sithole and Bozkus Kahyaoglu, in their "From Data to Decisions" chapter, emphasize the evolution of data from mere record-keeping to a sophisticated source of decision-making intelligence. It illustrates how efficient data utilization by financial institutions and markets informs strategic, operational and regulatory decisions.

Informed decision-making is expected to help enhance investment decisions too. Kalappa, Upadhyay and Ananda S's "Robo-Advisors for Investment Decision-Making" chapter provides an overview of the applications, characteristics, design and operations of robo-advisors, as well as the increasing trend of their adoption through a content analysis. It addresses the implications of robo-advisors' incorporation into decision-making processes for investors, service providers, policymakers, marketers and even researchers, providing suggestions for advancing their extensive use.

On the other hand, access to finances is surely a major priority concern particularly for the SMEs. Aykaş and Aydın's "Machine-Learning-based Financial Health Assessment" model proposes an analytical and machine-learning-based decision support framework to evaluate the financial health of SMEs from a creditworthiness perspective. The model is built based on key balance sheet ratios covering aspects such as liquidity, profitability and solvency, aiming to produce dynamic and accurate financial health scores for SMEs.

The AI revolution is effectively transforming investment decisions too. Sovbetov's "Algorithmic Morality" chapter explores the real-world performance of AI in investment decision-making and considers the future viability of AI-led asset management. It combines financial econometrics, behavioral insights and strategic implications, contributing both theoretical and empirical value.

Ethical, security-wise or risk management aspects are as crucial. Iyambo and Msimuko's "Ethical AI in Finance" chapter provides a clear, timely, and technically informed plan for integrating ethical considerations into AI development and deployment. It offers practical insights and strategies for financial institutions to proactively build trust, reduce bias, and ensure fair decision-making, thereby improving the utility and societal benefit of AI.

Risk management, ethical and security aspects of incorporating AI into decision-making processes shall matter as such. Ramuloo's "Decision Intelligence and Risk Management" chapter complements the book's focus on AI's transformative impact on financial decision-making by providing a deep dive into how decision intelligence enhances risk frameworks. The chapter bridges quantitative and qualitative investment approaches, emphasizing AI's role in data-driven strategies and risk mitigation, which are central themes of the book.

From a broader perspective, Stiefenhofer and Deniz's "Ethical Dilemmas of AI" chapter examines the ways AI is reshaping public administration. The chapter conducts a comparative interpretive analysis of European approaches to algorithmic tax administration, identifying four distinct moral configurations. It concludes that AI can exercise delegated administrative authority legitimately only when computational power remains embedded within frameworks of public justification, effective contestation and equal legal protection in the digital state.

Institutional or governance-related concerns are as consequential. Arora, Arora and Mehta's "Revolutionizing FinTech with AI" chapter examines the paradigm shift introduced by AI in the Fintech sector, and from the viewpoint of both the theoretical and practical applications, as well as the challenges it poses in effectively harnessing its benefits. The chapter presents a comprehensive analysis of state-of-the-art applications, underscoring their relevance and potential.

Bin-Armia's "AI-Enabled Smart Governance for Smart Money" chapter examines the integration of AI within the governance architecture of CBDCs, situating it in a global context of CBDC experimentation. It explores how AI-driven supervision and audit mechanisms enhance transparency, resilience and regulatory coherence, while the dual-ledger design supports secure issuance, programmability and advanced supervisory functions.

1.11 CONCLUDING REMARKS

AI is rapidly transforming finance. Yet, it also leads to countless possibilities, opportunities, risks and security issues. With the AI and related technologies accelerating, especially since the pandemic, business practices and the financial sector may also alter dramatically. Practical applications and integrated technologies are drawing ever-increasing attention.

Physical contact is eliminated, and simple tasks (as in the bill payments) or the type of simple but time-consuming jobs are usually left to be done by AI. AI will likely even increase efficiency of physical jobs. As an example, before starting a job or physically applying, AI could make it much easier to determine the most suitable options.

Meanwhile, social credit scores (like Klout or Soso) are emerging instead of conventional credit scores. Data-driven, industry-based operations and evaluation based on presence in the digital world, smart contracts instead of paper contracts, are gaining eminence. Blockchain technology will also likely eliminate intermediaries, financial advisors and financial consulting will probably be replaced by robots or quantum advisors or other similar calculation tools.

This book provides a unique focus on recently more practical, yet often underexplored area of AI in finance. In particular, the practical cases and application-focused chapters make the book unique amongst all the relevant options. AI applications and related ethical, security, and regulatory issues in finance serve as a recurring theme throughout the book.

The book discusses micro-foundations and practical applications of this recent technological transformation, and particularly on the AI-driven decision-making process in the post-AI era. It clearly differentiates itself by a distinct focus on the real world implications of AI and digital transformation in decision-making processes within finance.

However, short interviews with industry experts could also provide further real-world insight and credibility. Including toolkits or code snippets, such as Python or Jupyter notebooks, could benefit practitioners. Visual aids like diagrams and flowcharts could clarify complex ideas, while sidebars on ethical and regulatory issues would also add much more depth.

To further enhance the book's appeal, the book could include AI in Action case studies – featuring real or anonymized examples from the finance sector – that would demonstrate practical impact. This could expand the book's scope beyond banking and investments, highlighting its use in claims automation and risk modeling to appeal to a broader audience.

Yet, to enhance the RegTech framework, a comprehensive section that systematically examines evolving legal regulations alongside the ethical considerations surrounding AI applications is needed. This section could delve into specific regulations-wise rules, just as in new data protection laws and other anti-money laundering measures, while also exploring the potential ethical dilemmas posed by AI, like algorithmic bias and transparency issues.

The book might also benefit from a slight expansion, and deeper consideration of ethical implications, real-world partnerships and limitations related to model transparency and regulation. And finally, a few future-looking chapters would no doubt help.

Future research could focus more on further practical applications, efficiency focus and how generative AI or GenAI accelerates this process.

Challenges and risks associated with introduction of AI transformation, as well as implications for payments and e-bookkeeping technologies, prospective FinTech implications will all be worth contemplating.

A discussion on the geopolitical and cross-border impacts of AI could offer a more global perspective, showing how different regions adopt to and regulate AI in finance. Another section on future trends in AI and finance could offer a valuable forward-looking perspective.

More specifically, additions like "Future Trends and Strategic Implications," "Building Resilient, AI-Ready Financial Organizations" or "What's Next: A Practical Guide for Leaders" – highlighting generative AI, emerging regulations, and evolving global dynamics – could leave readers with actionable takeaways and a deeper forward-looking perspective.

NOTE

1. The workshop was organized as part of the Digital Workshops series (or AI and Digital Transformation Workshops). The workshop (jointly organized with HBKU, Qatar) encompassed over 60 participants and contributions from 7 different countries and 23 institutions.

REFERENCES

Adel, A. (2022). Future of Industry 5.0 in society: Human-centric solutions, challenges and prospective research areas. *Journal of Cloud Computing, 11*(1), 40.

Akman, E., Topçu, T. B. and Chiftchi, A. (2022). *Yapay Zekâ ve Kamu Politikası Ülke İncelemeleri*. Nobel: Ankara.

Aldasoro, I., Gambacorta, L., Korinek, A., Shreeti, V. and Stein, M. (2024). *Intelligent financial system: how AI is transforming finance*, Technical report, Bank for International Settlements.

Arf, C. (1959). Makine Düşünebilir mi ve Nasıl Düşünebilir? *Atatürk Üniversitesi 1958–1959 Öğretim Yılı Halk Konferansları*, 1, 91–103. https://mbkaya.com/hukuk/cahit-arf-makinedusunebilir-mi-orjinal.pdf

Bagis, B. (2022). Digital currencies and monetary policy in the new era, *Insight Turkey*, 24 (3), 189–211. doi: https://doi.org/10.25253/99.2022243.12

Bagis, B. (2025a). Digital Currencies and Financial Transformation. In: Gün, M., Kartal, B. (eds) *Machine Learning in Finance. Contributions to Finance and Accounting*. Springer: Cham.

Bagis, B. (2025b). "AI in Finance workshop successfully completed!", EcoPolitics Café, June 18, 2025. Link: https://bilalbagis.wordpress.com/2025/06/18/ai-in-finance-calistayi-gerceklesti/

Bağış, B. (2025). "Finance reimagined: Exploring AI's role in new digital age at a workshop", Daily Sabah, (June 24, 2025).

Boden, M. A. (ed.) (1996). *Artificial Intelligence*, Elsevier: New York, 1996.

Brennen, J. S. and Kreiss, D. (2016). Digitalization. *The International Encyclopedia of Communication Theory and Philosophy, 2016*, 1–11.

Bureau of Economic Analysis (2022). "How Big is the Digital Economy?", the U.S. Bureau of Economic Analysis. Link: bea.gov/data/special-topics/digital-economy

CBDDO (2021). "National Artificial Intelligence Strategy 2021–2025", Presidency of the Digital Transformation Office and the Ministry of Industry and Technology. Link: https://cbddo.gov.tr/en/nais

Citi Research (2024). *The Digital Transformation of the Global Economy Riding the Wave of Virtual Progress*, August 2024.

Cohen, J. and Morgan, S. (2025). *How to Know When a World Event Could Shock the Market*. NY Times, August 1, 2025. Link: https://www.nytimes.com/2025/08/01/opinion/economy-stocks-shock-patterns.html

Duggal, A. S., Malik, P. K., Gehlot, A., Singh, R., Gaba, G. S., Masud, M. and Al-Amri, J. F. (2022). A sequential roadmap to Industry 6.0: Exploring future manufacturing trends. *IET Communications*, *16*(5), 521–531.

Flasiński, M. (2016). *Introduction to Artificial Intelligence*, Springer International Publishing: AG Switzerland, Cham.

Harvey, C. R., Ramachandran, A., Santoro, J., Ehrsam, F. and Buterin, V. (2021). *DeFi and the Future of Finance*, Wiley: New Jersey.

Kaur, G., Lashkari, A. H. and Sharafaldin, I., Ziba Habibi Lashkari. (2023). *Understanding Cybersecurity Management in Decentralized Finance: Challenges, Strategies, and Trends* (Financial Innovation and Technology). Springer International Publishing: Cham.

Kiciński, J. and Chaja, P. (2021). Industry 4.0 - The Fourth Industrial Revolution. In *Climate Change, Human Impact and Green Energy Transformation* (pp. 115–140). Springer International Publishing: Cham.

Kshetri, N. (2022). *The Rise of Blockchains: Disrupting Economies and Transforming Societies*, Edward Elgar: Massachusetts.

Mastercard for Government (2025). *Digitalizing the Public Purse*, Mastercard for Government White Paper Series (January 2025).

Moloi, T. and Marwala, T. (2020). *Artificial Intelligence in Economics and Finance Theories: Advanced Information and Knowledge Processing*, Springer: Cham.

Moor, J. (2006). The Dartmouth college artificial intelligence conference: The next fifty years. *AI Magazine*, *27*(4), 87–91.

Nahavandi, S. (2019). Industry 5.0—A human-centric solution. *Sustainability*, *11*(16), 4371.

Negnevitsky, M. (2005). *Artificial Intelligence: A Guide to Intelligent Systems*, Pearson Education: London.

Nilsson, N. J. (2014). *Principles of Artificial Intelligence*, Morgan Kaufmann: Palo Alto.

OECD (2024), *OECD Digital Economy Outlook 2024 (Volume 1): Embracing the Technology Frontier*, OECD Publishing: Paris. https://doi.org/10.1787/a1689dc5-en.

Rossi, F. (2016). Artificial Intelligence: Potential Benefits and Ethical Considerations, *EPRS: European Parliamentary Research Service*. Belgium. Retrieved from https://policycommons.net/artifacts/1340375/artificial-intelligence/1950888/ on 11 Jun 2023.

Smith, S. S. (2024). *Blockchain, Artificial Intelligence, and Financial Services*, Springer: Cham.

Tsang, E. P. K. (2023). *AI for Finance*, CRC Press, Taylor and Francis: Boca Raton.

Türkiye Bilişim Derneği (2024). *Kamuda Yapay Zeka Uygulamaları*, Kamuda Yapay Zeka Uygulamaları Çalışma Grubu (Kasım 2024).

Ulnicane, I. (2022). Artificial Intelligence in The European Union Policy, Ethics and Regulation. In: Thomas Hoerber, Gabriel Weber, Ignazio Cabras (eds) *The Routledge Handbook of European Integrations*, Routledge: London, 254–269.

Wolfram, S. (2023). *What Is ChatGPT Doing:... and Why Does It Work?* Wolfram Media). (ChatGPT and AI)

Chapter 2

AI in central banking

Synthetic vs real world data in forecasting models

Nayif Sultan M A Al-Maadeed, Ahmet Faruk Aysan and Ibrahim Musa Unal

2.1 INTRODUCTION

The start of the COVID-19 pandemic in 2020 revealed a dangerous weakness of the analytical toolkit of central banks around the world. Earlier econometric models, which are developed using decades-old data, had a problem explaining the unprecedented economic shock in terms of simultaneous demand and supply shocks, large-scale government interventions, and shifts in consumer behavior.

Within the regime of central banking, it is not a matter of sentient machines carrying out autonomous policy making. Instead, it is defined as a set of newer computations such as machine learning (ML), natural language processing (NLP), and deep learning which can detect complex patterns, relationships and anomalies in large data sets that are far beyond the analytical capability of humans. This marks a shift from traditional, theory based causal explanation and prediction accuracy optimization, toward methods that prioritize direct learning and the optimization of predictive performance. The potential of AI is in revealing the presence of latent dynamics in economic activity that can be non-linear and could not be perceived by conventional theory, only that such a model would be more sensitive and more accurate in time.

The importance of the sound forecasting model in these fundamental operations cannot be underrated. In the case of monetary policy, the central banks take into account future possibilities. When they determine an interest rate today, it is so that it can affect the inflation and economic growth of the following 18–24 months. During the policy calibration, the precision of forecasts of inflation and the output gap is hence crucial. Likewise, financial stability can only be achieved by the identification of the systemic risks in their initiating stage. The duality of such processes can be found through both stress testing financial institutions as well as keeping the pulse on weak points within a complexly linked market They are to provide for modeling the processes through the system to infer non-linear dynamics-such as tail risks that reach up to a systemic event.

Here, we have created a true game changer, synthetic data algorithmically generated that is modelled according to statistical characteristics of real-world

 DOI: 10.1201/9781003656463-2

datapoints. Synthetic data can be manufactured through techniques such as Generative Adversarial Networks (GANs) to complement sparse data sets or create perfectly balanced samples for model training. Most importantly, these methods allow the simulation of catastrophic, extreme, or black-swan scenarios that do not exist in historical records, thereby enabling more robust and accurate model stress testing. Central banks can feed their AI model far-fetched results from simulated, endless hypotheticals of these extreme risks, which can instruct the model to identify warning signs that are way too intricate to be learnt by lived experience and thus augment their ability to prevent such risks. Second, the increased complexity and interconnectedness of the global financial system require progressively more advanced monitoring tools of systemic risks. Lastly, international organizations such as the Bank for International Settlements (BIS) are going out of their way to support technological innovation through dedicated programs such as the BIS Innovation Hub which expressly recommends that central banks use technologies such as AI and machine learning to modernize their business and address the challenges of tomorrow.

The given paper aims at discussing the changing collusion of AI, data, and forecasting in contemporary central banking. In this respect, it shall respond to the following fundamental research questions:

- What are the effects of synthetic data in development and implementation of AI-based forecasting models in central banking?
- What are the relative advantages and shortcomings of realizing synthetic data in contrast to real-life data to educate and approve models in the issues of monetary policy and financial stability?
- How might AI-driven models, especially the improved ones using synthetic data, enhance the identification of anomalies and tracking of the systemic risks in central banking processes?

To address these questions, the paper will make use of the secondary methods approach. It will start with a detailed literature review of existing applications of AI in all areas of finance and central banking and then will be a detailed comparison between the technical and practical difference between real-world and synthetic data.

2.2 LITERATURE REVIEW

This chapter summarizes the current landscape of knowledge on the methodologies of central banking and artificial intelligence (AI). It starts by tracing the history of AI in the financial policy world, going back to early rule-based AI systems and through to generative AI. It also takes a critical perspective on the two major data paradigms: the real-world and synthetic, analyzing pros and cons of their usage within the macroeconomic and financial forecasting area.

2.2.1 Evolution of AI in central banking

The adoption of AI by central banks is a slow but rapidly developing process that reflects the overall changes in the AI sphere. This development can be divided into three phases, each one of them being more complex, data-reliant, and analytically potent. To start with, the central banks utilized expert systems on a trial basis, in terms of rules. To give an example, a system may include rules such as, "IF inflation is more than 3% AND unemployment is less than 4%, THEN raise a flag of a possible tightening of the policy." These systems promised consistency and transparency, and yet, were very rigid in that they could not learn something based on new data and adjust to unexpected economic changes, which restricted their use to mere routine monitoring and compliance operations (Bholat, 2017). The second, less overwhelming but more significant phase was stimulated by the emergence of machine learning (ML) (Gogas & Papadimitriou, 2021).

Generative AI (GenAI), especially Large Language Models (LLMs) and diffusion models, presently characterize the frontier. Compared to the earlier AI that was mostly analytical, GenAI is creative, able to create new text, code, and, most importantly, consider the relation to the current research data.

The BIS has pointed out the opportunities of LLMs to central banks to act as assistants in areas such as summarizing the policy meetings and analyzing the supervisory reports but has also cautioned that the application of such systems is associated with various risks, such as factual hallucinations and increases in bias (BIS, 2023). IMF has created an AI Preparedness Index that, by evaluating the abilities of a nation to use AI by means of its digital infrastructure, human capital, and the quality of regulation, enables a measure of the preparation in a state in terms of institutions (Cazzaniga et al., 2024). On a technical basis, frameworks such as ISO/IEC 23053:2022 offer a set of recommendations for AI systems developed with machine learning in mind that focus on values such as transparency, explainability, and resilience that are paramount when it comes to the central banking arena.

2.2.2 Real-World data in forecasting

To understand economic policies and forecasting, real-world data which has been defined as data that is observed and is empirical have been the foundation of most economies. Its role regarding central banking is widespread and central.

Applications: The most important applications are in tracking inflation, with traditional consumer price indices being complemented by high-frequency scanner observations made by retailers, and web-scraped prices, which are now starting to be used to track inflation in real time (Cavallo, 2013). Detail is captured in loans, transaction and corporate balance sheets to formulate a model of the probability of credit default and estimate systemic financial risk in performing risk assessment

Table 2.1 Facts and figures of key real-world data sources

Data type	*Frequency*	*Publication lag*	*Key fact / figure*	*Core limitation*
GDP	Quarterly	~30 Days (Advance)	Avg. revision from advance to final estimate is ~0.6%.	Significant lag and revisions
CPI Inflation	Monthly	~15 Days	Tracks a fixed basket of ~80,000 items (U.S. BLS).	Infrequent; misses daily price dynamics
Bank Supervisory Data	Quarterly	~45 Days	Contains >2,000 data fields per institution.	Highly confidential; restricted access
Financial Crisis Data	Event-Driven	N/A	<15 major systemic crises globally since 1945.	Extreme data sparsity

(Table 2.1). In core macroeconomic forecasts, GDP, employment, and industrial production are the most reliable data that structural and time-series models are based upon to make decisions on direction to which monetary policy should run (Smets & Wouters, 2007).

Strengths: The main power of real-world data consists in its historical legitimacy and practicality. It presents what is existing which gives an impeccable empirical (scientific) groundwork. Its policy acceptance is based on this direct connection to the actual economic activity. The policymakers, financial markets, and the people would be more inclined at believing models that are based on verifiable and official data which is a key element of credibility of a central bank.

Limitations: Despite its strengths, real-world data presents significant challenges.

Privacy Risk: Many of the most desirable granular data (e.g., individual bank transactions, firm-level financials) is highly sensitive. Its application has significant privacy considerations, and its use is also restricted by privacy laws, such as the General Data Protection Regulation (GDPR), restricting the analysis.

Sparse Datasets: Most of the important economic phenomena, for example, financial crisis or deteriorated currencies are uncommon. That means having very sparse data sets and AI models do not get enough examples to learn, a typical class imbalance issue, which hinders significantly the capability of developing predictive early-warning systems.

Lag in Data Availability: Even official macroeconomic data can be published with a very long lag (e.g., quarterly GDP statistics are published weeks after the end of a quarter and are prone to revision). Such delay makes real-time policymaking very difficult, triggering central banks to deal with an old-fashioned image of the economy (Giannone, Reichlin, & Small, 2008).

2.2.3 Synthetic data in AI modelling

Synthetic data, which is defined as data artificially created to match the statistical characteristics and patterns of a real life dataset, has become a beneficial answer to the drawbacks of real-life data.

2.2.3.1 *Definition and generation techniques*

Synthetic data is algorithmically generated as opposed to data obtained by real-life events. Prominent generation techniques include GANs, where a "generator" network learns to create realistic data to fool a "discriminator" network that tries to distinguish real from fake data (Goodfellow et al., 2014). A formalization of this adversarial training is using a minimax objective function which the two networks are competing to solve.

$$\min D \max V(D, G) = Ex \sim pdata(x)[\log D(x)] + Ez \sim pz(z)[\log(1 - D(G(z)))]$$

Explanation: The discriminator (D) tries to maximize the probability of correctly identifying real data (D(x)→1D(x)→1) and fake data (D(G(z)) →0D(G(z)) →0). The generator (G) tries to minimize this by creating data so realistic that it fools D (D(G(z)) →1D(G(z)) →1).

Applications: It is innovative to have synthetic data in the context of a central bank. It passes a stern supervisory stress test wherein regulators can develop thousands of plausible yet unprecedented hypothetical scenarios of crisis to determine whether the banking system stands up to them (Cont, 2022).

Privacy Preservation: Based on the knowledge that the artificial data will be denied real people or firms as representatives, the topic of privacy will be essentially ruled out and it opens a door to a chance of data distribution and collaboration to which the projects would not have been able to achieve in real life.

A randomized algorithm MM provides (ϵ,δ) (ϵ,δ)-differential privacy if for any two adjacent datasets D1 and D2 (differing by one element) and for any set of outputs SS, the following inequality holds (Dwork, 2008):

$$P(M(D1) \in S) \leq e \in \cdot P(M(D2) \in S) + \delta$$

Explanation: This guarantees that the algorithm output is virtually the same when or whether data of any individual is in it, safeguarding the privacy of individuals. The budget of privacy is denoted by ϵϵ.

Simulation Flexibility: It then goes directly against the issue of sparse datasets in that the researcher can create balanced datasets or augment real data with examples of rare events, e.g. bank runs or market crashes, etc.

Cost Savings: It can reduce the significant costs associated with acquiring, cleaning, and labelling massive real-world datasets.

Concerns: Entering synthetic data is not risk-free. It is highly possible that overfitting will occur or a mode collapse state), when the generative model learns not the underlying distribution but memorizes and recreates some examples of the source data (Thanh-Tung & Tran, 2020). This results in absence of diversity in generated data. The second issue is false positives or low fidelity; without a perfect correspondence between synthetic and the real world, models trained with the data may not work on real-world data (Mehrabi et al., 2021).

2.2.4 Forecasting in central banking

The focus of modern progressive monetary policy is hitting that with forecasts. Banks have various modelling patterns, and the contrast between the modern and AI techniques is at their peak in this area. The old toolkit is made up of econometric models. These are dynamic Stochastic General Equilibrium (DSGE) models and Vector Autoregression (VAR) models, which have managed to take note of statistical relationships between fundamental macroeconomic variables (Christiano, Eichenbaum and Evans, 2005). The working horse of center bank forecasting, a standard VAR(p) model has the following mathematical structure: The Vector Autoregression (VAR) Model.

For a set of kk time-series variables YtYt (e.g., inflation, GDP growth), a VAR(p) model is expressed as:

$$Yt = c + A1Yt - 1 + A2Yt - 2 + \cdots + ApYt - p + \varepsilon t$$

Explanation: Each variable in the vector YtYt is modelled as a linear function of its own past values and the past values of all other variables in the system, up to pp lags. The AiAi matrices contain the model's coefficients.

They are strong as they are interpretable and coherent in theory. They are however based upon very simplifying assumptions and their accuracy in terms of out-of-sample forecasting has in many cases been criticized. By contrast, AI-based forecasting models are found to be mostly atheoretical and data-driven. Recurrent Neural Networks (RNNs including a specific class called Long Short-Term Memory (LSTM) networks are specifically built to learn long dependencies within time-series data (Smyl, 2020).

The Principle of RNN: The structure of a simple RNN contains a hidden state (h t) to which a more advanced model like LSTMs owes its greater complexity, using the following update rule:

$$ht = f(Whhht - 1 + Wxhxt + bh)$$

Explanation: The new hidden state (ht) is a function of the previous hidden state (ht–1ht–1) and the current input (xt). This allows the network to "remember" past information, making it ideal for sequential data.

Such ensemble methods as Random Forests and Gradient Boosting Machines have also shown to be effective when modelling something such as predicting recession (Masini et al., 2023). Forecasting is mostly done to guide policy (Alessi & Detken, 2018).

Recent advancements in AI and data-driven modeling have profoundly transformed central banking research, especially in forecasting, stress testing, and systemic risk assessment. Machine learning methods have shown that they are better than traditional econometric models at capturing non-linear macroeconomic dynamics. Medeiros et al. (2021) demonstrate that machine learning techniques surpass traditional DSGE and VAR models, particularly in the context of structural breaks. This supports the larger claim that AI-based methods work better in economies that change quickly. The addition of synthetic data makes these capabilities even better. Yoon et al. (2019) introduce TimeGAN, a generative framework that generates realistic time-series data while maintaining temporal dependencies, rendering it especially suitable for macro-financial simulations. Assefa et al. (2020) also show how synthetic data can make financial applications (such as credit risk modeling and AML systems) better. This shows that synthetic data is clearly useful for central bank stress-testing pipelines.

The significance of synthetic stress testing is underscored in the macro-financial literature. Cont (2022) emphasizes that synthetic scenarios facilitate a comprehensive evaluation of tail risks and systemic contagion mechanisms that cannot be deduced from restricted historical crises. This is in line with Aldasoro et al. (2023), who show that network models give us a structural basis for understanding systemic weaknesses. This lets synthetic data take the analysis to crisis pathways that we haven't seen before. At the same time, problems with real-world data, like delays in reporting and not being used very often, are still big problems. Giannone et al. (2008) were among the first to show that nowcasting methods can get real-time signals from high-frequency data. This is a partial solution to the problem of data latency, but it is still limited by the lack of empirical observations.

Deep learning applications in central banks also help us learn more about AI's strengths and weaknesses. The European Central Bank's recent study (ECB, 2024b) uses neural networks (NNs) to predict inflation and shows how models that are only trained on past macroeconomic data are still weak to new shocks. This shows how important it is to add synthetic data to models. Privacy restrictions make things even more complicated. According to Jordon et al. (2019), PATE-GAN can be used to make synthetic datasets that protect privacy, which can help organizations get around rules and privacy concerns when working with sensitive financial data. Masini et al. (2023) show that machine learning models are better at predicting recessions and assessing the economy in real time. These technical advances work well with more general advances in machine learning in forecasting. From an institutional standpoint, the initial integration of machine learning in central banking, as examined by Bholat (2017), offers significant insights into the operational, governance, and data-quality challenges that persist in the development of contemporary hybrid real-synthetic forecasting systems.

2.3 CONCEPTUAL FRAMEWORK

This section identifies the conceptual framework that shall be used to guide this research. The framework is formulated to compare the application of real versus synthetic data in the description of AI forecasting models in the context of a central bank in a structured scenery (Table 2.2).

While the detailed trade-off comparisons are presented in the table, it is much more intuitive to see the trade-offs in graphical form. Figure 2.1 presents a pictorial summary of these comparative profiles indicating the contrasting strengths of each data.

Table 2.2 Comparative framework of real vs. synthetic data in AI models

Dimension	*Real data AI models*	*Synthetic data AI models*
Accuracy	**Benchmark:** Represents the "ground truth." High accuracy on historical data but struggles with sparse, unseen events (e.g., crises).	**Proxy-based:** Accuracy is contingent on the fidelity of the synthetic data. Can improve model robustness by generating rare event data but risks introducing artifacts if the generative model is flawed.
Privacy	**High Risk:** Involves sensitive, personally identifiable, or commercially confidential information. Governed by strict regulations (e.g., GDPR), limiting data use and sharing.	**High Preservation:** Data is artificially generated, breaking direct links to real entities. Can be engineered with formal guarantees like differential privacy, enabling safer data sharing.
Cost	**High & Ongoing:** Dominated by the cost of collection, cleaning, labelling, and secure storage of vast, continuous data streams.	**High Upfront, Low Marginal:** Dominated by high initial computational costs and expertise for training generative models. However, the marginal cost of generating additional data is near-zero.
Explainability (XAI)	**More Direct:** Model outputs can be traced back to observable, real-world economic events, making policy justification more straightforward.	**More Abstract:** Introduces an extra layer of abstraction—the generative model itself. Explaining a forecast requires justifying both the predictive model and the synthetic data it was trained on.
Forecasting Efficiency	**Limited by Lags:** Efficiency is constrained by the inherent publication lags of official data (e.g., quarterly GDP), creating a reactive posture.	**High Efficiency:** Data can be generated on-demand, enabling rapid prototyping, real-time scenario analysis, and extensive stress testing without waiting for real-world data releases.

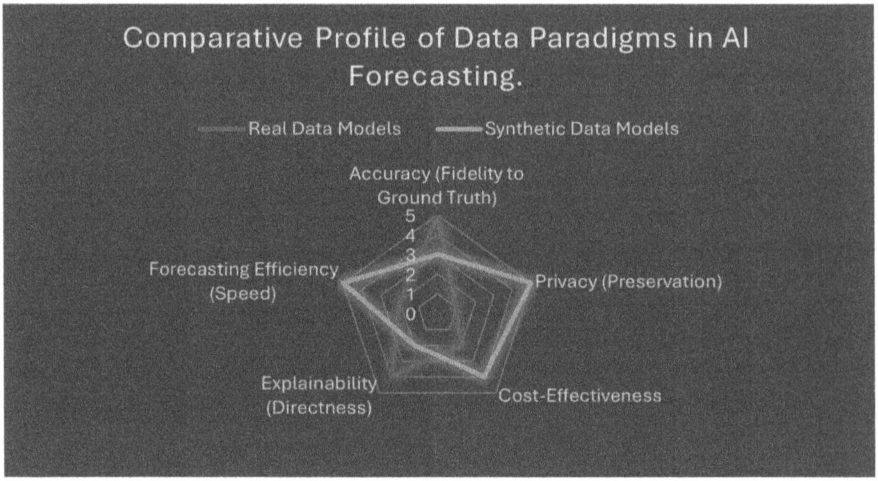

Figure 2.1 Comparative profile of data paradigms in AI forecasting (BIS, 2023)

2.3.1 Anchoring the framework in international standards

To give empirical weight to this comparison in the operational reality of central banking, the framework rests on two major institutional perspectives. The first is the Function Model of the BIS (2023) which conceives of forecasting as a pipeline from Data Ingestion to Model Training & Execution to Output Analysis & Policy Decision. This framework situates itself directly within the first two stages in which the choice between data and synthetic data becomes a very important choice at the Data Ingestion phase (Table 2.3).

Table 2.3 A unified framework for AI data strategy in central banking

	BIS stage: Data ingestion	*BIS stage: Model training*	*BIS stage: Output analysis*
High Preparedness	Dual Pipeline: Ingest both real data and validated synthetic data streams	Hybrid Models: Pre-train on synthetic, fine-tune/ validate on real.	Integrated Insights: Combine baseline forecast with synthetic stress-test distributions.
Medium Preparedness	Augmentation: Use synthetic data to fill gaps or for privacy in non-critical datasets.	Experimentation: Use synthetic data to train research models or test robustness of existing models	Comparative Analysis: Compare outputs from models trained on real vs. augmented data.
Low Preparedness	Foundation: Focus on cleaning and governing real-world data sources.	Baseline Models: Develop and master AI/ML models using only verified real-world data.	Forecast Validation: Focus on back-testing and validating the accuracy of the baseline forecast.

In terms of strategy, the matrix suggests an operational mode of displaying data interventions along the BIS pipeline (columns) against varying levels of institutional readiness determined by the IMF's AI Preparedness Index (rows).

Benefits of the Dual-Pipeline Architecture A dual-pipeline approach stands as the strategic solution to the original dilemma of speed versus accuracy. A central bank could maintain the credibility of its predictions and build that resilience against uncertainty by concurrently running two streams of engagement.

The Ground-Truth Pipeline delivering data toward an official anchor forecast. The **Simulation Pipeline:** Testing policy through risk and trial using synthetic data. The union of these pipelines would have the final payoffs.

Beyond Forecasting: A move from prediction drawn from one outcome. It is the capacity to stress-test the official model on thousands of realistically plausible scenarios that uncovers blind spots and tail risks that are not able to be seen with limited data.

Safe and Agile Policy Simulation: Constructs a "digital twin" of the economy against which different policy interventions can be tested in a consequence free environment before attempting implementation, resulting in better policy design.

Unlocking Constrained Data: Connecting the gap between privacy and scarcity. Generative models will generate massive amounts of "privacy safe" synthetic data from sensitive sources leading to pervasive research and model training that would not otherwise be achieved.

2.4 METHODOLOGY

This section lays the empirical framework for testing the main hypothesis: Incremental incorporation of synthetic data in forecasting would enable a central bank to forecast error-free especially during structural breaks.

2.4.1 Research design

Firstly, in order to ground the research in a real-world context we extract a failure in forecasting. The analysis of Federal Reserve inflation forecasts in Table 2.1 that we produced, serves as our motivating case study as it showcases the limits of traditional models in the face of the inflation following COVID.

Based on this, our research design is a structured comparative analysis using case-based approaches with the BIS sandbox environments. The experiment simulates the forecasting of a major macroeconomic variable through a structural break (e.g., core inflation) using three different scenarios that correspond to our Preparedness Maturity Model:

Scenario A (Low Prep): The baseline model uses only historical data.
Scenario B (Medium Prep): Model trained on historical data augmented with synthetic samples.
Scenario C (High Prep): Advanced model pre-trained on vast synthetic data and fine-tuned on historical data.

2.4.2 Data sources

The authenticity of our experiment hinges on relevant authoritative datasets. Last but not least, we will combine both synthetic data sources with examples.

Primary Real-World Data: Time series data collected over the years from the BIS Statistical warehouses and the ECB Statistical Data Warehouse. This includes macroeconomic indicators such as inflation, GDP, unemployment etc., and financial variables such as credit growth, interest rate spreads, etc.
Primary Synthetic Data: BIS synthetic datasets created from projects such as Project Gaia will be used. It is critical because it is designed explicitly to model realistic financial networks and economic scenarios where tail-risk events could plausibly occur though they have not previously occurred in history.
The Supplementary Data: IMF's International Financial Statistics will have additional data for cross-validation with respect to the extension of the geographical scope of analysis or the timeline of analysis.

2.4.3 Analytical techniques

Comparative analytical approach is meant to strictly compare the performance of models representing each preparedness level.

Model Training: A battery of machine learning models adaptable to the complexity presented by each scenario will be employed.
Scenarios A & B (Low/Medium Prep): Tree-based ensemble models such as Random Forest and XGBoost will be used. These models are powerful for capturing non-linear relationships in tabular data and serve as a strong baseline for the augmented data scenario.
In the third picture, High Prepare: The LSTM network is a sequential learning model. This design is suitable for time-series forecasting and works very well for large synthetic datasets in the pre-training/fine tuning.
Performance Evaluation: Reserving a comprehensive set of metrics for the performance evaluation of the models.

The predictive accuracy for point forecasts will be quantified using the Mean Absolute Error and the Root Mean Squared Error.

An example here would be event predictions, particularly forecasting an economic quarter in recession mode: In fact, the false positive rate is very important to understanding how a model likes to raise alarms. The compromise of precision and recall will be made with the use of the F1 Score.

2.5 AI FORECASTING MODELS IN CENTRAL BANKING

2.5.1 Use cases for AI forecasting

Public expectations have always been difficult to manage, and this in itself becomes one of the defining problems of new age policymaking. Central bank functions matched with AI could eventually allow algorithmic capabilities to address these challenges.

The other macro-variable is Nowcasting: AI algorithms perform nowcasting (e.g., inflation GDP) analyzing millions of high-frequency data points such as credit card transactions, mobility data, or online job postings. The Federal Reserve Bank of New York managed to project the collapse under COVID-19 with an index just days ahead of the official data-gathering effort which reduces the information lag from months to days altogether.

2.5.1.1 Dynamic stress testing and systemic risk identification

AI can dynamically stress test synthetic data allowing distinction from historical scenarios. The case in point is climate-related financial risk modeling by the BIS Innovation Hub under Project Gaia. Such an approach permits us to simulate new forward looking shocks (e.g., cyber-attacks on payment systems) in the course of identifying hidden systemic vulnerabilities that are inherently non-linear to the finance network.

2.5.1.2 Behavioral finance incorporated through NLP

By employing NLP techniques, central banks can assess textual content from the news and social media to produce real-time indices for measuring economic sentiment. ECB research has shown the sentiment from tweets can through a time lag lead official survey-based inflation expectations providing these authorities with an essential early warning signal of shifts in public perception (Figure 2.2).

2.5.2 Model architecture: From shallow learning to hybrid AI

The selection of model architecture is very important and relies on the task that is being performed and the maturity of the data at the central bank. We

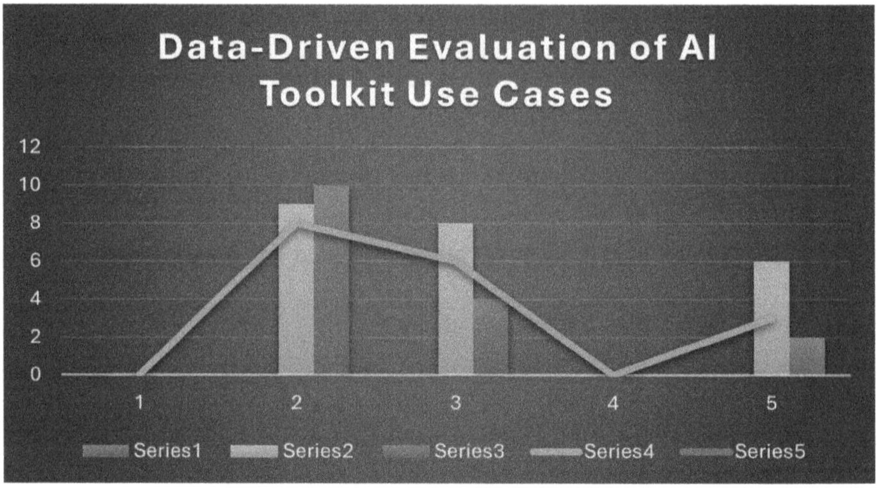

Figure 2.2 Data-driven evaluation of AI toolkit use cases (BIS, 2023)

can identify the relevant architectures in three broad categories that directly refer to our Preparedness Maturity Model.

2.5.2.1 An overview of AI architectures

Shallow Learning (e.g., XGBoost, Random Forest): These models are workhorses for structured, tabular data. In a central banking context they are excellent for the "Low" and "Medium Preparedness" scenarios. For example, improving a baseline inflation forecast by introducing a wider set of traditional economic variables. Some advantages are essentially high performance on standard tasks with moderate interpretability.

Deep Learning (e.g., LSTMs, Transformers): These NN architectures serve the "High Preparedness" tier. They are best able to learn from large, complex, and sequential data. LSTMs are specially built for time series data such as inflation while Transformers identify long range complex dependencies across many hundreds of economic indicators for the actual understanding of systemic risk root cause (Table 2.4).

In terms of what really counts in central bank forecasting models and their output this is the ultimate test. Now that we have defined the architectures for our three preparedness levels—Low/Model A, Medium/Model B, and High/Model C—we shall be comparing and contrasting their output based on the methodology we have proposed. The analysis is based on the practical dimensions that matter most for policymakers, which are accuracy, timeliness, stability, and interpretability (Table 2.5).

Table 2.4 AI model architectures for central banking

Architecture type	*Key models*	*Primary central bank role*	*Link to our framework*
Shallow Learning	XGBoost, Random Forest	Enhancing baseline forecasts with tabular data.	Low/Medium Preparedness
Deep Learning	LSTM, Transformers	Forecasting with complex, sequential data; crisis modelling.	High Preparedness
Generative AI	GANs, Agent-Based Models	Creating synthetic data for training and stress testing.	Powers High Preparedness

Table 2.5 Comparative evaluation of forecasting model outputs

Evaluation criterion	*Model A: Low prep (XGBoost on real data)*	*Model B: Medium prep (XGBoost on augmented data)*	*Model C: High prep (hybrid LSTM/transformer)*
Accuracy (Stable Periods)	High	High	Very High
Accuracy (Crisis / Structural Break)	**Low.** Fails to capture turning points; anchored to outdated historical patterns.	**Low-to-Moderate.** Shows some delayed reaction but still significantly underestimates the shock.	**High.** Captures non-linear dynamics and provides an early, more accurate signal of the break.
Timeliness	**Poor.** Acts as a lagging indicator, confirming a crisis only after it has occurred.	**Moderate.** Shows some leading capability but with a significant lag behind the initial shock.	**Excellent.** Designed to function as an early warning system, reacting to initial signs of instability.
Stability (Forecast Volatility)	**High (Inertial).** Forecasts are very stable but for the wrong reason—they fail to react to new information.	**Moderate.** More responsive than Model A but can exhibit some volatility as it tries to fit new data to old patterns.	**Responsive (Managed Volatility).** Reacts decisively to significant new information but is stabilized by its foundational pre-training.
Interpretability	**High.** Techniques like SHAP values can explain feature contributions, making it transparent to policymakers.	**High.** Same high level of interpretability as Model A.	**Low.** The model is a "black box," making direct causal attribution difficult. Trust is built via process, not direct inspection.

2.5.2.2 The Stability vs. Responsiveness Trade-off

This is called a content model. Policies are based on models that are completely inconsistent with every new data point that enters the model. Model A provides high stability but is extraordinarily inertial. This stability is frequently perceived as a disadvantage by the model for adjustment. Model C is exceedingly responsive under normal circumstances; it performs at an optimum, easily compensating under urgent deadlines when new data correlates with previously identified high-risk patterns from its training. The tuning phase is important here, as it regulates the model response to match particular local economic parameters and curb erratic behavior from the model.

2.6 COMPARING SYNTHETIC AND REAL-WORLD DATA UTILIZATION

At the heart of the preparedness model is its architecture, which is a strategic interplay between real-world and synthetic data. Understanding the distinctions between these two classes of data is essential in understanding how their mix provides advantages that aren't available from the use of either type alone. Real-world data are those sets of historical observations pertaining to the economy and finance, such as past GDP numbers, inflation rates, or market statistics. This data type is a direct representation of events in time.

Conversely, synthetic data is produced through algorithms that replicate statistical properties of real data. In this case, generative models from Project Gaia at BIS produce multiple plausible economic futures (Figure 2.3).

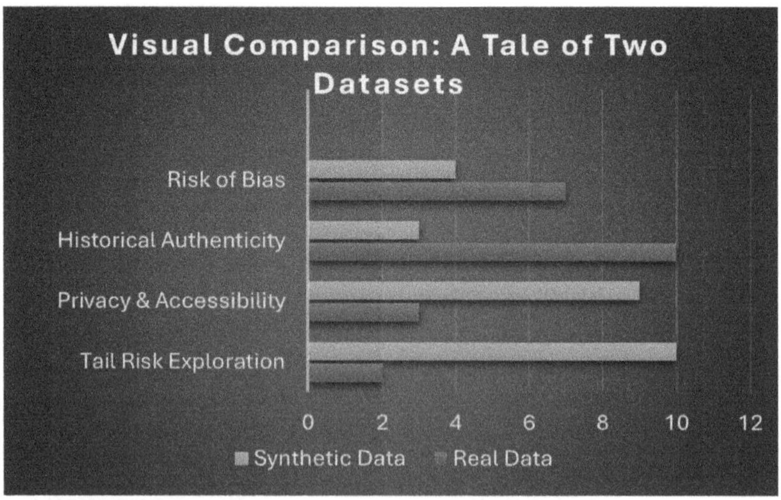

Figure 2.3 Visual comparison: A tale of two datasets (BIS, 2023)

2.6.1 Advantages and risks: A comparative view

The competence of one type of data is weakness for another data type. Strong complementarity is achieved.

Benefits of Synthetic Data, Exploring Tail Risks: The biggest advantage possible for central banks. With synthetic data it becomes possible to generate internally consistent crisis scenarios e.g., climate shocks or newly devised financial contagions) to have models extracting from occurrences that have never occurred before.

Overcoming Privacy & Regulatory Obstacles: Having zero real individual or firm-level information helps evade significant legal and reputational risks in using confidential data thus providing greater scope and safety for experimentation.

Accelerating Innovation: Research teams can have on-demand access to a huge volume of realistic datasets, thereby significantly shortening the development cycle for new models without waiting for clearance to use sensitive internal data.

2.6.1.1 Risks and limitations of synthetic data

'Model World' Overfitting Risk: The bias or artifact of the generative model itself can be learned by the AI model not necessarily the true dynamics of the economics. Fine-tuning is good in predicting a simulation, but it falls short when predicting real data.

Bias Amplification: The synthesized data is prone to exaggerating those biases and stereotyping in unreal simulation if the base data for training the generator is biased, for example, underrepresented by certain market behaviors.

No Real Signals: Synthetic data would not do anything new and prove to be just a better extrapolation rather than a new observation.

2.6.1.2 Real loses irreplaceable role of real-world data

This is also giving authentic unexpected signals, which is required for any model anchor but ground truth. She saves synthetic trained models from orbiting into sheer fantasy. That's why fine-tuning does not compromise in our "High Preparedness" model.

2.7 RISKS AND CHALLENGES OF SYNTHETIC DATA USE

2.7.1 Risk: Falsely positive and unreliable outputs

An AI model trained on crises would eventually get jittery with even the slightest real-world deviations, overreacting to provide false alarms and damaging policy decisions as a result.

An absolute "human-in-the-loop" type of intervention, whereby any model output becomes an input to expert analysis, rather than an automatic triggering of policy.

2.7.2 Risk: Embedded bias

Input or assumption biases present in the original real-world data or behind the generative model used could be biased and exacerbated via the model output leading to unjust or imprecise results.

Rigorous data governance and auditing of real and synthetic datasets to discover and to correct biases before subjecting them to training.

2.7.3 Risks: Ethical and explainability issues

The differentiation and deprivation of the public transparency and accountability might constitute the core of an assertion of the bank thus making it difficult to explain basically any policy decision made under the influence of AI.

Concentrate on process transparency that explains the rigorous validation, testing, and human oversight framework instead of trying to explain the internal mechanics of the model.

2.7.4 Risk: Loss of empirical grounding

If we become too reliant on synthetic data and ignore critical data from the real world, we might slowly increase the chance of our models diverging from economic reality.

2.8 SUPERVISORY AND ANOMALY DETECTION ROLE OF AI

After forecasting, AI's most imminent impact for the central banks is in the verification and detection of anomalies by automating the monitoring of huge transactional data for fraud prevention, Anti-Money Laundering or Combating Financing of Terrorism, and systemic risk.

2.8.1 How it works

Synthetic transaction data can be used for training AI models to recognize patterns of new illicit activities from complex money laundering typologies without compromising sensitive personal data. In a practical sense Graph Analytics and Generative AI can analyze transactional networks in real time to point out unusual clusters or behaviors diverging from established patterns.

Governing frameworks and key risks: All such impressive feats are under regulation by the EU AI Act 2024, BIS AI Principles, and ISO/IEC 42001 that seek to mitigate the following kinds of risks:

Bias: Because the model is trained on incorrect faulty data it may generate bias in flagging certain demographic or geographies, thus requiring comprehensive fairness audits to cover the effect.

Data Misuse & Surveillance: All transactions are constantly monitored, raising serious issues regarding calling for strict purposes for which data is collected and data minimization. Unexplainable Outputs ("Black Box"). This shows a legal and ethical quagmire rendering it impossible to justify by which actions (e.g., freezing an account) the supervisory authority will base its judgment on the averred untrustworthy outputs of the AI.

It becomes the central dilemma for all supervisors while it lessens privacy risks by decreasing the need for personal data in training synthetic data aggravates the transparency issue and complicates the justification of real AI decision making.

2.9 POLICY IMPLICATIONS AND REGULATORY CONCERNS

The impact of the incorporation of AI into the central banks does not occur in a vacuum, but is very much determined by the changing regulatory initiatives for its successful use across different nations.

2.9.1 Regulatory and responsible AI frameworks

A set of edicts and principles is in the process of being laid out in an attempt to create a de facto global standard applicable to AI concerning the financial industry.

Highlighted here are regulations: The EU AI Act 2024 sets a worldwide precedent characterizing high-risk AI systems whose application would most probably pertain to monetary policy or financial supervision. High-risk classification is subject to stringent data governance, risk management, transparency, and human oversight requirements.

Principles: These requirements are mirrored by the BIS AI Principles and the internal guidelines of the ECB which present the need for understanding and accountability from the lowest level of the models to the highest.

Responsible AI Practice: This essentially translates to three key responsibilities for every AI-inclined central bank. Modeling should be critically examined with respect to avoiding historic biases from bad data documented adequately with an audit trail even if the model behaves like a "Black Box" complexity is in direct proportion to the work that the AI aims to perform thus adding value.

2.9.2 Implementation: From research to reality

Connecting the Gap Between Theory and Practice: Some of the major projects include Gaia (for climate risk modeling) and Ellipse (NLP application for analyzing economic news). They exemplify the use of AI and synthetic data in dealing with risks that are difficult for older models to handle.

Developed vs. Developing Economies: Developed economies (e.g., ECB, BoE) proceed much more cautiously putting governance concerns first in the already established frameworks of employing AI. The regulators' challenge now consists in finding a space for emerging technologies in the legacy systems under a very tight regulatory system.

Developing economies like Saudi Arabia or India are more flexible, usually opting for leapfrogging new technologies to put up completely new systems. Here, AI is used in monitoring digital transactions financial inclusion with emphasis on speed and urgency.

2.9.3 Summary of comparative trade-off analysis

Opting for a hybrid AI strategy in lieu of conventional AI entails substantial trade-offs regarding performance, costs, and risks. The perspectives we have are given in Table 2.6.

Table 2.6 Comparative analysis of forecasting approaches

Criterion	*Traditional models (real data only)*	*Hybrid AI models (real + synthetic)*
Forecast Accuracy	High in stable periods. Low during structural breaks (e.g., misses crisis turning points).	Very High in stable periods. High during structural breaks (designed to anticipate novel shocks).
Cost of Implementation	Lower initial tech/talent cost. Higher ongoing compliance cost due to handling of sensitive real data.	Higher initial cost (compute power, specialized talent, model development). Lower ongoing compliance cost for parts using privacy-preserving synthetic data.
Risk Incidence	Lower "black box" risk. Higher risk of missing a crisis (e.g., the "transitory inflation" error).	Higher "black box" and "false positive" risk. Lower risk of being blindsided by a novel crisis.

2.10 CASE STUDIES

This concluding section proposes a hypothetical case for the twin pipeline model recommended and provides real time examples of how such concepts are adopted by genuine institutions.

2.10.1 BIS application of synthetic data: Project Gaia

This illustrates how one can generate synthetic data and investigate novel risks with it. Modeling is projected in the following manner, specifically with respect to systemic risk arising from climate change, a source that has no historical precedent.

Method: How BIS' Project Gaia will simulate unintended carbon tax spikes and natural disasters as shocks in public and private interconnected financial institutions using synthetic data, simulate insolvency events and simulate the impact on asset values as well.

Relevance: It provides the core technology necessary for synthetic streams, a classic example of exploring "black swan" events with synthetic data.

2.10.2 ECB real-data application: NN forecasting

This case study demonstrates how an organization uses contemporary models on conventional data. The goal is to increase core inflation forecasts' accuracy.

Method: To examine intricate, non-linear patterns in historical, real-world macroeconomic data (such as historical GDP, unemployment, and inflation) the ECB has conducted research using deep NNs.

Relevance: This is an advanced "Medium Preparedness" organization. It is susceptible to genuinely unprecedented structural breaks because it has sophisticated modelling capabilities but is still limited by historical data.

2.10.3 Dual pipeline model: A hypothetical inflation stress test

Here, we utilize the first two instances' advantages to demonstrate how our proposed "High Preparedness" model would work.

Goal: To give a thorough proactive assessment of inflation risk in the event of a geopolitical energy shock.

Approach: Synthetic pre-training. To learn the intricate dynamics of the supply shock and second-round effects on wages and prices a deep learning model is first trained on a large synthetic dataset representing thousands of simulated scenarios of an energy crisis.

Fine-tuning (Real): The outcome is calibrated on the most recent inflation and economic data coming from the central banks for the good of the pre-trained model.

Output: The model does not just estimate pointwise it gives a full risk assessment. Our base projection for inflation is 3.2%. Yet the model shows there is a 20% chance that inflation could be above 6%.

2.11 CONCLUSION AND RECOMMENDATIONS

The existing economic landscape is under multiplication by tremors of fast structural changes which have magnified the shortcomings of classical central bank forecasting. This paper proposes the ones we consider a very promising future, aimed at AI capabilities in combination with finely honed applications of real versus synthetic data. A Preparedness Maturity Model is suggested to chart an evolutionary pathway for central banks in an increasingly uncertain environment. AI models are to a greater or lesser degree well noted for their capability to identify complex non-linear patterns from contemporary economies particularly when deep-learning frameworks are employed. To this end, synthetic data will have to be used to ensure that models are trained not only on past crises but also to a limited extent on future crises.

2.11.1 Recommendations for central banks

The Dual-Pipeline Hybrid Model: We suggest that central banks adopt a high preparedness model with respect to investment in generative models to create artificial data for pre-training and conduct stress tests within the governance frameworks of the data used for fine tuning.

Regulation and Transparency to the Rescue: Organizations must commit to great governance with respect to the use of these tools on the basis of frameworks like BIS Principles and the EU AI Act. Further, the emphasis should change from an unattainable goal of model "transparency" to a more achievable goal of process "transparency," ensuring visibility and accountability at every stage of model validation and oversight.

Encouragement for Human to AI Collaboration: AI models must be regarded as instruments that assist decision-making rather than automated decision-makers. It should provide a necessary "human-in-the-loop" framework to interpret results, eliminate false positives, and ensure that final policy decisions are well-founded.

2.11.2 Future research directions

One of the many implications from findings in this study is that it immediately opens many avenues for research.

Generative AI in Simulation Policy: Shifting from full-fledged digital twin economies that can simulate and entirely demonstrate the impact of a policy before implementation is initiated.

Risk Forecasting: The refined hybrid model issues alerts for prospective debt crises through the combined use of unstructured geopolitical risk data together with economic data.

Real-Time Adaptive Regulation: Investigating how AI can assist whereby the supervisory standards are changed according to perceived risk levels in the financial system.

BIBLIOGRAPHY

Alessi, L., & Detken, C. (2018). Identifying excessive credit growth and leverage. Journal of Financial Stability, 35, 215–225.

Assefa, S. A., Dervovic, D., Mahfouz, M., Tillman, R. E., Reddy, P., & Veloso, M. (2020). Generating synthetic data in finance: Opportunities, challenges and pitfalls. In Proceedings of the First ACM International Conference on AI in Finance (ICAIF '20) (pp. 1–8). ACM.

Athey, S. (2019). The impact of machine learning on economics. In A. Agrawal, J. Gans, & A. Goldfarb (Eds.), The economics of artificial intelligence: An agenda (pp. 507–547). University of Chicago Press.

Bank for International Settlements (BIS). (2021). AI and the future of central banking. BIS Papers, No. 122.

Bank for International Settlements (BIS). (2022). Machine learning-based AML/CFT supervision. BIS Innovation Hub & Hong Kong Monetary Authority.

Bank for International Settlements (BIS). (2023). Project Gaia: For greener finance. https://www.bis.org/hub/projects/gaia.htm (Accessed: October 2025).

Bank for International Settlements (BIS). (2024a). About the BIS Innovation Hub. https://www.bis.org/hub/(Accessed: October 2025).

Bank for International Settlements (BIS). (2024b). Artificial intelligence (AI). https://www.bis.org/topic/artificial_intelligence.htm (Accessed: October 2025).

Bank for International Settlements (BIS). (2024c). BIS Statistics Explorer. https://stats.bis.org/ (Accessed: October 2025).

Bank for International Settlements (BIS) Innovation Hub. (2022). Project Ellipse: A platform for real-time economic insights from news.

Bank for International Settlements (BIS) Innovation Hub. (2023). Project Gaia: Climate related financial risk analysis.

Bholat, D. (2017). Machine learning at central banks. Bank of England Staff Working Paper No. 674.

Carstens, A. (2023). I, robot? Central banking in the AI era. Speech at the Federal Reserve Bank of San Francisco.

Cavallo, A. (2013). Online and official price indexes: Measuring Argentina's inflation. Journal of Monetary Economics, 60(2), 152–165.

Cazzaniga, M., Jaumotte, F., Li, L., Melina, G., Panton, A. J., Pizzinelli, C., Rockall, E., & Mendes Tavares, M. (2024). Gen-AI: Artificial intelligence and the future of work. IMF Staff Discussion Note SDN/2024/001. Washington, DC: International Monetary Fund.

Christiano, L. J., Eichenbaum, M., & Evans, C. L. (2005). Nominal rigidities and the dynamic effects of a shock to monetary policy. Journal of Political Economy, 113(1), 1–45.

Dwork, C. (2008). Differential privacy: A survey of results. In Theory and Applications of Models of Computation (TAMC 2008), Lecture Notes in Computer Science (Vol. 4978, pp. 1–19). Springer.

European Central Bank. (2024a). ECB Statistical Data Warehouse. https://sdw.ecb.europa.eu/ (Accessed: October 2025).
European Central Bank. (2024b). Neural networks for inflation forecasting. ECB Working Paper Series No. 2856.
European Central Bank. (2024c). Research. https://www.ecb.europa.eu/pub/research/html/index.en.html (Accessed: October 2025).
European Commission. (2024). The AI Act. https://digitalstrategy.ec.europa.eu/en/policies/ai-act (Accessed: October 2025).
Federal Reserve Bank of New York. (2024). Weekly Economic Index (WEI). https://www.newyorkfed.org/research/policy/weekly-economic-index (Accessed: October 2025).
Giannone, D., Reichlin, L., & Small, D. (2008). Nowcasting: The real-time informational content of macroeconomic data. Journal of Monetary Economics, 55(4), 665–676.
Gogas, P., & Papadimitriou, T. (2021). Machine learning in economics and finance. Computational Economics, 57(1), 1–4.
Goodfellow, I., Pouget-Abadie, J., Mirza, M., Xu, B., Warde-Farley, D., Ozair, S., Courville, A., & Bengio, Y. (2014). Generative adversarial nets. Advances in Neural Information Processing Systems, 27, 2672–2680.
Goodman, B., & Flaxman, S. (2017). European Union regulations on algorithmic decision making and a "right to explanation". AI Magazine.
International Monetary Fund. (2024). IMF Data. https://data.imf.org/ (Accessed: October 2025).
International Organization for Standardization (ISO). (2023). ISO/IEC 42001: Information technology Artificial intelligence Management system.
Jordon, J., et al. (2018). PATE-GAN: Generating synthetic data with differential privacy guarantees. International Conference on Learning Representations (ICLR).
Jordon, J., Yoon, J., & van der Schaar, M. (2019). PATE-GAN: Generating synthetic data with differential privacy guarantees. International Conference on Learning Representations (ICLR).
Lewis, D. F., et al. (2020). The New York Fed Staff Nowcast. Federal Reserve Bank of New York Staff Reports, No. 759.
Masini, R. P., Medeiros, M. C., & Mendes, E. F. (2023). Machine learning advances for time series forecasting. Journal of Economic Surveys, 37(1), 76–111.
Medeiros, M. C., Vasconcelos, G. F. R., Veiga, Á., & Zilberman, E. (2021). Forecasting inflation in a data-rich environment: The benefits of machine learning methods. Journal of Business & Economic Statistics, 39(1), 98–119.
Mehrabi, N., Morstatter, F., Saxena, N., Lerman, K., & Galstyan, A. (2021). A survey on bias and fairness in machine learning. ACM Computing Surveys, 54(6), 1–35.
Shapiro, A. H., Sudhof, M., & Wilson, D. J. (2022). Measuring news sentiment. Journal of Econometrics, 228(2), 221–243.
Smets, F., & Wouters, R. (2007). Shocks and frictions in US business cycles: A Bayesian DSGE approach. American Economic Review, 97(3), 586–606.
Smyl, S. (2020). A hybrid method of exponential smoothing and recurrent neural networks for time series forecasting. International Journal of Forecasting, 36(1), 75–85.
Thanh-Tung, H., & Tran, T. (2020). Catastrophic forgetting and mode collapse in GANs. In 2020 International Joint Conference on Neural Networks (IJCNN) (pp. 1–10). IEEE.
Tucker, A., et al. (2019). Generating Realistic Time Series Data with the Time-series Generative Adversarial Network (TimeGAN). NeurIPS.
Yoon, J., Jarrett, D., & van der Schaar, M. (2019). TimeGAN: Generating realistic time-series data. Advances in Neural Information Processing Systems (NeurIPS).

Chapter 3

A new innovative AI-based index

Anadolu University Economic Confidence Index

Hasan Murat Ertuğrul, Burçhan Sakarya, and Onur Polat

3.1 INTRODUCTION: BACKGROUND AND DRIVING FORCES

This chapter presents a novel, high-frequency Economic Confidence Index (ECI) constructed using natural language processing (NLP) and sentiment analysis on economic news articles for Turkish economy. Inspired by the S&P Twitter Sentiment Index, the model captures fluctuations in economic sentiment by analyzing public discourse in near real-time using large volumes of textual data scraped daily from Turkish news sites to create a web-based, artificial intelligence-driven index.

Confidence in the economy plays a critical role in shaping the real and financial outlook of the country. However, since many important economic indicators related to GDP, Industrial Production Index, Export, or Service Sector are published with substantial delays, confidence indices provide pioneering information to fill this gap. However, although there are different indices for measuring confidence in the national and international arena, there are various difficulties in terms of scope and method.

In classical approaches, methods based on a limited sample size, survey-based and limited to closed-ended questions are used. These approaches increase the "cost" burden as the sample size increases and bring with it the risk of "bias" in surveys and the problem of "respondent burden" as the number of questions increases.

In order to overcome such problems, news sites that include expert opinions stand out as an alternative and rich data source. By using texts obtained from news sites, the problems of "cost", "bias," and "respondent burden" encountered in classical trust index approaches can be largely eliminated.

3.2 LITERATURE

This literature survey is structured in twofold dimensions. One aims to provide an overview at the impact of confidence (sentiment) on business cycle. This question is also mentioned in the previous section to underline the

DOI: 10.1201/9781003656463-3

significance of the topic at hand. Second tier is built on to offer a survey of contemporary techniques, where this study's methodology is also a part.

Zarnowitz (1992), in his seminal work on business cycles points out that the interest in economic conditions, also displays a cyclical pattern, akin wave like movements in economic sentiment. Hence as described earlier new economic challenges of the global economy, it is evident that this recent interest is going to remain heightened for some foreseeable period. This wave of interest is most attached to the Keynes's (1937) "animal spirits" hypothesis. However, one can go even further as Beveridge (1917) that he posits that expectations are the main factor in economic fluctuations (see Dearle, 1909). The notion of business cycles and economic fluctuations was put on economic map by the works of Mitchell (1913). Building on this, Clarke (1917) has argued that changes in consumer confidence accelerate the mechanism that influences cyclical fluctuations. Parallel to this discussion, Pigou (1927) claimed that the psychological factors effects entrepreneurs in their decision-making process, as they become prone to making errors. These errors fluctuate the overall economy via rises and falls in investment decision. Along this literature of business cycles, these can be grouped as the theories of fluctuations based on sentiment, expectations and confidence of either consumers and/or entrepreneurs. We should also note that the deep literature on business-cycle measurement and conceptualization can be traced back to Juglar (1916), who demonstrated through extensive price and finance data that crises are merely brief phases in regular, wave-like fluctuations; Tugan-Baranovsky (1914), who identified swings in fixed-capital growth as the root cause; Wicksell (1907), who showed how mismatches between investment returns and the market interest rate drive cumulative boom-and-bust dynamics; Aftalion (2014), who emphasized the long lags in capital formation and the sensitivity of net investment to small consumption shifts; and Schumpeter (1939), who attributed cycles to clusters of innovations that disrupt old firms but ultimately improve resource use. Burns' (1969) paper is a foundational study in this field. Moreover, for measurement, the business cycles contributions of Burns and Mitchell (1946) must also be addressed.

Based on this perspective Shapiro et al. (2020) offers a line of causality from economic confidence (sentiment) to overall economic activity. This is tied to the notion that the economic state usually is influenced by an uncertainty—an uncertainty induced by out of system factors. This is the channel where Keynes's "animal spirits" comes into play. These animal spirits are basically the market psychology that should be captured, calculated or estimated via some tools. Moreover, since this spirit is not a numerical concept, this needs to be quantified and/or measures in some way. Furthermore, along with this main branch of thought, supplementary, and supporting vector of influence is also present. This channel captures the process through which expectations emerge from interactions across information nodes. This is somewhat like the self-fulfilling nature of markets. Spillover of information from one agent to another, hence placing economic confidence (sentiment) right at the center of the debate. Odendaal, et al. (2020) assesses these two channels as different lines of thought, while for both approaches sentiment and economic activity are highly correlated, making this a major indicator to monitor the economic activity.

In approaches that can be called the classical approach, limited by a narrow sample size, based on surveys, and constrained by closed-ended questions; as the sample size expands, the "cost" burden increases, "bias" occurs in question-and-answer responses, and "respondent burden" increases as the number of questions increases. The University of Michigan Consumer Confidence Index can be given as an example of confidence indices created with the classical approach. In the University of Michigan Consumer Confidence Index, telephone interviews are conducted with 500 families, asking 50 questions. The purpose of the survey is to obtain information about consumers' attitudes and behaviors, as well as their financial situations and expectations. On the 10th of each month, 60 percent of the survey results are announced in a preliminary report, and the final announcement is made on the first day of the following month. The questions relate to consumers' current and one-year-prior financial situations, their expectations for one year ahead, and the general economy's future 1 and 5 years ahead.

Important confidence indices in our country created according to the classical approach are the TURKSTAT ECI and the PMI Manufacturing Confidence Index.

The TURKSTAT ECI is a composite index that summarizes the evaluations, expectations, and trends of consumers and producers regarding the general economic situation, formed by weighing and combining the sub-indices of the consumer confidence index and the seasonally adjusted real sector, services, retail trade, and construction sector confidence indices. The sub-indices used in calculating the ECI are calculated using data compiled in the first two weeks of each month. An ECI greater than 100 indicates optimism regarding the general economic situation, while less than 100 indicates pessimism regarding the general economic situation.

The Purchasing Managers' Indices (PMI) created by IHS Markit are announced to the public in the form of monthly reports for sectors such as manufacturing, services, and construction (sector coverage varies from country to country) in over 40 developed and developing countries. In the survey organized to calculate the indices, participating companies are asked about the direction of development (increase/improvement or decrease/deterioration) of parameters such as production, new orders, stock levels, employment, supplier performance, and price trends. Diffusion indices are calculated for each of these parameters, and the PMI figure is reached using these indices. PMI values greater than 50 indicate an improvement or increase compared to the previous month, while values less than 50 are evaluated as deterioration or decrease compared to the previous month.

Despite the problems in the classical approach, web platforms emerge as an alternative data source. Additionally, in recent years, websites have developed with more people making comments/shares about the economy, financial markets, and stocks. Using these news sources, the problems of "cost," "bias," and "respondent burden" in classical confidence index approaches can be overcome to a very large extent.

The "S&P Twitter Sentiment Indices," first published globally by S&P Global at the end of 2021, aims to measure the performance of 200 S&P 500 companies. This index evaluates investors' and the general public's sentiment regarding the S&P 500 using large amounts of real-time data generated through tweets. The index, which classifies tweets as positive, negative, or neutral using NLP and machine learning (ML) techniques, provides insights into market sentiment that can influence trading strategies. The index is a valuable tool for investors who want to understand market trends, sentiment changes, and potential volatility in the S&P 500.

In the S&P Twitter Sentiment Index, the level of 100 generally represents neutral sentiment, indicating that the volume of positive and negative tweets related to the S&P 500 is balanced. Values above 100 indicate more positive sentiment, while values below 100 indicate more negative sentiment.

Recently, various researchers have been producing various indices using news-based and text mining methods. Among these indices, Caldara and Iacoviello (2022) produced a monthly geopolitical risk index starting from 1900 for the United States using six different newspaper reports. Economic policy uncertainty indices have been produced for different countries using similar methodology.

Avela and Lehmus (2020) created an economic uncertainty index for Finland using Finnish news sources with NLP (transformed naive-Bayes text classifier) and ML techniques. The index was found to have a strong and negative correlation with the Finnish consumer confidence index. Güneş et al. (2024) developed an index for Türkiye using sentiment analysis by utilizing 31,084 news items from Thomson Reuters and Financial Times and 12,900 reports from international organizations.

Utilizing AI-based indexes and use of semantics can be understood through the lens of sentiment analysis, which is a direct cross-section of NLP and ML, both of which are contained within the broader field of AI. The "use of semantics" is fundamental to understanding human language computationally, particularly in fields like Sentiment Analysis and NLP. They classify the existing literature into two main veins. The Early Research, where the study of the polarity and semantic orientation of words has been extensively explored, especially from the mid-to-late 1990s, citing works by Huettner and Subasic (2000) developed a cognitive linguistic model for sentiments based on fuzzy logic, while Hatzivassiloglou and McKeown (1997) propose a log-linear regression model to predict the orientation of two conjunctively joined adjectives. From these earlier initiatives to deeper semantic orientations models, one can say that the core goal of recent NLP approach is to "close the gap between what a computer understands, and sentiment expressed in a piece of text." This inherently involves semantic understanding, where challenges due to complexities like word disambiguation and syntactic ambiguity remains albeit diminishing rapidly.

In this study, taking an innovative step for the Turkish economy, a different and innovative confidence index from existing standard confidence indices, the Anadolu University Economic Confidence Index (ACI), will be introduced, created for the first time as a high-frequency web-based index using NLP models by utilizing texts from various news sites.

3.3 METHODOLOGY

The construction of the ECI in this study follows a multi-stage process combining data scraping, text preprocessing, sentiment classification, index normalization, and visualization. The following steps summarize the methodological framework:

3.3.1 Data collection and preprocessing

- **News Source Selection:** News articles containing predefined Turkish keywords related to economic and financial developments are scraped from Bloomberg website.
- **Text Cleaning:** The raw text is cleaned to remove irrelevant characters, HTML tags, and punctuation. Articles with invalid or missing timestamps are excluded.

3.3.2 Sentiment analysis using BERT

- **Model Setup:** We use the pre-trained model savasy/bert-base-turkish-sentiment-cased available from (HuggingFace: https://huggingface.co/savasy/bert-base-turkish-squad, Accessed: October 1, 2025). This BERT-based model is fine-tuned for Turkish sentiment classification and supports three classes: positive, neutral, and negative.
- **Tokenization and Prediction:** Each article is tokenized and fed into the model. The resulting logits are converted into probabilities using the SoftMax function.
- **Scoring Logic:** For each article, we extract the sentiment probabilities:
  - Positive sentiment score
  - Neutral sentiment score
  - Negative sentiment score

3.3.3 Daily sentiment aggregation

- For each day, the mean sentiment scores across all articles are computed:

$$Positive\,Score\,(PS) = \frac{Number\,of\,positive\,words\,in\,text}{Total\,number\,of\,words\,in\,text} \tag{3.1}$$

$$Nagative\, Score\,(NS) = \frac{Number\, of\, negative\, words\, in\, text}{Total\, numberof\, words\, in\, text} \tag{3.2}$$

$$Nautral\, Score\,(NES) = \frac{Number\, of\, neutral\, words\, in\, text}{Total\, number\, of\, words\, in\, text} \tag{3.3}$$

$$Confidence\, Index\,(CI) = PS - NS + \frac{NES}{2} \tag{3.4}$$

3.3.4 Weighting and Z-score calculation

Weighting:

Each news article is weighted based on its publication and popularity. For instance, let w_i denote the popularity weight of article i and CI_i be the confidence index of that article. Then the weighted confidence index is

$$CI_{weighted} = \sum_{i=1}^{n} w_i CI_i \tag{3.5}$$

Exponentially Weighted Average (EWA):

The EWA of daily indices for each topic is calculated as follows:

$$EWA_t = \alpha CI_t + (1-\alpha) EWA_{t-1} \tag{3.6}$$

where α is the smoothing coefficient.

Z-score Calculation and Normalization:

The Z-score of the monthly indices is calculated as follows:

$$Z = \frac{CI_{monthly} - \mu}{\sigma} \tag{3.7}$$

where μ is the monthly mean and σ is the standard deviation.

The Z-score is then normalized to the 0–100 range and the final confidence index is computed as follows:

$$CI_{final} = 50 + Z' \tag{3.8}$$

3.4 EMPIRICAL RESULTS

The ACI has a complementary nature to existing standard indices as an indicator that can react more quickly to economic events and has higher sensitivity to short-term developments compared to standard indices. Table 3.1

Table 3.1 ACI and TURKSTAT Economic Confidence Index

Date	*ACI**	*Change from previous month*	*TURKSTAT Economic Confidence Index**	*Change from previous month*
October 2024	97.50	1.30	98.00	3.00
November 2024	96.40	−1.10	97.10	−0.90
December 2024	95.20	−2.30	98.80	0.80
January 2025	97.90	+2.70	99.70	0.90
February 2025	97.60	−0.30	99.20	−0.50
March 2025	97.20	−0.40	100.80	1.60
April 2025	95.80	−1.40	96.60	4.20
May 2025	96.51	0.70	96.70	0.10
June 2025	96.53	0.02	96.71	0.01

Note: If the ACI and TURKSTAT Economic Confidence Index are above 100, confidence in the economy is at a positive level; if below 100, it is at a negative level. 100 indicates that confidence is neutral.

presents the trends of the ACI and TURKSTAT Economic Confidence Indices over the last 9 months.

As of June 2025, the ACI increased by 0.02 points compared to the previous month, reaching 96.53, below the critical threshold of 100. The TURKSTAT ECI showed an increase of 0.01 points in June 2025 compared to May 2025, also reaching 96.71, below the critical threshold of 100. The index has remained below the critical threshold of 100 for the last nine months and has largely moved in parallel with the TURKSTAT confidence index.

The relationship between the ACI and the TURKSTAT ECI was analyzed first through the traditional Granger causality test and then through the Quantile causality test. The Granger Causality Test Results are presented in Table 3.2.

According to the Granger causality test results, a unidirectional causality relationship was found from the ACI to the TURKSTAT Confidence Index.

Figure 3.1 presents the Quantile Causality relationship between the ACI and the TURKSTAT ECI.

Table 3.2 Granger causality test results

Direction of causality	*F statistic*	*Probability value*	*Result*
From TURKSTAT Confidence Index to ACI	1.87	0.14	No Causality
From ACI to TURKSTAT Confidence Index	4.26	0.02	Causality Exists

Note: The optimal lag length was determined as 1 using the Bayesian Information Criterion (BIC). All reported p-values are HAC (Heteroskedasticity and Autocorrelation Consistent) robust.

Figure 3.1 12-month rolling quantile causality: ACI to TURKSTAT Confidence Index

Figure 3.1 shows that quantile causality from the ACI to the TURKSTAT Confidence Index exhibits a dynamic structure over time. In the analysis conducted using 12-month rolling windows, it was determined that the causality relationship intensified in certain periods and differentiated depending on confidence levels (quantiles). Particularly during periods of economic stress (for example, the 2020 Covid-19 pandemic and the 2023 elections), causality was observed to strengthen. The causality effect became more pronounced in low and high confidence quantiles, highlighting the heterogeneous nature of economic confidence.

The results show that the ACI derived from news texts has a periodically strong explanatory effect on the TURKSTAT Confidence Index. However, it is understood that this relationship is not constant but rather varies according to time and confidence level. This situation reveals that the ACI can react more quickly to economic events and may be an indicator with higher short-term sensitivity compared to traditional indices.

3.5 CONCLUSION

These novel approaches also help policy makers not only to maneuver through mid-course of any policy implementation but also give them flexibility to investigate segmented insights. By appropriate tagging specifically, geography defined or demographic segments might be designed. With the help of this type of innovations in monitoring, policymakers could tailor stimulus or support programs with surgical precision, for instance, whether hospitality-sector sentiment rebounded after a particular wage-subsidy announcement.

Additionally, as mentioned earlier in countries with limited survey-capacity (both financially and adequate infrastructure for conducting surveys), authorities can immediately make use of such techniques to fill gaps—often at a fraction of the cost. This Türkiye-focused, LLM-based sentiment index is a prime example, leveraging news portals to track confidence when conventional surveys struggled with low and biased response rates. As geopolitical risks (e.g. Ukraine war, Middle East tensions) compounded pandemic uncertainty, high-frequency sentiment tools became a core part of "stress-testing" exercises—letting central banks simulate how a sudden narrative-shock (say, a spike in negative events, news) might ripple through economic confidence, credit spreads, or consumer spending.

In sum, the COVID crisis catalyzed a shift from slow, survey-centric metrics toward agile, text-driven sentiment indexes that increase the capacity of policymakers to see—and shape—expectations in near real time, adapt their narrative (*forward guidance*) dynamically, and design interventions targeted at the most vulnerable pockets of the economy.

ACKNOWLEDGMENTS

This study was supported by Anadolu University Scientific Research Project under the Grant Number SÇB-2024-2613. The authors thank Anadolu University Scientific Research Project Unit for their support.

REFERENCES

Aftalion, A. (2014). The theory of economic cycles based on the capitalistic technique of production (The Review of Economics and Statistics, vol. 9, no. 4, Oct., 1927, pp. 165–170). *Economia Politica*, 31(1): 93–102.

Avela, A. and Lehmus, M. (2020). It's in the News: Developing a Real Time Index for Economic Uncertainty Based on Finnish News Titles (No. 84). ETLA Working Papers.

Beveridge, W. H. (1917). *Unemployment: A problem of industry*. Longmans.

Burns, A. F. (1969). The Nature and Causes of Business Cycles. In *The Business Cycle in a Changing World* (pp. 3–53). NBER: Cambridge, Massachusetts

Burns, A. F. and Mitchell, W. C. (1946). *Measuring Business Cycles*, NBER: New York.

Caldara, D. and Iacoviello, M. (2022). Measuring geopolitical risk. *American Economic Review*, 112(4): 1194–1225.
Clark, J. M. (1917). Business acceleration and the law of demand: A technical factor in economic cycles. *Journal of Political Economy*, 25(3): 217–235.
Dearle, N. B. (1909). Review of unemployment: A problem of industry, by W. H. Beveridge. *The Economic Journal*, 19(74): 224–228. https://doi.org/10.2307/2221429
Güneş, D., Özkan, İ., and Erden, L. (2024). Economic sentiment and foreign portfolio flows: Evidence from Türkiye. *Central Bank Review*, 24(1): 100147.
Hatzivassiloglou, V. and McKeown, K. (1997, July). Predicting the semantic orientation of adjectives. In *35th Annual Meeting of the Association for Computational Linguistics And 8th Conference of the European Chapter of the Association for Computational Linguistics* (pp. 174–181).
Juglar, C. (1916). *A brief history of panics and their periodical occurrence in the United States*. Putnam.
Karmaniolos, S. and Skinner, G., (2019) A literature review on sentiment analysis and its foundational technologies *2019 IEEE 4th International Conference on Computer and Communication Systems (ICCCS)*, Singapore, 2019, pp. 91–95, doi: 10.1109/CCOMS.2019.8821771.
Keynes, J. M. (1937). The general theory of employment. *The Quarterly Journal of Economics*, 51(2): 209–223.
Mitchell, W. C. (1913). *Business Cycles*, University of California Press: Berkeley. https://archive.org/stream/cu31924003462680/cu31924003462680_djvu.txt.
Odendaal, H., Reid, M. and Kirsten, J. F. (2020). Media-based sentiment indices as an alternative measure of consumer confidence. *South African Journal of Economics*, 88: 409–434. https://doi.org/10.1111/saje.12261
Pigou, A. C. (1927). *Industrial fluctuations*. Routledge.
Schumpeter, J. A. (1939). *Business Cycles: A Theoretical, Historical, and Statistical Analysis of the Capitalist Process*, McGraw-Hill: New York.
Shapiro, A. H., Sudhof, M. and Wilson, D. (2020). Measuring News Sentiment. Federal Reserve Bank of San Francisco Working Paper 2017-01. https://doi.org/10.24148/wp2017-01
Subasic, P. and Huettner, A. (2000, August). Calculus of fuzzy semantic typing for qualitative analysis of text. In ACM KDD 2000, Workshop on Text Mining.
Tugan-Baranovsky, M. I. (1914). Periodic Industrial Crises. A History of British Crises. Excerpts from Part II, "The Theory of Crises." *The Annals of the Ukrainian Academy of Arts and Sciences in the US*, 3(9): 745–802.
Wicksell, K. (1907). The influence of the rate of interest on prices. *The Economic Journal*, 17(66), 213–220.
Zarnowitz, V. (1992). Front matter, business cycles: Theory, history, indicators, and forecasting. In *Business Cycles: Theory, History, Indicators, and Forecasting* (pp. 21–76). University of Chicago Press.

Chapter 4

From data to decisions

AI, data governance and the future of financial services

Sezer Bozkus Kahyaoglu and Lethiwe Nzama-Sithole

4.1 INTRODUCTION

In the volatile and aggressive landscape of modern business, big data emerges as a crucial element driving success and innovation. While traditional financial assessments such as balance sheets and electronic ledgers offer a snapshot of an organization's resources and economic health, they only tell part of the story. The true wealth of an organization lies in its information assets, which encompass the collective insights derived from various forms of data, including customer interactions, market trends, and operational processes (Ahmed et al., 2023).

An organization's ability to thrive in this data-driven era hinges on its capacity to leverage these information assets effectively. Success is measured not merely by profitability figures on a spreadsheet but by how adeptly an organization extracts actionable insights from its data reserves. Information is essentially the distilled knowledge derived from raw data, transforming it into a strategic asset that can drive informed decision-making (BIS, 2015, 2024). However, the journey from data to valuable information is fraught with challenges. Without strong data management practices, including meticulous data quality assurance, effective data integration across various systems, and a well-defined information lifecycle management strategy, organizations risk being inundated with information overload. This can lead to missed opportunities and poor strategic decisions (Breeden, 2024; NIST, 2023).

To fully leverage their data, organizations must prioritize a comprehensive approach that involves leveraging advanced analytics, adopting state-of-the-art data management technologies, and fostering a culture that values data-driven insights. In a world where information is king, those who can harness and optimize their data will not only survive but thrive, setting themselves apart in an increasingly competitive market (Bank of England, 2022, 2025).

The rapid expansion of data is revolutionizing the business world, with its volume doubling every 12 to 18 months (McKinsey, 2024). By 2025, the total amount of data generated globally is projected to exceed an astounding 175 zettabytes, a figure that illustrates the immense amount of information being created and collected. Importantly, a significant portion of this data is

DOI: 10.1201/9781003656463-4

unstructured, meaning it does not fit neatly into traditional databases (FMA, 2024). This includes a diverse array of formats, such as PDF documents, complex Excel spreadsheets, high-resolution images, and various forms of multimedia content, including audio recordings and videos (Bank of England, 2022; BIS, 2024; Breeden, 2024).

Additionally, geolocation data generated by GPS technology, along with a massive influx of emails, user-generated social media content, and information found on countless web pages, contribute to this expansive digital landscape. Machine data, including real-time outputs from sensors and connected devices, adds another layer of complexity (Aldasoro et al., 2024; BIS, 2024; Deloitte, 2018).

In today's competitive environment, effectively harnessing this vast and varied dataset is crucial. Companies that can analyze and leverage these insights will be better equipped to drive innovation, enhance customer experience, and make informed strategic decisions, ultimately positioning themselves ahead of the competition (EC, 2018; Fatas, 2019).

This paper is structured to effectively convey the power of data, which can be used to change and transform the finance sector as follows (Figure 4.1).

This work begins with an exploration of the data deluge we face today, underlining the essential role that big data plays in shaping informed decision-making. In the second section, we explore how big data directly impacts the finance industry, drawing insights from relevant literature. We shine a light on the pivotal role of artificial intelligence (AI) in revolutionizing finance, examining key applications such as credit scoring, portfolio

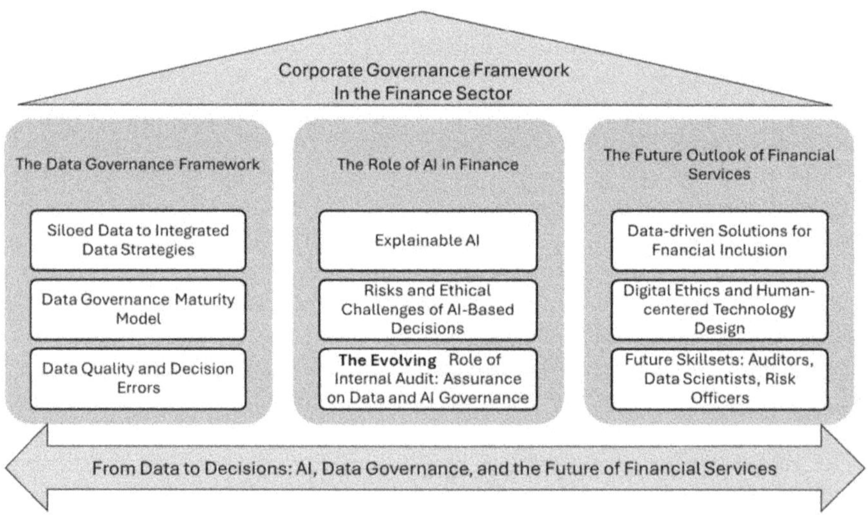

Figure 4.1 The organization of work.

Source: (Prepared by the Author.)

optimization, customer service automation, and fraud detection, all while considering the inherent data dependencies of these AI systems (Ahmed et al., 2023). Moving forward to the third section, we emphasize the paramount importance of robust data governance, particularly in relation to roles and functions, incorporating essential models of data governance and corporate governance maturity. The fourth section confronts the urgency for explainable AI, highlighting the risks, biases, and ethical dilemmas that, if ignored, can lead to detrimental decision-making outcomes. In the fifth section, we provide actionable recommendations to ensure the suitability, reliability, and accountability of data-driven AI systems as they navigate the complex regulatory landscape of the finance sector (BIS, 2024; Prenio & Yong, 2021). The final section envisions a future where the finance industry harnesses data-driven decision-making to its fullest potential. It presents compelling policy recommendations that address critical implications for policy, society, and future research, thereby enriching the ongoing discourse within the field. This paper not only contributes to the literature but also advocates a responsible and informed approach to integrating big data and AI in finance (Finance Watch, 2025).

4.2 THE DATA GOVERNANCE FRAMEWORK

The rapid integration of analytical processes and digital business models that harness the power of data is transforming every sector, resulting in profound and lasting changes. Historically, the exploration of large datasets was known as "data mining," but with the evolution of big data analytics, we are now entering a groundbreaking era. Considering the COVID-19 pandemic, the financial sector has experienced an unprecedented acceleration in digital transformation and the adoption of innovative technologies (Breeden, 2024; FMA, 2024). Big data analytics has made remarkable strides over the past decade, and its significance is poised to grow further with the introduction of five revolutionary technologies. These advancements big data, cloud computing systems, mobile applications, social networks, and sensors are not just enhancements; they are catalysts for change (Chukwuka et al., 2025). Each technology plays a crucial role in empowering businesses to make informed decisions, enhance performance, and manage the vast influx of data that is reshaping the financial landscape. Embracing these innovations could be the key to achieving a competitive advantage in today's data-driven business world (Finance Watch, 2025; Goertzel, 2014).

Big data is fundamentally defined by three key features: volume, velocity, and variety (Coforge, 2025). As digitalization accelerates across the business landscape, there has been an unprecedented surge in data generation. Recently, with the widespread adoption of digital business models and the integration of cutting-edge technologies into every product and service, the volume of stored data is skyrocketing, doubling annually (McKinsey, 2024).

The rapid pace of data production is further fueled by the explosion of mobile devices and social networks, making data more pervasive than ever (Hasan et al., 2020). The significant decrease in the cost and size of sensors, vital components of Big Data analytics, has made it possible to monitor and collect data continuously from diverse systems. With these smaller, more affordable sensors capturing vast amounts of information from people, the internet, and machines, we now face a daunting challenge: the sheer volume of data collected makes it difficult to draw meaningful insights and make informed decisions (Hasan et al., 2020). This phenomenon has given rise to what is known as the "big data problem"; the speed at which data accumulates is outpacing our ability to process and analyze it effectively (Hussain & Prieto, 2016). Nevertheless, rather than viewing this as a setback, we should see it as an incredible opportunity. The big data problem opens the door for advanced predictive analysis and data-driven decision-making, empowering businesses to harness the power of their data like never before. Embracing this challenge can lead to more informed strategies, innovative solutions, and ultimately, a competitive edge in today's digital world, which is the case for the finance sector (Finance Watch, 2025; Hasan et al., 2020).

By thoroughly exploring the structure of big data, we uncover a vast array of innovative information that can significantly enhance our understanding of the market. Central to this exploration are structured texts, such as databases and spreadsheets, which provide organized, easily analyzable data. In contrast, unstructured texts, including emails, reports, and social media posts, contain rich narratives and insights that require more complex analytical tools to dissect (FMA, 2024).

In addition to textual data, we must also consider the contributions from an array of devices. For instance, data generated by sensors from IoT devices, which monitor everything from environmental conditions to machinery performance, offers real-time insights into operations and consumer behaviors. Websites gather user interaction data, mobile and wearable devices, such as fitness trackers and smartwatches, track user habits and preferences, continuously generating valuable information to enhance customer engagement.

Moreover, the realm of social media represents an invaluable resource for understanding consumer sentiment. This encompasses vast volumes of content from platforms like X (former Twitter), where trending topics emerge; Instagram, which showcases visual preferences; and LinkedIn, where professional insights and connections flourish. Blogs and local Really Simple Syndication feeds also contribute to this dynamic dialogue, providing a rich source of feedback regarding organizations, employees, and products in various industries (Finance Watch, 2025).

Utilizing this extensive and diverse data ecosystem allows businesses to paint a detailed and well-rounded picture of customer needs and market dynamics. In today's fast-paced financial sector, harnessing these insights is not only advantageous but also essential for delivering exceptional value and fostering lasting relationships with clients. By adopting a data-driven approach, organizations can anticipate trends, tailor their offerings, and maintain a competitive edge, unlocking new pathways to innovation and success.

Traditional data warehouse strategies that rely on relational databases face significant challenges, including latency that can reach up to 24 hours. This delay makes relational databases and data warehouses less effective, particularly as the demand for scalable solutions increases amid the explosion of big data. Moreover, these methods impose strict limitations on data normalization and relational structures, constraining their overall effectiveness. While they offer valuable retrospective insights, they fail to provide the real-time or predictive analytics that businesses increasingly require. In contrast, big data analytics is evolving into a dynamic decision-support tool that empowers organizations to make informed, immediate decisions, moving beyond the outdated practices of traditional business intelligence that rely solely on aggregate reports. Embracing this evolution is crucial for staying competitive in today's fast-paced finance landscape (Goertzel, 2014).

When analyzed from a theoretical perspective, the discussed contexts highlight the necessity for restructuring corporate governance practices and control mechanisms. A key focus is on eliminating information asymmetry that can occur within corporate operations (Li & Li, 2025). Information asymmetry refers to the lack of timely access to accurate information, which can lead to potential losses due to managerial opportunism. Delayed and asymmetric information from existing data warehouses can result in inefficiencies and deficiencies in the internal control system. The development of real-time data analysis capabilities through big data analytics significantly enhances the accurate application of corporate governance principles. This advancement strengthens transparency, accountability, and audit mechanisms (Bozkus Kahyaoglu, 2024; Kahyaoglu & Aksoy, 2021). It plays a crucial role in corporate decision-making processes by identifying risks and opportunities, formulating responses, interpreting these responses, and implementing them effectively. Consequently, the shift from traditional data analysis to real-time analytics is not merely a technological enhancement; it presents an application that improves corporate risk management and performance, optimizes decision-making processes, and elevates the quality of decisions made. Ultimately, this transition establishes a foundation for the development of new management capabilities that promote ethical, evidence-based leadership in corporate operations, enabling high-quality corporate decision-making to become a competitive advantage (Li & Li, 2025).

Semantics is essential for optimizing the benefits derived from big data analytics (Finance Watch, 2025; McIlraith et al., 2001). This necessity is underscored by the fact that 60-80% of all data within big data environments comprises unstructured content, including narrative text, emails, and audio recordings. Extracting pertinent terms from unstructured data, while ensuring accuracy and relevance to industry-specific concepts, presents a significant challenge. Leveraging natural language processing (NLP) techniques in conjunction with specialized libraries and ontologies allows for the effective extraction of valuable insights from the extensive data repositories housed in the Data Lake. This method not only enhances the accuracy of data interpretation but also facilitates informed decision-making and drives innovation across various sectors (McIlraith et al., 2001).

Analyses within the realm of Big Data analytics can be categorized into three powerful temporal dimensions: retrospective analysis, real-time analysis and predictive analysis (Mühlhoff & Ruschemeier, 2024).

- Retrospective analysis serves as a deep dive into past events, illuminating them with comprehensive insights. By uncovering emerging trends and identifying root causes, this analysis empowers organizations to learn from history and make informed decisions.
- Real-time analysis is a game changer, providing immediate visibility into ongoing activities. It enhances situational awareness and allows for swift responses to changing circumstances. This capability is invaluable, especially in the financial sector, where timely alerts and reminders can mean the difference between success and failure.
- Predictive analysis takes a forward-thinking approach, offering a glimpse into future possibilities. By assessing financial risks, economic models, and market forecasts, it equips organizations with the foresight needed to navigate uncertainty. This strategic insight is crucial for effectively managing financial markets, instruments, and services, ensuring that companies remain one step ahead in an ever-evolving landscape.

The landscape of data governance is undergoing a remarkable transformation, driven by groundbreaking technological advancements and enhanced infrastructure. This evolution has led to a significant rise in the sophistication of data management practices. In the early days characterized by first-generation data management, companies predominantly relied on proprietary corporate data warehouses, which served as extensions of traditional databases (World Economic Forum, 2024).

These data warehouses were designed to produce domain-specific data formats for reporting, known as views, customized to meet the unique demands of various sectors. However, businesses often created separate views (or data warehouses) for different functions, such as marketing, operations and finance. This fragmented approach not only introduced substantial technical challenges but also resulted in an overwhelming number of unmanageable ETL (Extract, Transform, Load) jobs, tables and reports.

As a consequence, access to meaningful insights became the privilege of a small group of experts, while the majority struggled to effectively interpret the data. Although storing information on these platforms was relatively straightforward, extracting valuable insights proved to be a difficult task. Remarkably, the defining characteristic of this era was the reliance on relational and SQL-based databases, which underscored both the opportunities and limitations of data governance process at the time.

By recognizing the pitfalls of this first-generation approach, organizations can leverage advancements in technology today to create streamlined, intuitive data governance systems that empower all users to make informed decisions. This shift is not just a necessity it's a strategic imperative for businesses seeking to thrive in today's data-driven environment.

The second generation of data management transformed our approach to information through centralized, often open-source data lakes, enabling swift and simplified access to data. This era aimed to democratize data, fostering a "self-service" model that allowed users to explore and analyze information easily, often with minimal coding skills. Data engineers played a crucial role, creating automated programs that brought data analytics to life. Now, in the innovative realm of the third generation, we leverage cloud technology and containerization, incorporating cloud-managed data warehouses, real-time data streaming, and distributed data management. This evolution offers high-speed data storage and retrieval at significantly reduced costs compared to earlier methods.

Unlike outdated practices that required repeated data transfers between warehouses, the third generation shifts the focus: computations are now performed directly on the data itself. This streamlined approach not only enhances efficiency but also eliminates redundancy, enabling organizations to fully harness the potential of their data for rapid, informed decision-making.

In today's rapidly advancing landscape of data storage, data has emerged as the cornerstone of modern business, bringing to life the vision of "data as a service." This transformative approach extends beyond merely making data accessible everywhere and on demand; it aims to revolutionize how we manage that data to effectively meet our evolving needs. With the rise of smart data objects, we are entering a new era that promises to redefine the way we store and access information.

Data governance has transitioned from being a mere luxury to a fundamental competency that every organization must cultivate to thrive and sustain operations. The expression that "data is oil" or a treasure comparable to gold has never been more relevant. In an increasingly competitive marketplace and amid recurring economic challenges, mastering data quality, privacy, ethical usage, and usability is not merely advantageous; it is essential.

To truly differentiate themselves and ensure long-term success, businesses must focus on designing and implementing effective data governance processes. Those who excel in this area will not only enhance their brand value but also achieve outstanding financial outcomes. The benefits that arise, such as reduced operational costs, improved time efficiency, increased trust and confidence in data among stakeholders, accelerated adoption of new strategies, and faster returns on investment, are not just advantageous; they are vital for succeeding in today's financial markets. By embracing the power of data governance, financial institutions and all other organizations can unlock the potential for sustainable growth and a competitive edge.

The new generation of applications for data governance offers a significant advantage: robust data quality controls, which are essential for financial institutions and organizations operating within regulated industries (BIS, 2024; Scherer, 2016). By ensuring consistent and reliable data sets, these applications empower organizations to make quicker and more informed decisions, thereby enhancing their operational efficiency and competitive standing (Prenio & Yong, 2021).

Data governance extends beyond the mere act of storing, cleaning, or combining data; it encompasses a comprehensive framework that establishes clear policies, applications, and business rules for collecting, protecting, and effectively utilizing data. This strategic approach not only safeguards data integrity but also maximizes the value derived from data assets, supporting business goals.

Importantly, data governance is a continuous and repeatable process that ensures effective stewardship while minimizing potential risks. By adhering to the principles of corporate governance, well-structured management policies can strengthen the overall data strategy, driving organizational success. Investing in robust data management policies is essential for effective IT governance and serves as a foundational element of sound corporate governance practices. Harness the power of data management to unlock new opportunities and secure a competitive advantage in today's dynamic business environment.

The influence of technological advancements on financial markets is both profound and transformative (Bozkus Kahyaoglu, 2024). One of the key challenges faced by banks and financial institutions during this digital evolution is managing infrastructure amid the fragmentation of data sources. These sources include databases, data lakes, transaction systems (such as e-banking), and Online Analytical Processing systems (like customer data warehouses), which can hinder timely decision-making.

To address this significant issue, financial institutions are increasingly investing in robust data architectures that seamlessly integrate multiple data sources. A notable example of this innovative approach is the Bank of England's establishment of a "Single Bank Data Architecture," built on a centralized data management platform. This initiative enables banks to analyze much larger data sets effectively, streamlining their big data analytics processes and enhancing the speed and accuracy of decision-making. By adopting such transformative solutions, financial institutions not only improve their operational efficiency but also position themselves for success in a rapidly evolving financial landscape (Bank of England, 2024).

4.3 THE ROLE OF AI IN FINANCE

The recent turmoil in financial markets, marked by volatility and frequent crises, underscores the critical importance of effective data governance and big data analytics. It has become increasingly evident that reducing data fragmentation is not just a challenge, but a fundamental necessity. The lessons learned from the 2008 financial crisis highlighted this urgency. During that crisis, various financial institutions were exposed to a myriad of risks. However, the lack of a cohesive approach meant that low-interest loans and exchange-traded funds were tracked and reported through isolated systems (Sommers, 2023). This siloed methodology hindered comprehensive risk assessments and delayed the early detection of the crisis's impact, ultimately hampering sound decision-making (Bank of England, 2022).

Considering these significant challenges, the financial sector is now at a decisive moment. The acceleration of AI applications is not merely a trend; it is a vital requirement for navigating today's complex financial landscape. We must embrace innovative data architectures that break down silos and harness the power of AI. By integrating big data analytics and advanced machine learning (ML) techniques, including deep learning, we can transform the way risks are managed, and decisions are made, paving the way for a more resilient financial future. Now is the time to act decisively and reshape our approach to data in the financial markets.

The financial sector is uniquely positioned as a leader in data utilization, operating within a framework defined by stringent regulations and significant data requirements (Prenio & Yong, 2021; Scherer, 2016). This data dependency has evolved into a robust system capable of generating vast amounts of both structured and unstructured data, particularly as financial institutions undergo digital transformation and foster interconnections within a dynamic global finance ecosystem (Bozkus Kahyaoglu, 2024).

In this context, the rise of big data analytics and AI presents extraordinary opportunities for banks, financial institutions, and fintech companies. By effectively harnessing the power of big data, these organizations can transform their business processes and enhance decision-making capabilities, thereby gaining a significant competitive advantage (Cornelli et al., 2023; EC, 2018; Fatas, 2019).

For instance, financial institutions can tap into customer data to anticipate the behaviors of both current and prospective clients. This intelligence enables them to offer highly personalized banking solutions, tailored financial instruments, and customized services that meet individual needs. Moreover, by leveraging both internal and external data, these institutions can develop sophisticated investment strategies that not only align with their customers' unique preferences but also offer innovative approaches to bright, algorithmic trading and personalized asset management, all while minimizing costs.

With the evolution of business processes and digital models in financial institutions, a noticeable trend has emerged toward strategically integrating and processing various types of data. This includes operational databases, analytical databases, data warehouses, data lakes, and emerging distributed ledger technologies, such as blockchains. Institutions allocate substantial resources and IT efforts to develop these infrastructures (BIS, 2015; Treleaven et al., 2017).

However, the implementation of financial services, instruments, and market applications often faces challenges due to the need for semantic interoperability between isolated data sets across different systems. Additionally, as society evolves and customer expectations shift, the utilization of big data in banking applications becomes essential (McIlraith et al., 2001). The increasing significance of digital finance in branch banking and the demand for service data in physical environments further emphasize the need for pre-processing functions, such as anonymization, to enhance regulatory compliance (Scherer, 2016). Adhering to personal data protection laws and ensuring cybersecurity has both direct and indirect impacts, leading to concerns about transaction security in financial markets. As a result, finance professionals must make faster, more effective, and more accurate decisions. In this context, big data analytics and AI applications have become crucial (Bozkus Kahyaoglu & Caliyurt, 2018; World Economic Forum, 2024).

Despite advancements in big data technologies, new solutions are still necessary to overcome the aforementioned challenges and facilitate the large-scale development, deployment, and operation of big data applications for digital finance. In the rapidly evolving landscape of technology, the management of vast amounts of data, commonly referred to as big data, along with sophisticated analytical solutions, has paved the way for the integration of AI within the finance sector. AI fundamentally encompasses the capability of machines to replicate intelligent human behaviors, simulating decision-making processes typically attributed to human cognition (Aldasoro et al., 2024).

Currently, numerous AI applications exist that are engineered to think and reason similarly to humans, particularly in intricate environments. These systems evaluate various scenarios and generate optimal decisions based on their analyses. Understanding this, AI systems can be viewed as supporting two critical processes:

1. *Learning Process of AI:* Through this dynamic learning process, AI systems can develop rules and models that determine how they analyze and utilize incoming information, tailored to the specific requirements of the financial sector. This involves sophisticated algorithms that sift through and analyze big data, identifying patterns and trends that inform future actions relevant to the financial services and products.
2. *Reasoning Process of AI:* Once the AI systems have acquired and learned information, their reasoning capabilities come into play. This enables them to inform human decision-making by providing insights derived from the big data they have processed. Such reasoning not only aids in making informed choices but also enhances predictive capabilities, offering strategic advantages relevant for the finance sector.

It is a fact that AI technologies have already begun to transform the finance sector, influencing a variety of products and services, as well as practices related to financial market transactions. The implementation of these AI applications is often underpinned by a combination of advanced technologies. These advanced AI-based technologies can be summarized in Table 4.1 as follows:

Table 4.1 Type of AI-based technologies used in finance for improving decision-making

Type of AI-based technology in finance	*Scope of work*	*Impact on decision-making*
Video Processing	Video processing can leverage advanced visual data analysis, allowing for the rapid identification of suspicious transactions and behaviors.	This proactive approach greatly enhances security and builds trust.
Visual Scene Analysis	Harnessing the power of visual scene analysis significantly elevates risk assessment by effectively interpreting and analyzing visual information from diverse sources.	This enhanced capability empowers decision-makers to make more informed and strategic choices.
Speech Recognition	Transform customer service with robust automated systems that effectively understand and respond to verbal inquiries.	It helps to elevate your customer interactions and ensure every inquiry is addressed promptly and accurately. In this way, it will improve and enhance the service experience, making it easier to monitor discrepancies in service quality.
Natural Language Processing (NLP)	Natural Language Processing (NLP) is a groundbreaking technology that revolutionizes our understanding of market sentiment. By accurately analyzing vast amounts of textual data, ranging from the latest news articles and trending social media conversations to comprehensive financial reports, NLP empowers businesses and investors to uncover valuable insights.	These advanced analytics approach not only captures the nuances of language and tone but also identifies emerging trends, public opinions, and potential market shifts. With NLP, we can navigate the complexities of the financial landscape with precision, enabling smarter decision-making that responds to real-time sentiment and market dynamics.
Machine Translation	Imagine a world where language barriers vanish, and the flow of international business becomes effortless. Machine translation transforms the landscape of cross-border transactions and communications, delivering instantaneous translations of financial documents.	This remarkable technology not only bridges linguistic divides but also fosters trust and collaboration across borders, allowing enterprises to expand their reach and seize new opportunities in the vibrant global marketplace. Embrace this innovative tool to unlock a realm of possibilities where every word counts and every transaction matters for improved decision-making in the finance sector.

(*Continued*)

Table 4.1 (Continued)

Type of AI-based technology in finance	*Scope of work*	*Impact on decision-making*
Machine Learning and Deep Learning	Machine learning and deep learning harness the power of advanced algorithms to analyze historical data, significantly enhancing their predictive capabilities which are necessary in financial markets and services.	By refining their understanding of patterns and trends, these technologies not only empower organizations to anticipate future outcomes but also streamline decision-making processes, paving the way for increased efficiency and smarter strategies in the finance sector.
Cognitive Search	Cognitive search fundamentally transforms the landscape of information retrieval by equipping financial professionals with the tools to navigate and interpret intricate data sets with ease. By leveraging advanced algorithms and artificial intelligence, this approach allows users to interact with vast quantities of information more intuitively.	Financial analysts, portfolio managers, and other industry experts can swiftly uncover valuable insights, identify trends, and make data-driven decisions, all while minimizing the time spent shifting through overwhelming volumes of information. As a result, cognitive search not only enhances productivity but also fosters deeper analytical capabilities, ultimately driving better business outcomes.

Source: Compiled by the Author

Together, these technologies form a robust framework that empowers financial institutions to leverage AI, ultimately leading to improved efficiency, better risk management, and enhanced customer experiences.

It is crucial to acknowledge that, like any groundbreaking technology, the implementation of AI presents not only unprecedented opportunities but also significant risks that can challenge the financial sector's regulatory landscape. As we move forward, we must prioritize the design, implementation, reporting, and regular auditing of products and services with a keen awareness of these challenges (Aldasoro et al., 2024; BIS, 2024; Prenio & Yong, 2021).

It is necessary to take a closer look at how AI-driven products and services rely on pivotal data-dependent processes, namely data creation, processing, and analysis within increasingly interconnected technological ecosystems. These activities must be executed with transparency and accountability, adhering to robust corporate governance principles.

The security of these processes is fundamentally linked to the maturity of our institutions and their data management capabilities. In a financial landscape characterized by a strong need for trust and stability, addressing these aspects becomes essential for delivering services that hinge on effective data integration, analysis, and advanced algorithms. Moreover, it is a well-established fact that AI and Big Data offer transformative opportunities to enhance efficiency and elevate service quality within the financial sector. As we embrace these technologies, they are prepared to become the cornerstone of digital finance, driving innovation and progress for years to come (Deloitte, 2018; EC, 2018; OECD, 2023).

As the portability of financial data accelerates, we are approaching a significant transformation in the competitive landscape of the financial sector. The emergence of customer-centric approaches, enhanced by technological advancements, is poised to empower financial institutions with unparalleled market influence, leading to a consistent increase in profits (BIS, 2021).

In this evolving digital environment, it is evident that financial institutions that embrace innovation and adaptability will not only endure but also thrive. Their value is poised to rise as they leverage extensive customer data, utilizing AI-driven insights to make more informed and timely decisions. Furthermore, the potential of AI and Big Data extends well beyond individual banks; it can positively reshape the broader financial system. An increasing number of institutions are adopting an "open banking" framework, where consumer banking, transactions, and essential economic data are shared seamlessly with third-party financial service providers through Application Programming Interfaces (Wolska, 2024). These collaborative initiatives, grounded in data sharing, can significantly enhance the security of our economic system by improving the timeliness, accuracy, and effectiveness of critical information (Deloitte, 2018; KPMG, 2021).

We stand on the brink of a digital finance revolution, characterized by flourishing collaboration and a redefined approach to competition. Embracing these changes is not merely an opportunity; it is a necessity for those seeking to shape a more secure and prosperous financial future.

4.4 THE FUTURE OUTLOOK ON FINANCIAL SERVICES

Emerging technologies, particularly AI and Big Data, are poised to reshape the financial sector fundamentally. As these innovations gain prominence, they are transforming traditional business models and heralding a new era of disruptive innovation. Established financial institutions must recognize that embracing these technologies will allow them to redefine their roles and responsibilities in the industry.

AI algorithms, for instance, can analyze extensive datasets in real-time, enabling quicker decision-making and personalized customer experiences. Big Data analytics can draw insights from various sources, such as transaction histories, social media, and market trends, enhancing risk management and investment strategies (NIST, 2023). For example, "Quorum software created by JP Morgan Chase.

According to a 2018 report by the World Economic Forum, institutions that focus on the scale and complexity of their data capabilities, rather than just their capital size, are more likely to thrive. By leveraging these advanced technologies to create innovative, customer-centric services, financial organizations can secure a competitive edge. Hence, integrating AI and Big Data is essential for the future of finance. Institutions that actively adopt and apply these technologies will position themselves for success and sustainability in a rapidly evolving landscape (World Economic Forum, 2018).

The future vision for Digital Finance presents a compelling overview of a transformed financial landscape, where innovative policies are developed based on pioneering concepts and their anticipated roles in the market. These advancements are poised to revolutionize the financial ecosystem, fostering trust and confidence among users (US Department of the Treasury, 2024). The key components of this progress and future outlook on finance include the following instruments (Table 4.2):

Table 4.2 The future outlook on financial services/products and the value-added approach

Type of service/product	*Scope of work*	*Value-added approach*
Open Banking	Open banking is an innovative framework that allows customers to safely share their financial data such as account balances and transaction histories with licensed third-party providers, including fintech companies. This secure exchange enhances individual control and sparks competition, leading to creative financial solutions.	Customers benefit from tailored services, such as personalized budgeting tools and improved payment platforms, resulting in a more responsive and empowering banking experience.
Enhanced Anti-Money Laundering and Combating the Financing of Terrorism (AML/CFT)	Robust Anti-Money Laundering and Combating the Financing of Terrorism (AML/CFT) initiatives are crucial for navigating the intricate landscape of e-money and cryptocurrency.	These advanced measures are specifically designed to identify and mitigate risks associated with digital financial transactions, which can often be exploited for illicit purposes. By establishing stringent protocols, enhanced monitoring systems, and comprehensive regulatory frameworks, we can effectively protect the integrity and security of financial systems. Such proactive strategies will not only bolster consumer confidence but also promote transparency, making the digital economy safer for everyone involved.

Table 4.2 (Continued)

Type of service/product	*Scope of work*	*Value-added approach*
Cyber Resilience	Implementing comprehensive and robust defenses against cyber threats is crucial for safeguarding sensitive information such as personal data and financial records.	These proactive measures not only mitigate the risks of data breaches and cyberattacks but also empower financial institutions to foster and maintain trust within the communities they serve. By prioritizing cybersecurity, these institutions demonstrate their commitment to protecting their clients' assets and privacy, reinforcing public confidence in their services.
Biometric Authentication	Advanced fingerprint recognition technology provides seamless and secure access to financial services, effectively preventing unauthorized access.	By leveraging this advanced biometric solution, you can feel confident that your sensitive information is protected from unauthorized access, making your financial interactions not only secure but also incredibly convenient.
Robo-Advisors	Intelligent algorithms that deliver personalized investment recommendations, democratizing access to financial advice for investors of all experience levels.	By analyzing your risk tolerance, time horizon, and investment preferences, these automated advisors create a diversified portfolio designed to optimize returns. With robo-advisors, high-quality financial advice is no longer just for the wealthy; it's accessible to everyone.
Big Data and Machine Learning in Credit Scoring	Utilizing extensive data to create detailed credit assessments enables more accurate and equitable evaluations of borrowers. By harnessing the power of extensive datasets and cutting-edge machine learning algorithms, we are transforming the landscape of credit scoring. This innovative approach allows us to analyze a wide range of borrower information such as payment history, income levels, and spending habits to produce highly accurate credit assessments.	As a result, we can identify creditworthiness with greater precision, minimizing biases and ensuring a fairer evaluation process for all potential borrowers. This commitment to utilizing data-driven insights not only improves lending decisions but also promotes a more inclusive financial environment, giving individuals access to opportunities they deserve.

(*Continued*)

Table 4.2 (Continued)

Type of service/product	*Scope of work*	*Value-added approach*
Trade Finance through Distributed Ledger Technology (DLT) and Smart Contracts	Transforming trade finance through the integration of Distributed Ledger Technology (DLT) and smart contracts presents a groundbreaking opportunity to redefine how trade transactions are conducted. By leveraging DLT, all parties involved in a transaction can access a shared, immutable ledger that enhances visibility and accountability. Smart contracts further amplify this innovation by automating crucial processes such as payment approvals and compliance checks.	This transparency allows stakeholders to track the progress of transactions in real-time, significantly reducing confusion and disputes. These self-executing contracts eliminate the need for intermediaries, streamlining operations and accelerating transaction times. As a result, businesses can adapt more quickly to market changes and enhance their operational efficiency. This combination not only fosters a safer trading environment but also cultivates greater trust among participants, ultimately driving the growth of international trade.
Mobile Wallets Utilizing Near-Field Communication (NFC)	Revolutionizing the payment experience through quick and secure transactions via public cloud integration, making everyday purchases effortless. Mobile wallets equipped with Near-Field Communication (NFC) technology are transforming the payment experience for consumers and businesses alike.	These innovative platforms allow users to make transactions in seconds simply by tapping their smartphones or smartwatches against a payment terminal. With the added security of public cloud integration, sensitive financial information is safeguarded using advanced encryption techniques, ensuring peace of mind with every purchase. This seamless process eliminates the hassle of cash and cards, enabling users to complete everyday transactions.
Online Crowdfunding Platforms	Opening new pathways for entrepreneurs to connect with investors, stimulating innovation and supporting the growth of diverse projects. Online crowdfunding platforms are transforming the entrepreneurial landscape by providing a direct connection between innovators and investors.	These platforms allow startups to present their unique ideas to a global audience, harnessing community support to fund diverse projects, from technology and sustainability to the arts and social initiatives. By democratizing access to funding, crowdfunding fosters a dynamic ecosystem where varied voices can thrive, making it an essential tool for turning visions into reality.

Source: Compiled by the Author.

These components, along with many others, converge to redefine our interactions with financial services, paving the way for an exciting and secure future.

A diverse range of players is revolutionizing the financial industry, with prominent Big Tech companies such as "GAFA" comprising Google, Amazon, Facebook, and Apple alongside Alibaba, taking the lead. These powerhouse entities are not merely entering the financial sector; they are fundamentally transforming it by leveraging their extensive existing customer bases and integrating innovative digital solutions (Pisal, 2020).

By harnessing their technological expertise and vast data resources, these companies position themselves as indispensable partners for consumers, focusing on enhancing convenience and efficiency. For instance, Amazon's foray into payment processing and lending services demonstrates its intent to streamline transactions for its millions of users, while Facebook's digital wallet, Novi, seeks to simplify and secure online payments.

Moreover, telecommunications companies are making significant strides, incorporating cutting-edge technologies like the IoT and mobile payments into their offerings. With their ability to facilitate seamless transactions through smartphones and other connected devices, these firms are providing unique alternative banking solutions that challenge traditional financial institutions. As these sectors converge, we are witnessing a remarkable evolution in how financial services are delivered, promising a future where finance is more accessible, efficient, and user-centric than ever before (Bozkus Kahyaoglu, 2024).

4.5 CONCLUDING REMARKS

Financial markets and institutions, although inherently complex and risky, offer significant opportunities for substantial returns when supported by practical strategic approaches. To navigate these challenges successfully, it is vital to establish a state-of-the-art technological infrastructure tailored for early risk detection and robust protection against emerging digital threats, such as cyberattacks and data breaches. By investing in secure and resilient systems, financial institutions can deliver exceptional services, attract a broader range of clients, and substantially increase transaction volumes.

Moreover, mastering big data management and employing advanced data analytics, including ML and AI, are essential for formulating innovative investment strategies. These tools empower finance professionals to optimize portfolios based on real-time market trends and predictive insights, maximizing potential returns.

In this fast-paced environment, finance professionals must leverage these intelligent systems to make swift, informed decisions in the best interest of their clients. Additionally, a commitment to transparency and accountability enables institutions to demonstrate diligent compliance with legal regulations, fostering trust and credibility. As innovative technologies continue to be integrated across all sectors of financial markets, we stand on the brink of a transformative era that promises to redefine the future of finance and elevate the standards of service excellence.

The perspective on markets, financial tools, and business models has undergone a dramatic transformation, particularly in the wake of the 2008 financial crisis and the subsequent global pandemic. These pivotal events have accelerated the digital transformation process across the financial sector, creating numerous new opportunities for innovation and efficiency. However, this rapid change also presents significant challenges that AI has yet to fully address, such as the dissemination of asymmetric information and the emergence of ambiguous ethical compliance issues.

Addressing these challenges is vital for enhancing the transparency and accountability of financial markets. It is crucial for all stakeholders, including financial institutions, regulators, and consumers, to recognize their role in this evolving landscape; effective oversight cannot rest solely on the shoulders of regulatory bodies. The open banking framework, which promotes greater collaboration and data sharing among financial entities, is dismantling traditional barriers. This shift is fostering the development of innovative financial systems powered by blockchain technology, which operates on decentralized networks, enhancing both security and efficiency. For example, open banking applications in Europe that comply with PSD2).

In this context, institutions of higher education and research laboratories play indispensable roles. They are at the forefront of creating and promoting responsible finance applications that align with the technological advancements necessary for the future of financial markets. These institutions act as hubs of innovation, conducting research and developing solutions that not only advance the industry but also cater to ethical standards and societal needs. Therefore, it is imperative for governments and educational bodies to actively support these innovations while rigorously assessing their social implications and benefits.

While the dynamics of financial markets may constantly shift, one foundational principle remains unchanged: the necessity for robust oversight. This supervision must integrate various aspects of the financial system to ensure stability, fairness, and effectiveness in a rapidly changing environment.

REFERENCES

Ahmed, N., Wahed, M., & Thompson, N. (2023). The growing influence of industry in AI research. *Science*, 379(6635), 884–886.

Aldasoro, I., Gambacorta, L., Korinek, A., Shreeti, V., & Stein, M. (2024). Intelligent financial system: How AI is transforming finance, BIS Working Papers, no 1194, June. Available at: https://www.bis.org/publ/work1194.htm (Date Accessed 08.06.2025)

Bank for International Settlements (BIS) (2015). Corporate Governance Principles for Banks, Basel Committee on Banking Supervision, ISBN 978-92-9197-126-8 (online). Available at: https://www.bis.org/bcbs/publ/d328.pdf (Date Accessed 08.06.2025)

Bank for International Settlements (BIS) (2021). Enabling open finance through APIs Report on payment initiation, Available at: https://www.bis.org/publ/othp41.pdf ISBN 978-92-9259-507-4 (online) (Date Accessed 08.12.2025)

Bank for International Settlements (BIS) (2024). Regulating AI in the Financial Sector: Recent Developments and Main Challenges by Juan Carlos Crisanto, Cris Benson Leuterio, Jermy Prenio and Jeffery Yong, Available at: https://www.bis.org/fsi/publ/insights63.pdf (Date Accessed 08.06.2025)

Bank of England (2022). Artificial Intelligence and Machine Learning. Discussion Paper 5/22, Available at: https://www.bankofengland.co.uk/prudential-regulation/publication/2022/october/artificial-intelligence (Date Accessed 08.06.2025)

Bank of England (2025). Financial Stability in Focus: Artificial intelligence in the financial system, Financial Policy Committee April 2025, Available at: https://www.bankofengland.co.uk/-/media/boe/files/financial-stability-in-focus/2025/financial-stability-in-focus-artificial-intelligence-in-the-financial-system.pdf (Date Accessed 08.06.2025)

Bozkus Kahyaoglu, S. (2024). Digital transformation cycle in business landscape: The managerial perspective. *EDPACS*, 69(2), 22–29. https://doi.org/10.1080/07366981.2024.2310341

Bozkus Kahyaoglu, S., & Caliyurt, K. (2018). Cyber security assurance process from the internal audit perspective. *Managerial Auditing Journal*, 33(4), 360–376. https://doi.org/10.1108/MAJ-02-2018-1804

Breeden, S. (2024). Engaging with the machine: AI and financial stability – speech by Sarah Breeden, Available at: https://www.bankofengland.co.uk/speech/2024/october/sarah-breeden-keynote-speech-at-the-hong-kong-monetary-authority (Date Accessed 08.06.2025)

Chukwuka, M. O., Anuoluwapo, J. S., Andrew, C. N., Temitope, K., Tewogbade, S. A., & Oluwole, F. (2025). AI in green financing: Catalyst for change or overstated promise? *World Journal of Advanced Research and Reviews*, 26(03), 2626–2633. Article DOI: https://doi.org/10.30574/wjarr.2025.26.3.2477.

Coforge (2025). Understanding the 3 Vs of Big Data - Volume, Velocity and Variety. Available at: https://www.coforge.com/what-we-know/blog/understanding-the-3-vs-of-big-data-volume-velocity-and-variety (Date Accessed 08.12.2025)

Cornelli, G., Frost, J., Gambacorta, L., Rau, R., Wardrop, R., & Ziegler, T. (2023). Fintech and big tech credit: Drivers of the growth of digital lending, *Journal of Banking & Finance*, 148,106742. https://doi.org/10.1016/j.jbankfin.2022.106742

Deloitte. (2018). Open banking – Privacy at the epicentre [online]. Deloitte. Available at: https://www2.deloitte.com/content/dam/Deloitte/au/Documents/financial-services/deloitteau-fs-open-banking-privacy-epicentre-170718.pdf. (Date Accessed 08.06.2025)

European Commission (EC) (2018). Fintech Action Plan: For a More Competitive and Innovative European Financial Sector. Available at: https://finance.ec.europa.eu/publications/fintech-action-plan-more-competitive-and-innovative-european-financial-sector_en (Date Accessed 08.06.2025)

Fatas, A. (2019), The Economics of Fintech and Digital Currencies, CEPR, Available at: https://cepr.org/publications/books-and-reports/economics-fintech-and-digital-currencies (Date Accessed 08.06.2025)

Finance Watch (2025). Artificial intelligence in finance: how to trust a black box? Available at: https://www.finance-watch.org/wp-content/uploads/2025/03/Artificial_intelligence_in_finance_report_final.pdf (Date Accessed 08.06.2025)

Financial Market Authority (FMA) (2024). Understanding Artificial Intelligence in Financial Services. Occasional Paper series, Available at: https://www.fma.govt.nz/assets/Research/Understanding-Artificial-Intelligence-in-Financial-Services.pdf (Date Accessed 08.06.2025)

Goertzel, B. (2014). artificial general intelligence: Concept, state of the art, and future prospects., *Journal of Artificial General Intelligence*, 5(1), 1–48. https://doi.org/10.2478/JAGI-2014-0001.

Hasan, M. M., Popp, J., & Oláh, J. (2020). Current landscape and influence of big data on finance. *Journal of Big Data*, 7, 21. https://doi.org/10.1186/s40537-020-00291-z

Hussain, K., & Prieto, E. (2016). Big Data in the Finance and Insurance Sectors. In *New Horizons for a Data-Driven Economy: A Roadmap for Usage and Exploitation of Big Data in Europe* (pp. 209–223). Springer International Publishing, Cham.

Kahyaoglu, S. B., & Aksoy, T. (2021). Artificial Intelligence in Internal Audit and Risk Assessment. In Hacioglu, U., & Aksoy, T. (eds) *Financial Ecosystem and Strategy in the Digital Era. Contributions to Finance and Accounting.* Springer, Cham. https://doi.org/10.1007/978-3-030-72624-9_8

KPMG. (2021). Open banking opens opportunities for greater customers [online]. Available at: https://home.kpmg/ph/en/home/insights/2019/07/open-banking-opens-opportunitiesfor-greater-value.html. (Date Accessed 08.06.2025)

Li, J., & Li, Z. (2025). Mechanisms of corporate digital transformation on asymmetric capital structure adjustment: The mediating role of information asymmetry and financial stability. *Heliyon*, 11(3), e41745. https://doi.org/10.1016/j.heliyon.2025.e41745

McIlraith, S. A., Son, T. C., & Zeng, H. (2001). Semantic web services. *IEEE Intelligent Systems.* 16(2), 46–53.

McKinsey (2024). Tech services and generative AI: Plotting the necessary reinvention, [online]. Available at: https://www.mckinsey.com/industries/technology-media-and-telecommunications/our-insights/tech-services-and-generative-ai-plotting-the-necessary-reinvention#/ (Date Accessed 08.12.2025)

Mühlhoff, R., & Ruschemeier, H. (2024). Predictive analytics and the collective dimensions of data protection. *Law, Innovation and Technology*, 16(1), 261–292. https://doi.org/10.1080/17579961.2024.2313794

NIST (2023), Artificial Intelligence Risk Management Framework (AI RMF 1.0), https://doi.org/10.6028/NIST.AI.100-1.

OECD (2023). Generative Artificial Intelligence in Finance. OECD Artificial Intelligence Papers. https://www.oecd.org/en/publications/generative-artificial-intelligence-in-finance_ac7149cc-en.html

Pisal, S. (2020). Rise Of Facebook, Amazon, Apple, Netflix, Google During COVID-19 PANDEMIC. Electronic Theses, Projects, and Dissertations. 1311. https://scholarworks.lib.csusb.edu/etd/1311 (Date Accessed 08.06.2025)

Prenio, J., & Yong, J. (2021). Humans keeping AI in check – Emerging regulatory expectations in the financial sector, FSI Insights on Policy Implementation no 35, August. https://www.bis.org/fsi/publ/insights35.htm (Date Accessed 08.06.2025)

Scherer, M. U. (2016). Regulating artificial intelligence systems: Risks, challenges, competencies, and strategies. *Harvard Journal of Law and Technology.* 29(2), 1–48.

Sommers, F. (2023). Exchange-Traded Funds - Operations Tracking Profile (April 7, 2023). http://dx.doi.org/10.2139/ssrn.4412521 (Date Accessed 08.12.2025)

Treleaven, P., Brown, R. G., & Yang, D. (2017). Blockchain technology in finance. *Computer*, 50(9), 14–17.

U.S. Department of The Treasury (2024). Artificial Intelligence Report on the Uses, Opportunities, and Risks of Artificial Intelligence in the Financial Services Sector. https://home.treasury.gov/system/files/136/Artificial-Intelligence-in-Financial-Services.pdf (Date Accessed 08.06.2025)

Wolska, A. (2024). Open Banking and the Catalysts for Digital Transformation in the Financial Ecosystem (December 29, 2024). http://dx.doi.org/10.2139/ssrn.5075577
World Economic Forum (2018). The Global Competitiveness Report 2018, https://www3.weforum.org/docs/GCR2018/05FullReport/TheGlobalCompetitivenessReport2018.pdf (Date Accessed 08.06.2025)
World Economic Forum (2024). Global cybersecurity outlook 2024, Insight Report in collaboration with Accenture, January. https://www3.weforum.org/docs/WEF_Global_Cybersecurity_Outlook_2024.pdf?bcs-agent-scanner=3d6200b9-6784-8640-a1fa-bd235ef7292d (Date Accessed 08.06.2025)

Chapter 5

Artificial intelligence in finance

Application of robo-advisors for investment decision-making

Bharath Kalappa, Deepika Upadhyay, and Ananda S Upadhyay

5.1 INTRODUCTION

The implementation of artificial intelligence is transforming human functioning systems in nearly all industries. It has now been transferred from supporting industries, including travel, health, education, and communication, into wealth management. Artificial intelligence-based applications have been utilised by various wealth management companies to provide their customers with investment decision advice tailored to their needs (Singh & Kaur, 2017). A key trend in online integration, artificial intelligence can transform various industries, notably the financial sector (Barile et al., 2024). To offer financial services more productively and cost-effectively, the financial sector regularly adopts modern technologies. On the heels of the 2007–2008 global financial crisis, when high regulations on conventional banks and innovations in computer science created opportunities to build non-bank, digital-based financial organisations, the integration of these innovations exclusively advanced (Hou et al., 2025). Transactions, investments, insurance, loans and advances are the essential financial services that engage technology (Warchlewska & Waliszewski, 2020).

The notion of investing and safeguarding money is advancing gradually. Digital investments in stocks, derivatives, bonds, commodities, mutual funds, and other forms of assets are gaining strength moderately as they introduce computerised portfolio selection that meets each investor's demands and optimises profits (Singh & Kaur, 2017). Automated teller machines, digital payments, and blockchain-based trade financing are examples of innovative technology in the financial services sector (Hou et al., 2025). Besides, with advances in data processing capabilities and advanced digital systems, investors have begun applying software programming to robotise their investing approaches; this is termed as algorithmic investing and trading (Prasad & Seetharaman, 2021). Computerised financial advisors, also known as robo-advisors, have become fundamental devices in the portfolio management service sector due to this technological revolution. They present programmed, algorithm-machine-based financial advisory services without human engagement (Hou et al., 2025; Syed & Janamolla, 2024).

 DOI: 10.1201/9781003656463-5

Robo-advisors, which are forecasted to displace conventional investments, are among the numerous financial innovations that have emerged in response to the 2008 global financial crisis, often referred to as an ideal storm (Nguyen et al., 2023). Stock investors require advice to achieve their investment intentions (Warchlewska & Waliszewski, 2020). In recent times, robo-advisors have emerged as an exciting buzzword in the scientific technology and financial markets. The digital portfolio management programs identified as robo-advisors deliver automated investment decisions that are mainly based on economic and passive investments. Robo-advisors also successfully handle these divisions through investment restructuring (Uhl & Rohner, 2018). They are user-friendly and enable 24/7 accessibility to modest investment advising services. Conventional investment providers, such as banks, insurance agencies, and portfolio managers and brokers, are also adapting to modern trends by introducing robo-advisory services in their investment offerings (Huang et al., 2022; Nain & Rajan, 2024). It is a leading-edge service that enhances both community improvements and robust economic development. Particularly, by building and refining robo-advisor components, emerging technologies such as cloud computing, big data, and market segmentation will be expanded and more proficiently employed globally, predominantly increasing digital upgrades across investment industries (Cheng et al., 2019). A current generation of investors has emerged in the portfolio management industry recently. These investors are sophisticated, open to modern innovations, and seek ongoing and operational supervision over their wealth, and rely on insights from a selection of avenues instead of a single conventional advisor. Besides this demographic transformation, past generations are also shifting and progressing more tech-aware, so they think and command modern wealth services that are equal to those delivered by tech innovators (Beketov et al., 2018). As an outcome, robo-advisory services have a comprehensive prospect market segmentation. Nevertheless, stock investors have only recently started to welcome robo-advisory services for investment decisions (Nain & Rajan, 2024).

5.1.1 Rationale of the study

The current evaluation fills a significant research gap in the implementation of robo-advisors in stock investment decisions, hence increasing the pool of work in the domain. Because conceptual discoveries are fundamental to the sustainability of any domain, there have not been numerous studies in the literature on robo-advisors that emphasise the theoretical basis and practical implementations. By expanding on contemporary understanding and giving clarity on how robo-advisors impact portfolio investment decisions, this study stands in contrast to the previous studies. This study offers an in-depth examination of how robo-advisors perform and proposes a conceptual model for future research. In addition to bridging the existing study gap, this work provides a TCCM (Theory, Context, Characteristics, Methodology) framework for prospective research avenues on robo-advisors in investment decisions, upgrading theoretical and operational knowledge in the realm.

5.1.2 Objectives of the study

RO1. To explore the overview of robo-advisors for investment decision-making in stock markets.
RO2. To examine the application design and operational process of robo-advisors for investment decision-making in stock markets.
RO3. To assess the key challenges, regulatory disputes, and major remedies related to robo-advisors for investment decision-making in selected nations.
RO4. To illustrate the case study in understanding robo-advisors for investment decision-making.
RO5. To present the TCCM framework and conceptual model for future empirical studies on robo-advisors in investment decision-making.

5.2 METHODOLOGY

This chapter conducts a structured conceptual literature review, methodically investigating existing studies that apply content analysis to identify common themes, theories and research gaps. In addition, the case study presentation and the TCCM framework are implemented to arrange and categorise the research outcomes. The chapter establishes an accurate conceptual model grounded on this review to direct future researchers on the platform of robo-advisory services in the equity market investment decision-making process.

5.3 INVESTMENT DECISION-MAKING THROUGH ROBO-ADVISORS

5.3.1 What are robo-advisors?

The word "robo-advisor" is an integration of two words: "robo" is a short form of "robot", which indicates "a device handled by a computer implemented to accomplish tasks mechanically", and "advice", which indicates "a view provided on what decision to make or how to respond in a specific situation". Predominantly named as "robo-advisors" that deliver "robo advice", they may also be called as "algorithmic investment advisors" (Barile et al., 2024).

By integrating modern technology with machine learning algorithms, robo-advisors authorise investment decision services for investors by creating artificial-based investment strategies. Robo-advisors promote access to portfolio management tools by making risky decisions, rationalising and reducing

Table 5.1 Characteristics of robo-advisors in investment decision-making

Characteristics	*Outcomes*
Immaterial	Robo-advisors reform the investor-advisor engagement into a cost-effective investor intellectual platform.
Configured	Robo-advisors are grounded on algorithmically encrypted data that can be more finely tuned to the requirements of investors over time at a premium rate.
Logical Calculation	Robo-advisors make it evident that they present unbiased data, rather than the emotions and sentiments of conventional advisors concerning an investment.
Investor-Controlled	Robo-advisors enhance investor control because the investor is the individual who upgrades their profile in the robo-advisor algorithm and begins the data search.
Contemporary	The information concerning robo-advisors is the latest, most accurate, and relevant as of the date of accession of a conventional advisor's skills.
Reliable	The algorithmic control, deeply rooted in expertly generated content on the robo-advisor forum, is authentic in the sense that it is provided by robo-advisors rather than the trading-investor relationship.
Big Data Analytics	Robo-advisors also form trust by relying on big data, which offers a vast diversity and richness, and ignoring scant local data sets that are often used in advisor and client engagements.
Machine-Learning Algorithms	Robo-advisors encourage investors to follow machine-learning algorithms; the platforms handle, offset, and smooth investment portfolios periodically, in addition to exhibiting significant information.

Source: Adapted from study (Wexler & Oberlander, 2021).

the value of financial knowledge, and enhancing readiness (Potdar & Pande, 2021). This paves the way for the characteristics of robo-advisors in investment decision-making outlined in Table 5.1 (Wexler & Oberlander, 2021).

5.3.2 Overview of robo-advisors in investment decision-making

At the start of the 2000s, robo-advisors were known as computerised platforms that delivered investment decision services based on algorithms with modest support from individuals. Based on easy, fixed algorithms and user data, these early models were aimed to provide fundamental investment advice and wealth management (Syed & Janamolla, 2024). Nearly 200 robo-advisors are readily available on the stock market, offering services related to investment decision-making concerning portfolio management (Potdar & Pande, 2021). In the last decade, the robo-advisory platform has witnessed remarkable growth. The United States became the first nation to have robo-advisors when the two cutting-edge companies, Betterment and Wealthfront, were started in 2008 (Huang et al., 2022). They developed mixed portfolios by applying modern portfolio theory, tailored to the investor's investment horizon and risk tolerance level. This digitalisation offers a fair substitute for conventional financial advisors through a robotics-driven process, such as tax optimisation and rebalancing (Syed & Janamolla, 2024). This innovative application was performed on an online interface and was user-friendly. Adjusting investor avenues within the targeted dates was the objective. As the targeted dates, such as retirement age, approach, the fund becomes risk-averse, with fewer securities and high bond investments (Singh & Kaur, 2017). Despite being first launched as financial technology start-ups during the global financial crisis, their prominence has increased recently, particularly as conventional investment institutions have begun to offer their own personal robo-advisory services. For instance, in 2015, one of the top brokerage companies in the United States, Charles Schwab, announced robo-advisors and creative portfolio advice. The biggest wealth manager in the world, BlackRock, acquired a robo-advisory firm in 2015. Major banks such as Bank of America and Wells Fargo have also taken notice of robo-advisors and have begun to offer their own algorithmic advisory services (Hou et al., 2025).

The robo-advisors are digital applications that understand investor inclinations and generate investment decisions on the investor's behalf, which appear to be appropriate at any time (Warchlewska & Waliszewski, 2020). Rogers in year 2003 stated that when a key group of investors is realised, the speed of technology by specific communities either grows quickly (Effective innovation) or falls slowly (Ineffective innovation). As stated by Rogers, these social communities are characterised as slow learners, forward thinkers, pioneers, the primary adopters, and the late adopters. The first two communities comprise a mass of robo-advisory users, mainly younger investors with major investment experience (Digmayer, 2024). Authentically estimating stock market levels is intense, but executing these machine learning algorithms will clearly aid in shrinking those gaps (Potdar & Pande, 2021).

Several robo-advisory forums are customising their platforms due to the age class they influence in investment decision-making. Generation Y seeks direction for high-risk, performance-driven portfolios, while Generation X seeks consultation for less risky, conservative growth portfolios (Potdar & Pande, 2021). Industries have been trying to encourage robo-advisors to various investor communities, primarily those with less experience in securities and those who are conservative with moderately low savings (Digmayer, 2024).

Robo-advisors have also manifested in developing countries. In particular, the rise of a middle class and the integration of advanced technology are driving the significant increase in robo-advisors in Asian countries. Several countries, namely China, Hong Kong, India, Japan, Singapore, Thailand, and Vietnam, have begun using robo-advisors. Although robo-advisors are still in development, they are also offered in other emerging countries. In the next few years, it is projected that robo-advisors will endure global expansion (Hou et al., 2025).

5.3.3 Application, design and operations of robo-advisors in investment decision-making

A robo-advisor develops a digital application to accomplish stock investor self-evaluation and security management procedures by employing artificial intelligence (Cheng et al., 2019). In an effort to support the other sections of the investment process, the establishment of a portfolio investment and its management are integrated with a financial information provider who offers instant data on investment avenues and market movements (Shanmuganathan, 2020). The buying and selling of securities required for investment advice is produced mechanically by the robo-advisors. Gently pressing the button on the robo-advisor screen enables an investor to enter securities instantly in batch mode (D'Acunto et al., 2019). Robo-advisors typically take the form of mobile-based applications and web portals that enable investors to complete a scheduled questionnaire (Shanmuganathan, 2020). Four generations are incorporated in the board division of robo-advisors that have been recommended in Deloitte documents. By applying scheduled online questionnaires and drafts, the first-and second-generation robo-advisors offer both online access to conventional investment management advice and services. The third and fourth generations of robo-advisors perform fully digitalised security management by creating and realigning securities by applying quantitative models and algorithms (Beketov et al., 2018).

Using a chat window, stock investors might engage with and seek investment guidance from robo-advisors in the forum. The robo-advisors' web chat function is linked to the Microsoft Bot Framework, which offers its base. Additionally, Figure 5.1 was presented, which depicted an avatar that possessed a human form. The robo-advisor applied human pronouns like "I" and "me" and showed itself as Charles. Its connectivity skills comprised attending to questions like "How are you?" "What can you do?" and "How much is my stock worth?" Likewise, Table 5.2 presents the sample questions and responses from robo-advisors, specifically those that allow investors to ask for assistance. Demo questions that investors might ask Charles, which facilitated the source for investment decision advice, are presented in Table 5.3. The robo-advisor consistently advised investing in premium assets; if investors had other, modest assets in their securities, it also advised selling them (Back et al., 2021).

Figure 5.2 highlights robo-advisors with and without community design components that deliver advice instantly at the onset of each trading phase (subsequently referred to as push advice) and those that perform upon demand (subsequently called as pull advice). The robo-advisor without community design components lacks a distinct identity, confining investors without a name or identity. The robo-advisor with community design components has a name, conveys its purpose through operating in a universal language, and delivers investment advice through requests like "Can you please help me?"(Back et al., 2021).

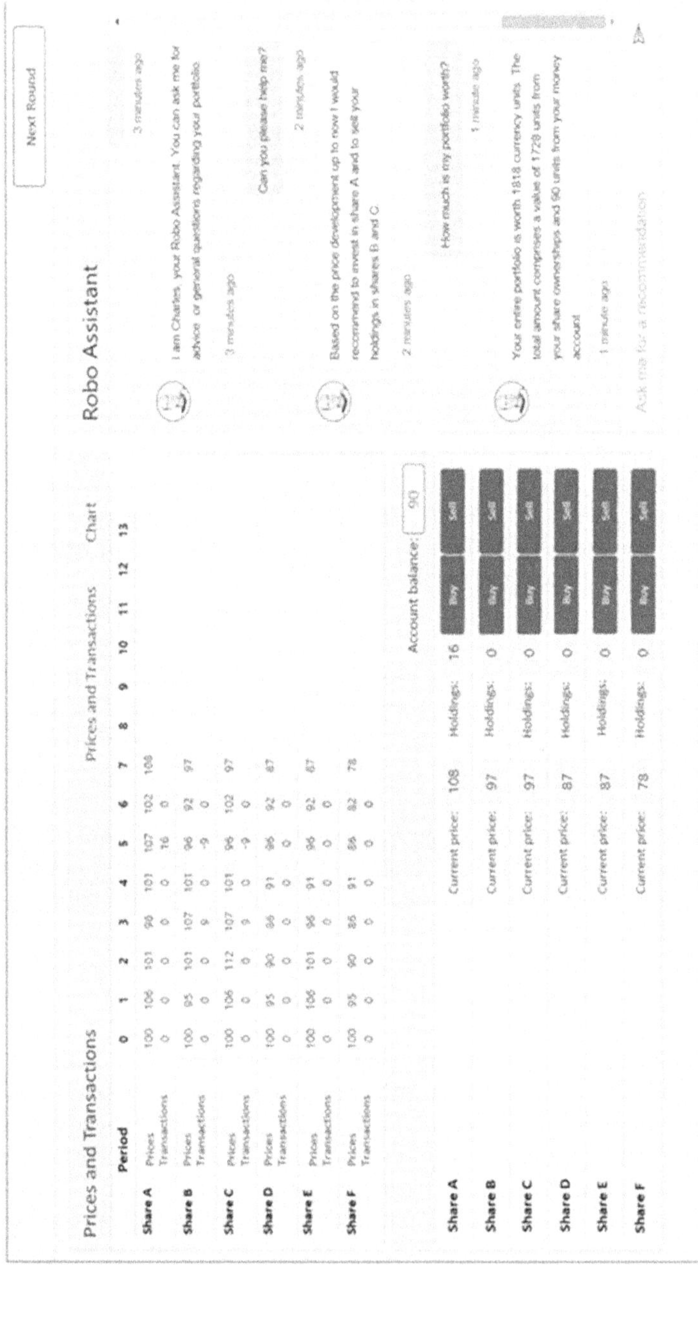

Figure 5.1 Investors interface with the robo-advisor's application.

Source: (Adopted from Back et al., 2023.)

Table 5.2 Investors and robo-advisors sample queries and replies

Investors queries	*Robo-advisors replies*
Hi	Hello.
How are you feeling?	I am good. Glad for asking.
Who are you?	I am your robot helper, Charles. I am ready to address any questions and offer advice concerning your portfolio management.
What is your age?	I was primarily formed in the summer of 2019 with a software code, and I have been growing since then.
Who designed you?	I have been designed by highly committed researchers, and I am endlessly developing unique discoveries and expanding.
Thank you	It's my Pleasure.

Source: Adapted from study (Back et al., 2021).

Table 5.3 Demo queries that investors can ask robo-advisors

Demo Queries that Investors ask in Robo-advisors for Portfolio Investment Decisions
Which stock has earned the highest worth?
Which stock has lost the lowest value?
If stock A rises in price, how much will it cost in the subsequent period?
How often did share B earn in cost?
How much is my stock rate?
How many money units would I obtain if I sold all my stocks?
Who are you?
What are your strengths?
Can you please assist me?
I want some guidance.
Can you provide me with some suggestions?
What stocks should I purchase?
What stocks should I trade?

Source: Adapted from study (Back et al., 2021).

Figure 5.2 The robo-advisor with community design components (right) and without community design components (left).

Source: (Adopted from Back et al., 2023.)

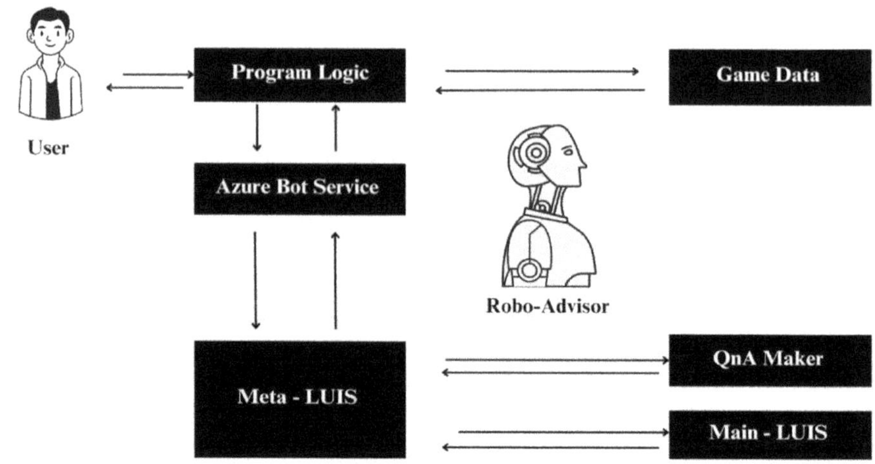

Figure 5.3 Components of the robo-advisors.

Source: (Author' own creation.)

As shown in Figure 5.3, the robo-advisor is composed of six components. The web forum features trading algorithms, a dialogue system, a comprehensive collection of all gaming data, and the incorporation of the robo-advisor chatbot, which forms the outstanding four components. These components generate the program logic and game data. The program logic generates texts that are sent to the Azure Bot Service, which analyses them and then transmits the outcomes again to the program logic. Microsoft's Language Understanding Intelligence Service (LUIS) is launched by the meta-LUIS component, which determines whether the newly arrived investor text should be processed by the main-LUIS or QnA Maker, which are two machine learning language components. Exclusively, both components examine each arriving text, and the findings provide an additional level of trust. Meta-LUIS determines which of the two findings is transmitted to the Azure Bot Service based on the trust level (Back et al., 2021). Finally, robo-advisors aid in enhancing financial stability, improving community spirit, and promoting wealth management, and stock markets are being attached to sustainability (Cheng et al., 2019).

5.3.4 Steps, building blocks of robo-advisors in the investment decision-making

Quantitative algorithmic models termed rob-advisors are engineered to support investment decisions and manage investors' stocks (Liu et al., 2023). Robo-advisory encompasses a range of investment services, comprising risk assessment, mortgage lending, credit evaluation, and investment guidance. Likewise, many financial institutions, notably the banking sector, have merged smart forums that operate as robo-advisors (Chhatwani, 2022). Therefore, a robo-advisor's directing process replicates the conventional investment advising approach. The three robo-advisory steps are stock configuration, comparison and management, which are reproduced in this system's six main steps: initiation, identification, idea, offer, completion, and management (Jung et al., 2018). Notably, there are three standard models of robo-advisors: (1) full automation, in which the robo-advisors function alone without human engagement; (2) advisor assisted, in which the investors have a choice to call a human financial advisor when essential; and (3) guided advice, in which the human financial advisors employ the robo-advisors essentially as a task planner during their data analysis (Huang et al., 2022).

The five key building blocks of a robo-advisor are generally portfolio selection, investor profile assessment, risk-return optimisation, tracking and reshuffling assets, and performance analysis. In simple terms, a robo-advisor creates an appropriate portfolio and makes gradual revisions by inquiring about its investors' investment intentions (Liu et al., 2023). Fortunately, robo-advisors appear to be a rising trend that mitigates the need for human advisors' engagement, allowing investors and conventional financial advisors to adopt a passive approach without closely monitoring the stock markets (Huang et al., 2022).

5.3.5 Theoretical framework of robo-advisors in investment decision-making

The Technology Acceptance Model (TAM), the Unified Theory of Acceptance and Use of Technology (UTAUT), and Innovation Diffusion Theory (IDT) are key theories that underline the adoption of robo-advisors in equity investment decision-making (Nain et al., 2024). TAM, which claims that perceived utility and perceived simplicity are the two key elements that motivate technology adoption, is the reason for the growing appeal of robo-advisors (Yeh et al., 2023). One of the most prominent theories of technology adoption is UTAUT, which was designed to investigate investors' readiness and inclination to welcome emerging technology (Nain & Rajan, 2024). Additionally, IDT attributes such as proportional advantage, intricacy, suitability, feasibility, and transparency encourage investors to use new technologies (Nguyen et al., 2023). As a result, all these robo-advisory theories are founded on technology and innovation that is perceived to surpass human skills, mostly in relation to storage and immediate processing of data.

5.3.6 Popular robo-advisory companies for investment decision-making

5.3.6.1 Betterment

Betterment, one of the top and largest robo-advisory companies in the United States, was launched in 2008. As computerised financial operations expanded gradually, COVID-19 had a positive influence on Betterment. Betterment disclosed a 25% surge in account openings in the first three months of 2020. Betterment facilitates an affordable, transparent, and rational portfolio allocation technique, along with a wide range of investment decision-making tools, according to a 2022 Morningstar Inc. research of sixteen robo-advisors. Betterment, a prominent robo-advisor, offers two service options: Betterment Premium, which incurs a yearly fee of 0.40% and gives unlimited phone access to registered financial advisors, and Betterment Digital, which delivers securities management for a yearly management fee of 0.25%. Furthermore, it differentiates itself from other robo-advisors by proposing an array of customised securities choices, covering BlackRock Target Income, Goldman Sachs Smart Beta, adjustable portfolio, and community-oriented investments. Betterment commonly distinguishes its investors into three groups: individual, institutional, and aged investors. Each of these groups obtains services from Betterment alone, namely Betterment for Advisor (B4A) and Betterment for Business (B4B). They can provide services that include tax deduction strategies, individual retirement accounts, investment planning, and even more. Concerning investment avenues, Betterment facilitates investors in apportioning stocks and bonds and directs on generating advice for portfolio investment decisions. In recent times, Betterment has garnered significant attention from venture capital firm investors. As a result, Betterment is notable globally and a gold standard in the United States' robo-advisor industry (Di, 2023).

5.3.6.2 *Wealth front*

Wealthfront is another leading company in the robo-advisor realm and claims to be the finest robo-advisors in 2022. With over 480,000 investors in the United States and approximately $27 billion in assets under management as of 2022, Wealthfront will be acquired by UBS Group AG for $1.4 billion in cash. Although it offers outstanding machine-driven management as well as other tax-saving tactics, it has apparently not been fully implemented, as few investors opt to look outside due to the absence of conventional financial advisors. Additionally, Wealthfront enables investors to make cryptocurrency investments, currently restricting them only to bitcoin and ether (Di, 2023).

5.3.6.3 *Charles Schwab*

In the long run, Charles Schwab has evolved into a comprehensive investment forum and has invited external portfolio investment companies. As stated on Charles Schwab's authorised website, its screening criteria for exchange-traded funds in securities, which largely include mitigating risk, dimensions, standardisation, tracking, and working expense ratios, can help in diminishing the number of exchange-traded funds exceeding 2,000 that may be added to an investor's smart portfolio account. In the event that portfolio allocation deviates significantly from the objectives, Charles Schwab has a fully computerised rebalancing technique (Di, 2023).

5.3.7 Evaluation of key challenges, regulatory disputes and major remedies on robo-advisors in selected nations

The primary challenges for robo-advisors include artificial intelligence bias, regulatory disputes, and cybersecurity. Some governing authorities, such as the Securities and Exchange Commission in the United States, the Financial Conduct Authority in the United Kingdom, the Securities and Exchange Board of India in India, etc. As illustrated in Table 5.4, a nation establishes accountability. To encourage better and higher transparency among

Table 5.4 Outlining the robo-advisor's usage risks, regulatory problems, and significant solutions across selected countries

SL No.	*Nations*	*Key challenges*	*Regulatory disputes*	*Major remedies*
1	United States	• Fraudulent AI allegations • Algorithm bias • Cybersecurity	• Securities and Exchange Commission supervision under the Investment Advisors Act • State-level rules	• Transparent AI usage standards • Common algorithm checks • Privacy safety
2	United Kingdom	• Technical bugs creating losses • Weak reaction to market fluctuations	• Financial Conduct Authority regulatory control • Investors' safety standards	• Restoration plans • Real-time market loss tracking • Increased transparency
3	Germany	• Legal insecurity due to changing policies • Investors' safety issues	• Germany's Federal Financial Supervisory Authority • General Data Protection Regulation	• Proper regulatory framework • Powerful investor rights implementation • Algorithm anxiety checking
4	Japan	• Strong reliance on algorithms risks organisational breakdowns • Limited adjusting to market variations	• Financial Services Agency • Strong cybersecurity laws	• Elastic adaptive methods • Rigorous data protection measures
5	India	• Regulatory uncertainty • Data privacy risks • Less financial literacy	• Securities and Exchange Board of India • Conditions on fee structures • No combined financial technology model	• Proper combined rules • Powerful data security policies • Financial education campaigns

Source: Author's own creation.

robo-advisors internationally, major remedies focus on online security, the development of moral artificial intelligence, investor financial literacy, and regulatory clarity.

5.3.8 Benefits and risks associated with robo-advisors in investment decision-making

5.3.8.1 Benefits

The robo-advising companies emerged as a transformational move by newcomers who identified a way to deliver advice to investors who were previously underserved by conventional human advisors. A sight to shift to robo-advisors is the decreased cost of retaining a full level of conventional human advisors (D'Acunto et al., 2019). In addition to the price reductions secured by innovations, there are several reasons why robo-advisors may appear to be more expensive than human advice. Transferable algorithms centred on financial models are widely used by robo-advisors (Huang et al., 2022). Automation can also improve communication with investors more rapidly and conveniently. For instance, in response to updates or progress in the stock markets, robo-advisors can instantly inform investors (Di, 2023).

Furthermore, robo-advisors are transparent. The improved speed and efficacy of executing plans generated by machine-driven algorithms, which are integrated into robo-advisors, is an added advantage. For example, automated processing empowers tax-saving loss harvesting, a core service delivered by robo-advisors, notably Betterment and Wealthfront (D'Acunto et al., 2019). From another angle, conventional human advisors and investors routinely engage in conversations that are identical to retail transactions, where the advisor has a desire to optimise personal benefits that might not match the investor's foremost interest. Investors may be subjected to the disputes, biases, and mental constraints of conventional human advisors. As a result, investment planning is increasingly being conducted in online forums, where robo-advisors are being considered as a solution for major legal reforms (Chhatwani, 2022).

5.3.8.2 Risks

Robo-advisors do not necessarily have downsides. The incorporation of programmed tools regularly demands that the tool enable stock investors a certain level of control, such as the power to approve any trade and examine portfolio decisions. Offering stock investors this kind of control helps address the algorithm model, which is a point of caution for investors, as it provides algorithms full power over investment decision-making (D'Acunto et al., 2019). Despite this, offering investors full power also re-establishes imperfect behaviour, such as excessive trading and indiscipline. Likewise, few robo-advisors have been criticised for mostly putting company revenues over the goals of stock investors (Huang et al., 2022). With respect to financial rewards, competitors and newcomers may employ diverse tactics when accessing the robo-advisor industry. It is the obligation of competitor companies to meet their existing investors. It is challenging for them to launch an innovative product from a commercial standpoint since it could impact their existing investors (D'Acunto et al., 2019).

Holding investors is the greatest difficulty encountered by robo-advisor companies. Stock investment decision-making is influenced by evolving market conditions and requires allocating time to offer constructive outcomes (Nain & Rajan, 2023). When investors do not see their investment objectives being accomplished in the near future, they quickly lose enthusiasm and discontinue employing the robo-advisors (Di, 2023). To retain active investors during their waiting period and offer them a greater return on investment, robo-advisors must provide additional services beyond advice services (Nain & Rajan, 2023).

The investment planning industry uses several robot genres. Privately owned companies that are not engaged in the investment industry are the entities that provide robo-advisory services (D'Acunto et al., 2019). Multiple companies have associated online forums to educate investors on their cash flow habits and how they influence their pension funds, in addition to issuing notifications after each transaction. These lending company-provided forums are typically designed to promote the independent business and its own proposed investment planning and schemes. As an outcome, not all robo-advisory companies are unbiased (Chhatwani, 2022).

5.4 CASE LET ON UNDERSTANDING THE USAGE OF ROBO-ADVISORS IN THE INVESTMENT DECISION-MAKING

Priyanka, a 35-year-old IT professional based in Pune, wanted to retire at the age of 55 with enough savings in her account to maintain her current lifestyle. She approached her close friends and colleagues in the office for suggestions regarding investments. They all suggested different investment avenues, including fixed deposits, Public Provident Fund, Monthly Income Scheme from the Post Office, Mutual funds, Treasury Bills, company shares, and Bonds issued by public sector companies, among others. When she asked her parents and relatives who had good experience with investments, they advised her to invest in gold, silver, and other precious metals, and also suggested that she consider investing in real estate. Although it required a substantial upfront payment, it would yield a steady income in the form of rentals, equivalent to receiving a pension. She liked the idea, but unfortunately, the real estate prices were so high that it was out of her budget. So, she started reading newspaper columns and blogs by famous writers about which investment to prefer. Based on the advice of her friends, she selected a few books to learn the science of investing, such as The Psychology of Money by Morgan Housel, The Intelligent Investor by Benjamin Graham, and Rich Dad Poor Dad, written by Robert Kiyosaki. After reading these best-selling novels, she remained uncertain about how to begin her investment journey. Then she started searching on the internet. This experience was mind-boggling; she was overwhelmed with the volume of information available to prospective investors. Her boss suggested seeking expert advice from investment advisors. They would charge fees. He also shared the contact details of an investment advisor whom he had consulted. Going through different financial and investment portals. she was introduced to Robo-advisors. These Robo-advisors were AI-based investment advisors, which is why they were named as Robo-advisors. They are relatively new in the market. When Priyanka entered all her details into a robo advisory platform, it curated a ready-made investment plan for her. She was happy as the plan was quite close to what she wanted to do with her money. Deep within, she understood it was based on some algorithm.

5.5 RESULTS

In line with earlier work, the outcomes of this research reveal the growing impact of robo-advisors on portfolio investment decisions. Robo-advisors are digital platforms that deliver investment advice based on machine learning algorithms with limited human involvement. To manage financial portfolios in accordance with investors' risk tolerance, investment targets, and choices, they typically employ cutting-edge algorithms and modern portfolio theory. The operation of robo-advisors in portfolio investment decisions has reshaped wealth management, expanding it to a broader market because of their convenience and price reductions. Initiation, identification, idea, offer, completion, and management are important steps of a robo-advisor's design. Operations typically include collecting investor information, testing their financial position, and indicating personalised investment approaches. Portfolio selection, investor profile assessment, risk-return optimisation, tracking and reshuffling assets and performance analysis are the building blocks of robo-advisors. Famous robo-advisors with affordable costs and a broad spectrum of portfolio selections include Betterment, Wealthfront, and Charles Schwab. The selected nations' key challenges for robo-advisors comprise artificial intelligence bias, regulatory disputes, and cybersecurity. To encourage better and higher transparency among robo-advisors internationally, major remedies focus on online security, the development of moral artificial intelligence, investor financial literacy, and regulatory clarity. Benefits include low cost, manageable, and customised investment advice. Despite this, complications persist, including risks such as a lack of uniformity, limited human engagement, and possible artificial intelligence biases. Despite the fact that case studies have been proven to help understand robo-advisors as an essential element in rationalising stock market investment decisions.

5.6 LIMITATIONS AND THE AGENDA FOR FUTURE RESEARCH DIRECTIONS

A substantial amount of literature has been generated by robo-advisor researchers in the previous decade. The information applied in this research was obtained from previous studies. Grounded in the exhaustive review of robo-advisors in the literature on stock market investment decisions, researchers outline avenues for future study. As in earlier studies, researchers segregated the proposed research lines into theory, context, characteristics, and technique, adhering to the outline of the TCCM framework. Model research questions for future studies are compiled for each theme in Table 5.5. While this review study has provided informative and constructive inputs, future studies must consider distinct boundaries. This paper is conceptual in nature; therefore, it is challenging to generalise its outcomes. Future studies can centre on applying quantitative, qualitative and mixed approaches to empirically verify the research's constructs. With the support of interviews and group brainstorming, future researchers may also explore investors' opinions of machine learning services to determine what discourages investors from engaging with robo-advisors. Figure 5.4 illustrates a fascinating path for future study, assessing the independent, dependent, mediating, and moderating variables in the framework of the suggested conceptual model. Despite the mentioned shortcomings, the outcomes of this research will provide investors, service providers, financial advisors, policymakers, marketers,

Table 5.5 TCCM framework for future research paths on robo-advisors in investment decisions

SL No.	*TCCM component*	*Significant future research paths*
1	Theory	• What are the requirements of investors in the adoption of robo-advisors in investment decision-making? • What abilities do robo-advisors need to be ambitious in the stock markets?
2	Context	• How do robo-advisors influence investment decisions in emerging markets? • How does the pre-and post-robo-advisory adoption behaviour of stock investors vary?
3	Characteristics	• What are the socio-economic factors that influence the usage of robo-advisors by small-scale investors? • How can robo-advisors be customised for a better investment decision?
4	Methodology	• Applying a qualitative research approach to understand the stock investors in robo-advisory usage. • Assessing the impact of advanced technologies in robo-advisors on stock investors through a quantitative approach by considering large samples.

Source: Author' own creation through literature.

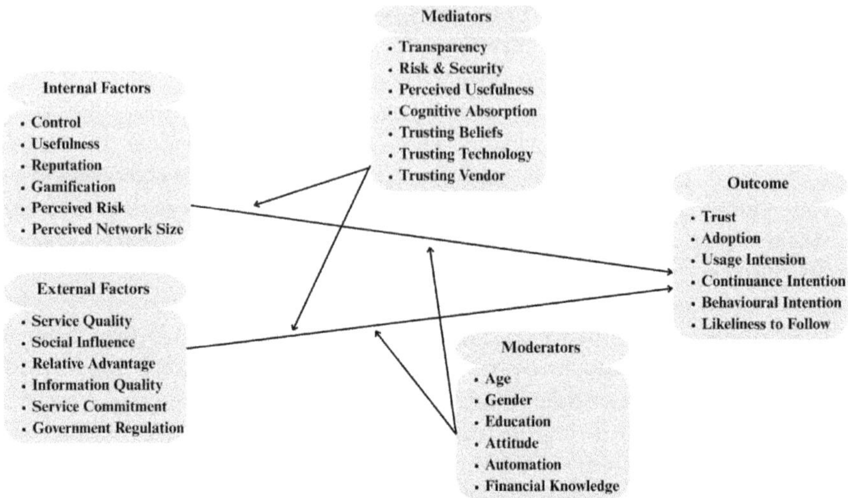

Figure 5.4 Conceptual model for future research.

Source: (Author' own creation through literature.)

academicians, and researchers with constructive information for the efficient global implementation of sophisticated robo-advisory services.

5.7 CONCLUSION

In the domain of stock markets and other financial resources, machine learning algorithms are a broad and expanding topic of research. Advice is crucial for achieving financial goals and making investment decisions within a given time frame. Yet, not all investors are able to hire a human financial advisor to assist them in making investment decisions. Artificial intelligence contributed to the establishment of robo-advisory itself due to technological enhancements in the investment world. Robo-advisors are online applications that utilise neural networks to offer investment advice without human engagement. The wealth management industry is evolving due to the global growth of the robo-advisory market. The objective of this research is to examine the role of robo-advisors in global investment decisions. The three core aspects of robo-advisors, namely clarity, simplicity, and user-friendliness, are emphasised in the main results. Furthermore, it is stated that robo-advisory services are continuing in their infancy and need substantial reforms to succeed in the investment industry. According to a review of previous literature, robo-advisory services are expected to experience significant growth over the next five years, as efforts are made to educate stock investors and to set regulations that currently supervise investment decisions. In conclusion, this research has crucial uses for financial technology experts and wealth managers.

5.8 IMPLICATIONS

Stakeholders in the financial investment industry can achieve significant gains by utilising robo-advisors. For stock investors, they offer affordable, simplified security management and equalising financial services. Service providers can connect with more digital natives, thereby boosting flexibility for growth and a competitive landscape. Financial advisors can combine robo-advisors' models to serve a greater variety of investors or give more attention to advanced services for wealthy investors. Policymakers must regulate robo-advisors to secure stability, disclosure, and investor welfare. Marketers can target budget-conscious, technology-centric investors. Academicians and researchers have the opportunity to explore the influence of robo-advisors on stock market behaviour, investors' cognitive psychology, and social implications in investment decision-making.

REFERENCES

Back, C., Morana, S., & Spann, M. (2021). Do robo-advisors make us better investors? *SSRN Electronic Journal*. https://doi.org/10.2139/ssrn.3777387

Back, C., Morana, S., & Spann, M. (2023). When do robo-advisors make us better investors? The impact of social design elements on investor behavior. *Journal of Behavioral and Experimental Economics*, *103*, 101984. https://doi.org/10.1016/j.socec.2023.101984

Barile, D., Secundo, G., & Bussoli, C. (2024). Exploring artificial intelligence robo-advisor in banking industry: A platform model. *Management Decision*. https://doi.org/10.1108/MD-08-2023-1324

Beketov, M., Lehmann, K., & Wittke, M. (2018). Robo advisors: Quantitative methods inside the robots. *Journal of Asset Management*, *19*(6), 363–370. https://doi.org/10.1057/s41260-018-0092-9

Cheng, X., Guo, F., Chen, J., Li, K., Zhang, Y., & Gao, P. (2019). Exploring the trust influencing mechanism of robo-advisor service: A mixed method approach. *Sustainability*, *11*(18), 4917. https://doi.org/10.3390/su11184917

Chhatwani, M. (2022). Does robo-advisory increase retirement worry? A causal explanation. *Managerial Finance*, *48*(4), 611–628. https://doi.org/10.1108/MF-05-2021-0195

D'Acunto, F., Prabhala, N., & Rossi, A. G. (2019). The promises and pitfalls of robo-advising. *The Review of Financial Studies*, *32*(5), 1983–2020. https://doi.org/10.1093/rfs/hhz014

Di, X. (2023). Regulatory leadership in struggling – The US path in robo-advisors governance. *Law and Financial Markets Review*, *17*(2), 116–135. https://doi.org/10.1080/17521440.2024.2313473

Digmayer, C. (2024). Automated economic welfare for everyone? Examining barriers to adopting robo-advisors from the perspective of explainable artificial intelligence. *Journal of Interdisciplinary Economics*, *36*(2), 224–245. https://doi.org/10.1177/02601079221130183

Hou, J.-R., Li, Y.-H., & Kankham, S. (2025). The service attributes of robo-advisors: A choice-based conjoint analysis. *Information Technology & People*, *38*(1), 338–362. https://doi.org/10.1108/ITP-04-2023-0375

Huang, R. H., Wang, C. C., & Zhang, O. X. (2022). The development and regulation of robo-advisors in hong Kong: Empirical and comparative perspectives.

Journal of Corporate Law Studies, 22(1), 229–263. https://doi.org/10.1080/14735970.2021.2012884

Jung, D., Dorner, V., Weinhardt, C., & Pusmaz, H. (2018). Designing a robo-advisor for risk-averse, low-budget consumers. *Electronic Markets*, *28*(3), 367–380. https://doi.org/10.1007/s12525-017-0279-9

Liu, C., Yang, M., & Wen, M. (2023). Judge me on my losers: Do robo-advisors outperform human investors during the COVID-19 financial market crash? *Production and Operations Management*, *32*(10), 3174–3192. https://doi.org/10.1111/poms.14029

Nain, I., & Rajan, S. (2023). Algorithms for better decision-making: A qualitative study exploring the landscape of robo-advisors in India. *Managerial Finance*, *49*(11), 1750–1761. https://doi.org/10.1108/MF-01-2023-0055

Nain, I., & Rajan, S. (2024). A scoping review on the factors affecting the adoption of robo-advisors for financial decision-making. *Scientific Papers of the University of Pardubice, Series D: Faculty of Economics and Administration*, *32*(1). https://doi.org/10.46585/sp32011884

Nain, I., Rajan, S., Natchimuthu, N., & Shivanna, G. (2024). An empirical analysis of the antecedents and barriers to adopting robo-advisors for investment management among Indian investors. *Macroeconomics and Finance in Emerging Market Economies*, 1–18. https://doi.org/10.1080/17520843.2024.2341530

Nguyen, T. P. L., Chew, L. W., Muthaiyah, S., Teh, B. H., & Ong, T. S. (2023). Factors influencing acceptance of robo-advisors for wealth management in Malaysia. *Cogent Engineering*, *10*(1), 2188992. https://doi.org/10.1080/23311916.2023.2188992

Potdar, A., & Pande, M. (2021). Comprehensive analysis of machine learning algorithms used in robo-advisory services. *Journal of Physics: Conference Series*, *1964*(6), 062105. https://doi.org/10.1088/1742-6596/1964/6/062105

Prasad, A., & Seetharaman, A. (2021). Importance of machine learning in making investment decision in stock market. *Vikalpa: The Journal for Decision Makers*, *46*(4), 209–222. https://doi.org/10.1177/02560909211059992

Shanmuganathan, M. (2020). Behavioural finance in an era of artificial intelligence: Longitudinal case study of robo-advisors in investment decisions. *Journal of Behavioral and Experimental Finance*, *27*, 100297. https://doi.org/10.1016/j.jbef.2020.100297

Singh, I., & Kaur, N. (2017). WEALTH MANAGEMENT THROUGH ROBO ADVISORY. *International Journal of Research -GRANTHAALAYAH*, *5*(6), 33–43. https://doi.org/10.29121/granthaalayah.v5.i6.2017.1991

Syed, W. K., & Janamolla, K. R. (2024). How AI-driven robo-advisors impact investment decision-making and portfolio performance in the financial sector: A comprehensive analysis. *11*(07).

Uhl, M. W., & Rohner, P. (2018). Robo-advisors versus traditional investment advisors: *an unequal game. The Journal of Wealth Management*, *21*(1), 44–50. https://doi.org/10.3905/jwm.2018.21.1.044

Warchlewska, A., & Waliszewski, K. (2020). Who uses robo-advisors? The Polish case. *European Research Studies Journal*, *XXIII*(Special Issue 1), 97–114. https://doi.org/10.35808/ersj/1748

Wexler, M. N., & Oberlander, J. (2021). Robo-advisors (RAs): The programmed self-service market for professional advice. *Journal of Service Theory and Practice*, *31*(3), 351–365. https://doi.org/10.1108/JSTP-07-2020-0153

Yeh, H.-C., Yu, M.-C., Liu, C.-H., & Huang, C.-I. (2023). Robo-advisor based on unified theory of acceptance and use of technology. *Asia Pacific Journal of Marketing and Logistics*, *35*(4), 962–979. https://doi.org/10.1108/APJML-07-2021-0493

Chapter 6

A machine learning-based financial health assessment and credit scoring tool for start-ups and SMEs

Kübra Aykaş and Nadi Serhan Aydın

6.1 INTRODUCTION

Small- and medium-sized enterprises (SMEs) play a pivotal role in the sustainable growth of national economies and in shaping the dynamics of socio-economic development from production to employment, and from employment to financial stability. Due to their vulnerable and fragile structures against market instabilities, these enterprises have a constant need for cash flow to sustain their commercial activities. This ongoing need often drives SMEs into a continuous search for financing opportunities. Financial institutions, on the other hand, determine the activation of support mechanisms for SMEs based on specific eligibility criteria. One of the most significant indicators of such eligibility is the enterprise's financial strength and its capacity to maintain that strength over time. The main barriers to SME financing include high cost, physical distance, and lack of proper documentation, which deter banks from managing the risks in servicing SMEs (Huang et al., 2020). Consequently, in order to benefit from financial support mechanisms, SMEs must regularly monitor and evaluate their own financial health. Within this framework, one of the most crucial determinants of financial health is creditworthiness, making credibility a key indicator of an enterprise's overall financial well-being.

6.2 REVIEW OF MACHINE LEARNING APPLICATIONS IN FINANCIAL HEALTH PREDICTION AND CREDIT SCORING FOR SMEs

In today's financial literature, machine learning (ML) methods, which are gaining increasing momentum in terms of their practical applications, significantly enhance banks' ability to distinguish between good and bad customers from a financial health perspective. As financial institutions increasingly adopt AI-driven credit scoring, the real-world implications are profound, impacting financial inclusion, revolutionizing risk management strategies, and influencing decision-making processes while concurrently influencing consumer trust (Addy et al., 2024). At the same time, they enable SMEs to identify potential

DOI: 10.1201/9781003656463-6

risks in advance and to benefit more effectively from personalized, finance-oriented services that promote financial health. SMEs often face challenges in obtaining credit due to their perceived high credit risk, and financial institutions have tightened their lending criteria, underscoring the need for more accurate and unbiased credit risk assessment methodologies (Intharasompong et al., 2025). In this context, Moscato et al. (2021) provided a comprehensive benchmark of ML approaches for credit score prediction, demonstrating that ensemble methods such as Random Forest and Gradient Boosting outperform traditional statistical models due to their superior ability to capture nonlinear relationships and complex interactions in financial data. Similarly, Malakauskas and Lakstutiene (2021) explored the use of AI tools in modeling SME creditworthiness and emphasized that AI-based models leveraging neural networks and data-driven feature extraction can enhance predictive accuracy and offer more dynamic assessment frameworks compared to conventional methods. Expanding this perspective, Nguyen et al. (2025) proposed a hybrid approach combining knowledge-based systems with ML techniques to predict the financial health of SMEs, highlighting improved interpretability and robustness while mitigating the "black-box" problem common in purely ML-based models. Likewise, Provenzano et al. (2020) developed a comprehensive ML-based credit rating and default prediction framework integrating natural language processing (NLP), gradient boosting, and genetic algorithms, achieving strong performance on test data. In a similar vein, Dumitrescu et al. (2022) introduced the Penalised Logistic Tree Regression (PLTR), a hybrid credit scoring model that merges the interpretability of logistic regression with the flexibility of decision tree-based feature engineering, thereby improving predictive accuracy while preserving transparency in credit risk assessment. Furthermore, Li et al. (2016) proposed a hybrid credit risk evaluation model for SME lending that integrates traditional logistic regression with artificial neural networks (ANNs), emphasizing that this improvement in model accuracy reduces credit assessment errors, enhances portfolio performance, and potentially lowers both capital requirements for banks and interest rates for firms. In another study, Wu and Pan (2021) applied the PDC-RF algorithm to the Lending Club dataset, reducing the feature dimension from 145 to 22. After performing WOE encoding, they compared the performance of RF, SVM, and logistic regression models. The study concluded that the logistic regression model was more suitable in terms of both performance and interpretability, and a credit scorecard was developed based on this model.

6.3 DATASET STRUCTURE AND FEATURE SPACE

In this chapter, the dataset utilized for the empirical assessment of SMEs' financial health is formally introduced. The dataset, sourced from Kaggle,[1] encompasses 7,805 observations pertaining to 1,334 companies and 24 distinct features, each of which has been derived from the credit evaluation criteria employed by leading international credit rating institutions. Designed to capture the multidimensional nature of financial health, the dataset incorporates key financial indicators such as liquidity ratios, profitability metrics, leverage measures, and sector-specific descriptive attributes. As detailed in Table 6.1, these variables collectively represent the fundamental determinants that shape the financial health profile of firms and serve as the analytical foundation for the subsequent modeling stages.

Table 6.1 Corporate credit rating data summary

Variable	*Name*	*Explanation*	*Data type*
Y	Rating	Credit score or grade assigned to the company.	object
X1	Rating Agency	Organization providing the credit rating	object
X2	Corporation	Name of the company being rated.	object
X3	Rating Date	Date when the credit rating was issued.	object
X4	CIK	Unique identifier number for financial assets	int64
X5	SIC Code	Industry classification used to evaluate financial metrics.	float64
X6	Sector	Industry sector of the company.	object
X7	Ticker	tock ticker symbol of the company.	object
X8	Current Ratio	Measures short-term liquidity.	float64
X9	Long-term Debt / Capital	Assesses long-term financial leverage.	float64
X10	Debt/Equity Ratio	Indicates the proportion of debt to equity used in financing.	float64
X11	Gross Margin	Measures the percentage of revenue remaining after deducting cost of sales.	float64
X12	Operating Margin	Shows profitability from core business operations.	float64
X13	EBIT Margin	Percentage of earnings before interest and taxes relative to revenue.	float64
X14	EBITDA Margin	Earnings before interest, tax, depreciation, and amortization as a percentage of revenue.	float64
X15	Pre-Tax Profit Margin	Indicates profitability before taxes	float64
X16	Net Profit Margin	Shows overall profitability.	float64
X17	Asset Turnover	Measures efficiency of assets in generating revenue.	float64
X18	ROE—Return On Equity	Efficiency of generating profit from shareholders' equity	float64
X19	Return On Tangible Equity	Profitability generated from tangible equity assets.	float64
X20	ROA—Return On Assets	Efficiency of asset utilization.	float64
X21	ROI—Return On Investment	Overall efficiency of investment returns.	float64
X22	Operating Cash Flow Per Share	Operating cash flow allocated per share.	float64
X23	Free Cash Flow Per Share	Cash flow remaining per share after capital expenditures.	float64

Table 6.2 Distribution of credit ratings and class labels

Credit Score	*Frequency*	*Class*	*Total*
AAA	90		
AA+	73		
AA	185		
AA–	254		
A+	478	Class 1 Total	5099
A	836		
A–	722		
BBB+	846		
BBB	910		
BBB–	705		
BB+	545		
BB	453		
BB–	427		
B+	422		
B	310		
B–	288		
CCC+	151	Class 0 Total	2076
CCC	65		
CCC–	10		
CC+	**1***		
CC	18		
C	11		
D	**5***		

*Indicates extremely rare minority class.

In the dataset as well as the present model, the *Rating* variable acts as the target variable. Within this framework, firms with a credit rating of BBB— were classified as financially risky and unsuitable for lending. However, as seen in Table 6.2, the number of financially risky firms was considerably lower compared to other classes, leading to a class imbalance problem. In evaluating financial health, such imbalances can adversely affect the ability to accurately and reliably classify firms based on their financial condition. Therefore, in this study, we also employ resampling techniques to improve data quality and balance model performance. Through the implementation of these methods, it was aimed to mitigate class imbalance and, consequently, to achieve significant improvements in evaluation metrics particularly in those representing the minority class, such as recall and the F1-score.

6.4 EVALUATION METRICS

As our sample exhibits data imbalance, the effects of resampling techniques were investigated to improve the representation of the minority class, which comprises financially risky and non-creditworthy firms. The evaluation of model performance was conducted based on four fundamental metrics: Accuracy, Precision, Recall, and F1-Score.

Accuracy represents the proportion of correctly classified observations among all samples. However, in an imbalanced dataset, where the majority class (e.g., financially healthy companies) is overrepresented, this metric may fail to reflect the true performance of the model. A high accuracy value does not necessarily indicate that the model can correctly identify the minority class that is, financially distressed and non-creditworthy companies. Therefore, Recall becomes the most critical evaluation metric for accurately detecting the minority class. Recall measures the proportion of actual financially distressed cases that the model correctly identifies. In other words, it evaluates the model's ability to avoid overlooking risky companies.

The following are well-known equations to calculate these metrics:

$$Accuracy = \frac{TP + TN}{TP + FP + FN + TN} \tag{6.1}$$

$$Precision = \frac{TP}{TP + FP} \tag{6.2}$$

$$Recall = \frac{TP}{TP + FN} \tag{6.3}$$

$$F1 - Score = 2 \times \frac{Precision \times Recall}{Precision + Recall} \tag{6.4}$$

In our case, TP (True Positive) refers to companies that are financially distressed and correctly identified as such; FP (False Positive) represents companies that are financially healthy but incorrectly classified as risky; and FN (False Negative) denotes financially distressed companies that the model fails to detect. A high Recall value indicates that the model is more successful in identifying financially risky companies meaning it reduces the likelihood of overlooking cases with default risk. However, focusing solely on Recall may increase the rate of false alarms (FP). Therefore, to achieve a balanced evaluation of model performance, metrics such as the F1-Score, which considers both Recall and Precision components, should be jointly assessed.

6.5 DATA PREPROCESSING AND FEATURE ENGINEERING

In constructing predictive models aimed at assessing the financial health of companies, the primary prerequisite is to transform the available data into a structure suitable for analytical processing and modeling. In this regard, data preprocessing can be considered a preparatory stage that enhances the quality of model output. This stage is not only one of the most critical steps affecting the model's ultimate accuracy and generalizability but also a fundamental component that directly influences the efficiency, stability, and computational speed of the entire learning process.

On the dataset where the target variable was defined as *Rating*, the initial step involved analyzing missing and outlier values. No missing observations were detected in the dataset, thereby preserving the integrity of the variables. In addition, categorical variables were converted into numerical form using transformer classes such as LabelEncoder and OneHotEncoder. Through this process, all variables were made compatible with numerical processing, enabling the learning algorithms to be applied directly and efficiently.

Following the transformation procedures, standardization was applied to eliminate imbalances arising from differences in the scales of numerical variables. This process is based on rescaling the variables so that their mean equals zero and their standard deviation equals one. Mathematically, the standardization procedure can be expressed as follows:

$$z = \frac{x - \mu}{\sigma} \tag{6.5}$$

where x represents the original (raw) value of the variable, μ denotes the mean of the variable, and σ indicates its standard deviation. The resulting value, z, corresponds to the standardized form of the variable.

After the standardization process, we examine the relationships among the standardized variables to identify potential interdependencies. As illustrated in Figure 6.1, a correlation analysis is conducted, which reveals a high level of association among certain financial indicators. This situation brought the issue of multicollinearity to attention. To mitigate the effect of shared variance among variables and enhance the model's generalizability, we apply Principal Component Analysis (PCA).

PCA is a sophisticated dimensionality reduction method used in the data preprocessing stage to minimize the negative effects caused by high dimensionality and random noise. As known, dimension reduction algorithms convert data from higher dimensions to lower dimensions according to particular specified requirements. PCA is primarily used to condense a huge set of variables into a manageable number while retaining the majority of their information (Bharadiya, 2023). PCA generates new, composite, and mutually independent (orthogonal) components by optimizing the linear combinations of the original features, thereby redefining the information content of the dataset within a more compact yet highly representative subspace. PCA provides additional strategic benefits such as discriminative feature extraction, noise filtering, mitigation of multicollinearity, and more intuitive visualization of high-dimensional data. Consequently, ML models gain advantages not only in computational efficiency but also in stability of accuracy metrics, improved generalizability, and optimized processing times.

The steps of PCA are presented in Table 6.3.

In this study, PCA is applied to the initial 23 numerical variables in the dataset. By retaining 95% of the total variance, the dimensionality of the data is reduced from 23 variables to 12 principal components with minimal information loss. Figure 6.2 presents the variance structure of the PCA results,

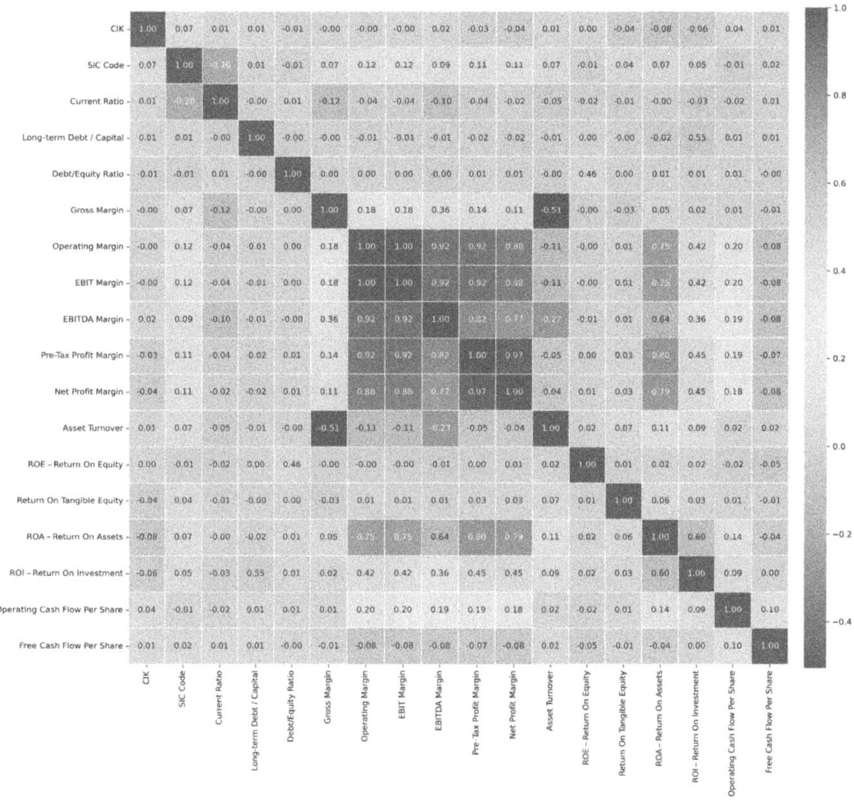

Figure 6.1 Correlation analysis of financial indicators

Table 6.3 Principal component analysis (PCA) methodology

Steps	*Formulas*
1. Constructing the Data Matrix	$X = \begin{bmatrix} x^{1T} \\ x^{2T} \\ \vdots \\ x_n^{T} \end{bmatrix}$, Each row represent a data point $X \in R^{nxd}$
2. Mean Centering	$X' = X - \overline{x}$, where $\overline{x} = (1/n)\Sigma^{(i=1)n} x_i$
3. Computing the Covariance Matrix	$\Sigma = (1/(n-1))(X')^T X'$
4. Finding Eigenvalues and Eigenvectors	$\Sigma v_k = \lambda_k v_k$
5. Selecting Eigenvectors with the Largest Eigenvalues	$PC = [v_1, v_2, v_3, \ldots, v_m], (\lambda^1 > \lambda^2 > \cdots > \lambda_m)$

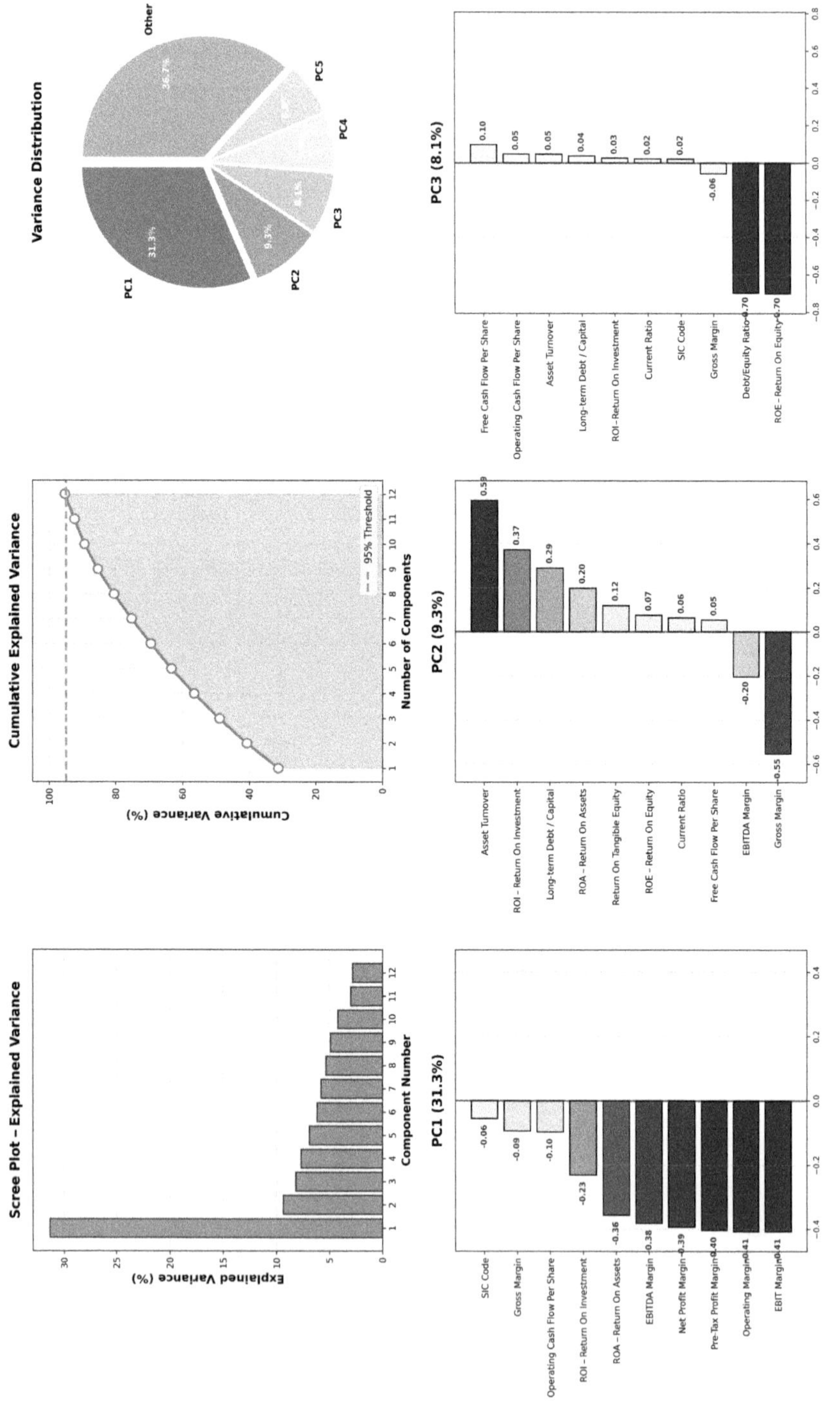

Figure 6.2 Principal component analysis (PCA) results and variance structure

including the scree plot, cumulative explained variance, and the distribution of variance across components. The figure indicates that the first principal component (PC1) accounts for a substantial portion of the total variance, while the remaining components progressively capture the residual variance. In addition, the loading plots of the leading components reveal the financial ratios that contribute most significantly to the formation of each principal component.

The first principal component (PC1) is primarily characterized by profitability and performance-related financial ratios. These include Operating Margin, Pre-Tax Profit Margin, Net Profit Margin, EBITDA Margin, Return on Assets (ROA), Return on Investment (ROI), and Return on Equity (ROE), with Gross Margin contributing to a lesser extent. Collectively, these variables reflect firms' operational efficiency, profitability, and return-generating capacity, indicating that PC1 captures the core financial performance dimension of the dataset. As such, PC1 plays a critical role in the model's decision-making process for distinguishing financially at-risk enterprises.

Overall, the findings indicate that components driven by profitability and efficiency serve as decisive indicators in assessing firms' financial health and creditworthiness.

6.6 HANDLING CLASS IMBALANCE WHEN FALSE NEGATIVES ARE COSTLY

In datasets used in critical areas such as credit rating, class imbalance is one of the most common issues. Such imbalance can prevent minority classes from being adequately learned, causing models to entirely overlook these classes. This situation biases the model toward the majority class and results in skewed predictions. While the model may show high accuracy for the majority class, its predictive performance for the minority class is often poor. Class imbalance adversely affects the learning process, typically producing classifiers with low accuracy for the minority class and assigning most new instances to the majority class (Blagus & Lusa, 2013). In financial decision-making, misclassifications in the minority class can be costly. A single misclassified firm in the minority class may lead to significant errors in credit allocation or investment strategies.

To mitigate the negative effects of this imbalance, various oversampling techniques have been developed in the field. The literature includes numerous resampling methods commonly used to represent minority classes. In this study, compared to other methods, the Synthetic Minority Over-sampling Technique (SMOTE), the Adaptive Synthetic Sampling approach (ADASYN), and SMOTE-based hybrid approaches—which better preserve the original structure of the minority class while generating balanced data—were applied during the preprocessing stage to address class imbalance and improve model performance. Although these resampling techniques serve the same purpose of enhancing the minority class, they differ in their implementation methods.

SMOTE increases the representational power of the minority class by generating synthetic samples based on existing minority instances. Rather than simply duplicating samples, it creates new synthetic examples by interpolating between minority class instances within a given neighborhood (Fernández et al., 2018). This process provides a more balanced data distribution, enabling ML models to achieve better discriminative performance across all classes.

In the operation of the SMOTE algorithm, after selecting a minority class instance x_i, one of its 5 nearest minority neighbors is randomly chosen, and this point is denoted as x_{nn}. SMOTE generates a new synthetic data point at a random location along the line segment between x_i and $x_{nn.}$ The new point x_{new} is follows:

$$x_{new} = x_i + \delta \times (x_{nn} - x_i), 0 < \delta < 1 \tag{6.6}$$

The improved version of SMOTE, called ADASYN, generates synthetic data in a way that is sensitive to sample density. The primary idea behind ADASYN is to use a weighted distribution for different minority class examples based on their learning difficulty, with more synthetic data created for minority class examples that are harder to learn than minority class examples that are easier to learn (Ahmed et al., 2022). This approach enables a more imbalance-aware sampling process, thereby enhancing the model's ability to learn from the minority class.

First, the degree of class imbalance is calculated:

$$d = \frac{m_s}{m_l}, d \in (0,1] \tag{6.7}$$

Then, the required number of synthetic samples for the minority class is then calculated by defining the desired balance ratio, β, within the range of [0,1] in the dataset:

$$G = (m_l - m_s) \times \beta \tag{6.8}$$

For each x_i, the K nearest neighbors are identified. Let Δ_i denote the number of neighbors belonging to the majority class. Then, the local class imbalance ratio $r_i \in [0,1]$, representing the proportion of majority-class neighbors around x_i, is obtained as follows:

$$r_i = \frac{\Delta_i}{K} \tag{6.9}$$

which is normalized as follows:

$$\hat{r}_i = \frac{r_i}{\sum_{i=1}^{m_s} r_i} \tag{6.10}$$

The number of new synthetic samples to be generated are then given by

$$g_i = \hat{r}_i \times G \tag{6.11}$$

Each minority sample x_i is repeated g_i times, and a random sample x_{zi} is selected from among its K nearest neighbors. Then, a new synthetic data point is generated as follows:

$$s_i = x_i + (x_{zi} - x_i) \times \theta,\ \theta \in [0,1] \tag{6.12}$$

One of the hybrid methods used alongside SMOTE is SMOTE-Tomek (SMOTE + Tomek Links). During the SMOTE process, some synthetic samples may be generated very close to the majority class regions. To prevent this, Tomek links are applied to identify the closest pairs belonging to the majority and minority classes, and the majority class instances in these pairs are removed from the dataset. This helps to make the class boundaries clearer. However, this approach may also lead to the removal of some valid data points while sharpening the boundaries.

Another hybrid method, SMOTE-ENN (SMOTE + Edited Nearest Neighbors), filters out observations that do not agree with the majority of their k-nearest neighbors, along with the synthetic samples generated by SMOTE. This method stands out for its strong ability to clean noise from the dataset, though its aggressive nature can result in a certain degree of data loss.

As shown in Table 6.4, the dataset exhibits an imbalanced distribution, with companies carrying default risk being underrepresented. To model creditworthiness based on credit ratings and mitigate the effects of the imbalanced class structure, the present study applies resampling methods such as SMOTE, ADASYN, SMOTE-Tomek, and SMOTE-ENN to enhance the learning of minority classes.

As shown in Figure 6.3, our imbalanced dataset goes through various preprocessing steps, including the detection of missing values, outlier checks,

Table 6.4 Class distributions before and after resampling

Class distributions (with train/test split)			
Dataset	*Class 1*	*Class 0*	*Total*
Full Data	5099	2706	7805
Train (80%)	4079	2165	6244
Test (20%)	1020	541	1561
Train (before vs after resampling)			
Technique	Class 1	Class 0	Class Ratio
Original Train	4079	2165	1.88:1
SMOTE	4079	4079	1:1
ADASYN	4079	4023	1.01:1
SMOTE+Tomek	4068	4068	1:1
SMOTE+ENN	3297	3362	0.98:1

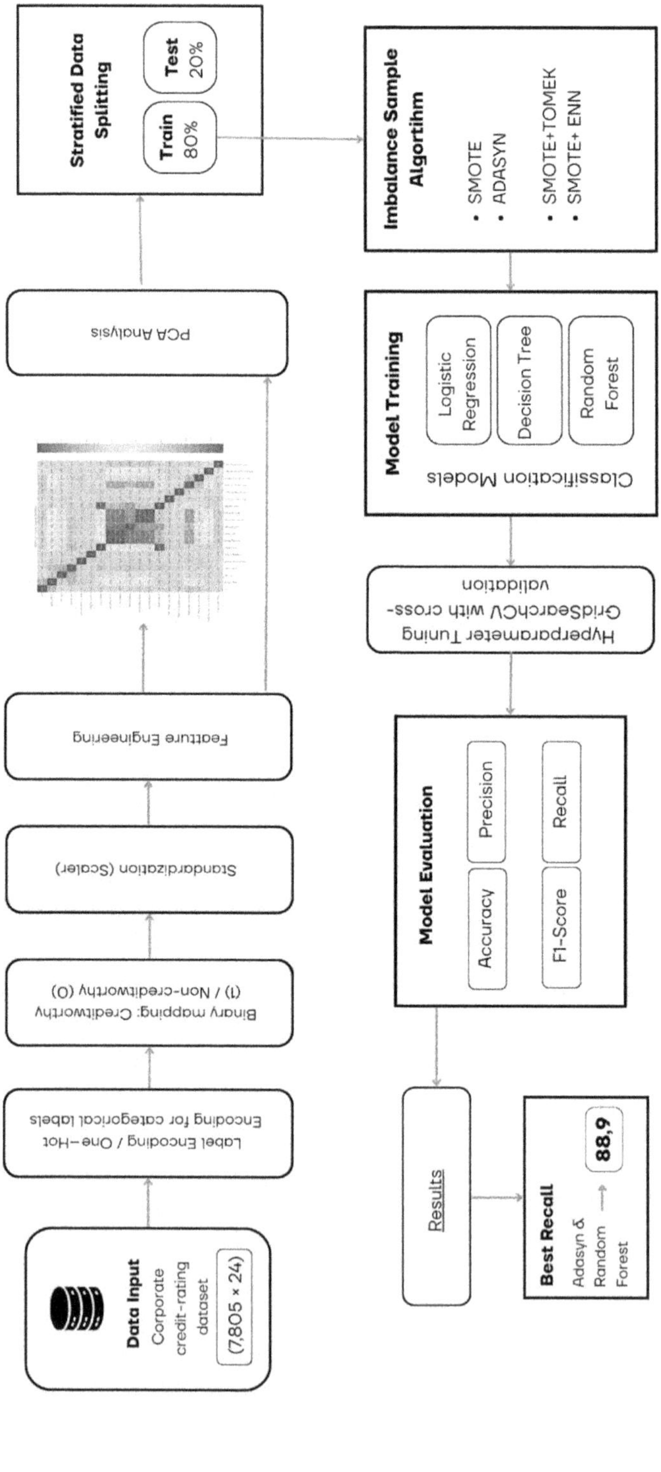

Figure 6.3 End-to-end pipeline for financial health and credit scoring framework

conversion of categorical variables to numerical format, and scaling of numerical variables using normalization or standardization techniques. To address class imbalance and improve model performance, SMOTE, ADASYN, SMOTE-ENN, and SMOTE-Tomek methods are employed. Following these preprocessing steps, three different ML models, namely, Decision Tree, Logistic Regression, and Random Forest, are trained and tested for financial health prediction. Hyperparameter optimization for each model is conducted using GridSearchCV: for Logistic Regression, the regularization parameter (C = [0.01–100]) and class weights; for Decision Tree, maximum depth (5–15), minimum samples split (2–100), and minimum samples per leaf (1–5); and for Random Forest, the number of trees (2–100) along with the Decision Tree parameters were systematically explored. To enhance the model's ability to generalize, a Stratified K-Fold Cross-Validation strategy (k = 5) is employed, preserving the original class distribution in each fold and minimizing bias caused by the imbalanced dataset. Model performance on both train and test sets is evaluated using accuracy, precision, recall, and F1-score metrics. This comprehensive approach enables a comparative analysis of 12 different model configurations (3 algorithms × 4 sampling methods) and facilitates the identification of the most optimal model for financial health assessment.

As shown in Table 6.5, the obtained results indicate that the resampling (oversampling) techniques used for imbalanced datasets play a decisive role in the overall model performance.

Table 6.5 Comparative performance of models with different resampling techniques

		Accuracy		*Precision*		*Recall*		*F1-Score*	
Model	*Resample*	*Train*	*Test*	*Train*	*Test*	*Train*	*Test*	*Train*	*Test*
Decision Tree	Actual	0.946	**0.894**	0.942	**0.882***	0.901	**0.802**	0.921	**0.840**
Decision Tree	Adasyn	0.963	**0.898**	0.960	**0.848**	0.966	**0.861***	0.963	**0.855**
Decision Tree	Smote	0.964	**0.900**	0.965	**0.845**	0.962	**0.850**	0.964	**0.857**
Decision Tree	Smote-Enn	0.991	**0.862**	0.997	**0.774**	0.986	**0.844**	0.991	**0.808**
Decision Tree	Smote-Tomek	0.960	**0.902***	0.962	**0.858**	0.958	**0.851**	0.960	**0.859***
Logistic Regression	Actual	0.783	**0.774***	0.827	**0.813***	0.474	**0.452**	0.602	**0.581**
Logistic Regression	Adasyn	0.711	**0.741**	0.714	**0.600**	0.698	**0.761***	0.706	**0.671**
Logistic Regression	Smote	0.752	**0.762**	0.761	**0.635**	0.735	**0.739**	0.748	**0.683***
Logistic Regression	Smote-Enn	0.792	**0.760**	0.810	**0.631**	0.769	**0.741**	0.789	**0.681**
Logistic Regression	Smote-Tomek	0.750	**0.760**	0.755	**0.632**	0.742	**0.737**	0.748	**0.680**
Random Forest	Actual	0.961	**0.915**	0.958	**0.913***	0.928	**0.839**	0.943	**0.874**
Random Forest	Adasyn	0.971	**0.912**	0.964	**0.867**	0.958	**0.889***	0.971	**0.875**
Random Forest	Smote	0.972	**0.911**	0.972	**0.879**	0.951	**0.863**	0.972	**0.871**
Random Forest	Smote-Enn	0.998	**0.872**	1.000	**0.801**	0.998	**0.841**	0.998	**0.820**
Random Forest	Smote-Tomek	0.970	**0.916***	0.972	**0.889**	0.970	**0.866**	0.970	**0.878***

*Maximum score achieved per metric.

For each model, the training and test sets were analyzed separately, enabling a clear evaluation of the effects of resampling techniques. In model comparisons, test set values were reported, as they reflect the models' true performance. Considering the test recall scores of the three models, the ADASYN method provides the most pronounced improvements. In the Decision Tree model, the recall performance after applying ADASYN increased from 80.2% to 86.1%. For the Logistic Regression model, ADASYN raised the recall value from 45.2% to 76.1%. In the Random Forest model, the recall score improved from 83.9% to 88.9%.

Using the same logic to examine F1 scores, the SMOTE-Tomek method provides the most notable improvements for the Decision Tree and Random Forest models, while in the Logistic Regression model, SMOTE application increases F1 performance.

6.7 RESULTS AND CONCLUSION

In this study, a methodology was introduced to assess the financial health and credit scores of SMEs and startups and facilitate their access to finance. The study, conducted using an open-source dataset, incorporated data preprocessing, feature engineering (via PCA), class imbalance handling, as well as resampling techniques. With PCA applied during preprocessing, 95% of the total variance was retained, reducing the number of features from 24 to 13. The findings showed that profitability- and efficiency-related ratios explained the majority of the variance, providing significant insights into financial health from a creditworthiness perspective. To address the common issue of class imbalance in financial datasets, widely used resampling techniques that preserve the structure of the minority class and contribute to improved model performance, namely, SMOTE, ADASYN, and hybrid approaches (SMOTE+ENN, SMOTE-Tomek), were applied to robust ML models such as Decision Tree, Logistic Regression, and Random Forest, and their performance was analyzed in a comparative manner. The primary rationale for selecting these resampling methods was their ability to generate synthetic data while preserving information in the minority class. Considering the scarcity of financially unhealthy companies within the dataset, recall score was considered particularly important. Experimental results indicated that resampling techniques can have significant positive effects on the classification model performance. In terms of recall, ADASYN provided the most consistent improvements across all three models. In the Decision Tree model, recall increased from 80.2% to 86.1% after applying ADASYN. In the Logistic Regression model, the effect of ADASYN was more pronounced, with recall rising substantially from 45.2% to 76.1%. In the Random Forest model, recall improved from 83.9% to 88.9%. These findings demonstrate that ADASYN is particularly effective in addressing class imbalance in linear models such as Logistic Regression. When examining F1-score performance, a different pattern emerged: SMOTE+Tomek produced the most notable improvements in the Decision Tree and Random Forest models, while basic SMOTE application yielded the highest F1 improvement in the Logistic Regression model.

This indicates that different resampling strategies may be preferred depending on model complexity. Overall, the Random Forest + SMOTE+Tomek combination exhibited the most balanced performance with 91.6% test accuracy and 87.8% F1-Score, while Random Forest + ADASYN stood out in capturing the minority class with 88,9% recall. Overfitting analysis revealed that SMOTE+ENN increased the train-test performance gap above 0.12, particularly in Decision Tree and Random Forest models, suggesting that hybrid methods that over-clean should be applied with caution.

In conclusion, in financial health and credit scoring applications where correct identification of the minority (at-risk) class is critical, combining robust data preprocessing and resampling techniques with ensemble learning models such as Random Forest enhances model accuracy and reliability, which is essential for financial risk assessment.

NOTE

1. https://www.kaggle.com/

REFERENCES

Addy, W., Ajayi-Nifise, A., Bello, B., Tula, S. T., Odeyemi, O., & Falaiye, T. (2024). AI in credit scoring: A comprehensive review of models and predictive analytics. Global Journal of Engineering and Technology Advances, 18(2), 118–129.

Ahmed, G., Er, M. J., Fareed, M. M. S., Zikria, S., Mahmood, S., He, J., Asad, M., Jilani, S. F., & Aslam, M. (2022). DAD-net: Classification of Alzheimer's disease using ADASYN oversampling technique and optimized neural network. Molecules, 27(20), 7085.

Bharadiya, J. P. (2023). A tutorial on principal component analysis for dimensionality reduction in machine learning. International Journal of Innovative Science and Research Technology, 8(5), 2028–2030.

Blagus, R., & Lusa, L. (2013). SMOTE for high-dimensional class-imbalanced data. BMC Bioinformatics, 14, 106.

Dumitrescu, E., Hué, S., Hurlin, C., & Tokpavi, S. (2022). Machine learning for credit scoring: Improving logistic regression with non-linear decision-tree effects. European Journal of Operational Research, 297(3), 1178–1192.

Fernández, A., García, S., Herrera, F., & Chawla, N. V. (2018). SMOTE for learning from imbalanced data: Progress and challenges, marking the 15-year anniversary. Journal of Artificial Intelligence Research, 61, 863–905.

Huang, Y., Zhang, L., Li, Z., Qiu, H., Sun, T., & Wang, X. (2020). Fintech Credit Risk Assessment for SMEs: Evidence from China. IMF Working Paper No. 2020/193. International Monetary Fund.

Intharasompong, S., Wongwiwat, P., & Phaphan, W. (2025). Stacked Ensemble Models for SME Credit Risk Assessment: Integrating Data Balancing and Feature Selection Techniques. Preprints.

Li, K., Niskanen, J., Kolehmainen, M., & Niskanen, M. (2016). Financial innovation: Credit default hybrid model for SME lending. Expert Systems with Applications, 61, 343–355.

Li, Y., & Chen, W. (2020). A comparative performance assessment of ensemble learning for credit scoring. Mathematics, 8(10), 1756.

Malakauskas, A., & Lakstutiene, A. (2021, August). The application of artificial intelligence tools in creditworthiness modelling for SME entities. In 2021 IEEE International Conference on Technology and Entrepreneurship (ICTE) (pp. 1–6). IEEE.

Moscato, V., Picariello, A., & Sperlí, G. (2021). A benchmark of machine learning approaches for credit score prediction. Expert Systems with Applications, 165, 113986.

Nguyen, H. D. V., Vu, S., Pham, U., Nguyen, D., & Dinh, D. (2025, July). A hybrid knowledge-based and machine learning approach for financial health prediction in small and medium-sized enterprises. In International Conference on Industrial, Engineering and Other Applications of Applied Intelligent Systems (pp. 390–402). Singapore: Springer Nature Singapore.

Provenzano, A. R., Trifirò, D., Datteo, A., Giada, L., Jean, N., Riciputi, A., Le Pera, G., Spadaccino, M., Massaron, L., & Nordio, C. (2020, August 4). Machine learning approach for credit scoring (arXiv:2008.01687 [q-fin.ST]). arXiv.

Wu, Y., & Pan, Y. (2021). Application analysis of credit scoring of financial institutions based on machine learning model. *Complexity*, *2021*(1), 9222617.

Chapter 7

Algorithmic morality

AI-Driven investing across industries and crises

Ihlas Sovbetov

7.1 INTRODUCTION

The growing adoption of artificial intelligence (AI) in asset management has generated intense academic debate regarding the capacity of algorithms to outperform human decision-making. The appeal of algorithmic strategies rests on their ability to process large datasets, detect nonlinear patterns, and implement emotionless decisions that are free from the behavioural biases documented in behavioural finance (Kartini & Nahda, 2021; Oechssler et al., 2009). From robo-advisors for retail investors to AI-based ETFs in institutional portfolios, automation has begun to reshape the boundaries of traditional asset management (D'Acunto et al., 2019; Kofman, 2025). Yet, evidence on whether algorithmic decision-making consistently translates into superior investment outcomes remains inconclusive.

Recent contributions highlight both the potential and limitations of AI-driven financial models. Fischer and Krauss (2018) and Gu et al. (2020) demonstrate that advanced machine learning methods, such as Long Short-Term Memory networks and tree-based models, can improve asset pricing forecasts, capturing momentum, volatility, and liquidity effects more effectively than linear models. However, Smith and Wyatt (2025) observe that AI-powered ETFs often fail to deliver persistent outperformance despite their early promise. Similarly, Chen and Ren (2022) find that while AI-powered mutual funds outperform their human-managed peers through lower transaction costs and reduced behavioural biases, they do not systematically outperform the market itself. These mixed results suggest that algorithmic funds may excel in efficiency and volatility management, but their ability to consistently generate excess returns is less clear.

The literature also highlights the behavioural dimension of automation. D'Acunto et al. (2019) show that robo-advisors help investors avoid common biases and improve diversification. Grobys et al. (2022) find that hedge funds with higher levels of automation perform better than discretionary funds. By contrast, Miguel and Chen (2021) argue that human managers still outperform machines at the top of the performance distribution, which indicates a limit to algorithmic skill. These studies highlight an important distinction:

DOI: 10.1201/9781003656463-7

algorithmic investing may mitigate human biases and smooth portfolio risk, but its relative advantage could depend heavily on market conditions and industry contexts.

Beyond performance metrics, scholars also stress the importance of transparency, interpretability, and trust in algorithmic finance. Cerneviciene and Kabasinskas (2024) note that limited interpretability can undermine confidence in algorithmic decisions, and Duarte and Campos (2024) show that human cognitive biases can reappear in AI-assisted decision processes. Complementary evidence by Cao et al. (2024) shows that while AI analysts can surpass humans in processing vast, transparent, and voluminous information, human expertise remains crucial in contexts requiring institutional knowledge or the valuation of intangible assets. Their results suggest that hybrid models that combine human expertise with machine efficiency reduce extreme errors and perform well in complex financial environments. These concerns reflect a broader debate on what may be described as algorithmic morality. The central question is whether investors and regulators are willing to rely on opaque systems whose decision logic often remains inaccessible.

Although the literature on AI in finance has expanded considerably (Bahoo et al., 2024), two gaps remain. First, most studies focus on the aggregate performance of AI-based funds without considering how performance varies across industries. Sectors shaped by high information asymmetry or strong sentiment, including technology or sin industries, may behave differently from sectors where fundamentals dominate, such as industrials or finance (Sovbetov, 2025a). Second, limited evidence exists on how algorithmic versus non-algorithmic ETFs responded to systemic shocks. The COVID-19 crisis provides a natural setting to evaluate whether emotionless investing offers resilience when human judgment is most strained. Prior work suggests that automated funds may mitigate downside risks during downturns (Anuar et al., 2025). Related studies show that complementary assets such as gold or tokenized gold improve crisis performance for AI-intensive stocks (Dammak et al., 2024). Yet, the sectoral resilience of algorithmic versus discretionary ETFs has not been systematically evaluated.

This chapter addresses these gaps by comparing the performance of algorithmic ETFs with non-algorithmic ETFs across six industries: technology, industrials, financials, healthcare, energy, and sin industries. Using monthly data from 2013 to 2025, we apply Fama–French five-factor models and pooled panel regressions to assess whether algorithmic ETFs deliver superior returns, lower volatility, or enhanced resilience. The results show that algorithmic ETFs deliver consistently lower volatility but do not outperform high-growth or cyclical sectors, such as technology, finance, and energy, in terms of returns. During COVID-19, healthcare ETFs emerged as the strongest performers, while technology, industrials, and finance showed varying degrees of contraction. The findings demonstrate that the value of algorithmic investing is conditional on sectoral characteristics and macroeconomic conditions.

The chapter makes two contributions. It provides the first comprehensive industry-level analysis of algorithmic versus non-algorithmic ETF performance. It also integrates a crisis-period assessment to evaluate whether emotionless strategies provide resilience under stress. In doing so, the chapter advances the debate on algorithmic morality by showing that while algorithms excel at smoothing volatility and mitigating behavioural biases, they do not uniformly dominate in generating abnormal returns. The findings have implications for investors, fund managers, and regulators, underscoring the need for a balanced approach that recognizes both the strengths and limitations of algorithmic decision-making in financial markets.

7.2 DATA AND METHODOLOGY

7.2.1 Data and sample

The empirical analysis is based on a comprehensive dataset of exchange-traded funds (ETFs) spanning the period from January 2013 to July 2025. The sample is constructed to distinguish between algorithmic ETFs, which employ AI and machine learning for portfolio construction and rebalancing, and non-algorithmic ETFs, which are managed through conventional discretionary or rule-based strategies. To evaluate whether the performance advantages of algorithmic investing are universal or sector-specific, the sample is further disaggregated into six industry groups: technology, industrials, financials, healthcare, energy, and sin industries, the latter defined as funds with exposure to alcohol, tobacco, gambling, and defense. Table 7.1 presents the annual composition of the ETF sample. The total number of funds grows steadily

Table 7.1 Sample by years

	Sample	*Algorithmic*	*Technology*	*Industrials*	*Financials*	*Healthcare*	*Energy*	*Sin*
2013	52	10	7	12	15	2	5	1
2014	60	11	7	14	16	3	8	1
2015	62	11	7	15	16	4	8	1
2016	72	11	7	16	20	8	9	1
2017	83	13	7	18	22	12	10	1
2018	97	14	12	19	24	14	12	2
2019	109	15	18	20	24	15	15	2
2020	127	15	19	20	30	25	16	2
2021	146	14	24	24	30	32	20	2
2022	173	13	25	28	34	45	24	4
2023	195	12	29	32	36	50	32	4
2024	228	16	39	40	42	50	36	5
2025	248	16	42	40	50	50	45	5
TOTAL	**270**	**21**	**44**	**47**	**53**	**52**	**48**	**5**

Table 7.2 Descriptive statistics of monthly returns of ETF

	Mean	*Median*	*Max.*	*Min.*	*St.Dev.*	*Skewness*	*Kurtosis*	*Obs.*
Algorithmic	0.928	1.198	8.705	–8.534	3.051	–0.460	3.613	151
Energy	0.746	0.880	32.310	–34.470	8.104	0.209	6.886	151
Financials	1.271	1.970	16.340	–20.200	5.303	–0.408	4.320	151
Healthcare	1.014	1.330	13.450	–10.120	4.224	–0.237	2.944	151
Industrials	1.001	1.270	13.960	–16.910	4.810	–0.379	3.924	151
Sin	1.190	1.080	15.533	–12.437	3.877	–0.150	4.718	151
Technology	1.726	1.930	14.920	–12.600	5.153	–0.303	3.015	151

from 52 in 2013 to 248 in 2025, with notable increases in energy, healthcare, and technology ETFs. The representation of algorithmic ETFs rises gradually over time, reflecting their growing importance in asset management.

ETF-specific data, including monthly adjusted prices, dividends, and net asset values, are obtained from LSEG Datastream. All return series are expressed in US dollars and computed on a total return basis, inclusive of dividends. Descriptive statistics in Table 7.2 summarize the distributional properties of monthly ETF returns. Technology ETFs deliver the highest average returns at 1.73 percent per month, though they also display substantial risk with a standard deviation of 5.15 percent. In contrast, algorithmic ETFs provide lower mean returns of 0.93 percent, yet they exhibit the lowest volatility across all categories, with a standard deviation of just 3.05 percent. The energy sector shows the most extreme swings, with returns ranging from 32.3 percent to –34.5 percent and a volatility of 8.10 percent, reflecting exposure to oil price collapses and pandemic-related shocks. Healthcare and financial ETFs record intermediate performance, with mean returns of 1.01 and 1.27 percent, respectively, accompanied by moderate volatility. Industrial and sin ETFs display similar average returns, around 1.0–1.2 percent, with volatility levels between 3.9 and 4.8 percent. Overall, these patterns suggest that algorithmic ETFs deliver smoother and less volatile performance profiles than traditional sector ETFs, even if they do not dominate in terms of raw returns.

7.2.2 Empirical strategy

The core empirical strategy relies on time-series and panel regressions. To estimate risk-adjusted performance, we apply the Fama–French (2015) five-factor model, augmented with additional global anomalies where appropriate. The specification is expressed as follows:

$$R_{it} = \alpha + \beta_1 \cdot MKT_t + \beta_2 \cdot SMB_t + \beta_3 \cdot HML_t + \beta_4 \cdot RMW_t + \beta_5 \cdot CMA_t + \varepsilon_{it}$$

where R_{it} is the excess return of portfolio i in month t that is calculated over the risk-free rate proxied by the one-month US. Treasury bill yield. The market factor *MKT* represents the excess return of the global market portfolio, while SMB, HML, RMW, and CMA capture the size, value, profitability, and investment effects, respectively. The intercept α measures abnormal performance unexplained by common risk factors, interpreted as Jensen's alpha. Factor sensitivities β_j quantify the exposures of each portfolio to systematic risks. Estimation is conducted using Newey–West standard errors to account for heteroskedasticity and serial correlation. A positive and statistically significant alpha indicates that the portfolio delivers persistent abnormal returns, while a negative alpha suggests underperformance.

The risk-free rate and monthly risk factor (MKT, SMB, HML, RMW, CMA) are obtained from Kenneth R. French's online library for developed markets.[1] Firms are first divided into two size groups using the regional median of market capitalization, classifying stocks as small or big. Within each size group, independent 2×3 sorts are then conducted on book-to-market equity, profitability, and investment using the 30th and 70th percentiles of the respective variables as breakpoints. The size factor, SMB (Small Minus Big), is obtained as the average of three return spreads, each measuring the difference between small and big firms within the value, profitability, and investment sorts. The value factor, HML (High Minus Low), reflects the return differential between firms in the highest and lowest book-to-market groups. The profitability factor, RMW (Robust Minus Weak), contrasts firms with robust operating profitability (above the 70th percentile) against those with weak profitability (below the 30th). The investment factor, CMA (Conservative Minus Aggressive), compares firms with conservative investment policies (below the 30th percentile of asset growth) against aggressively investing firms (above the 70th percentile). In addition, the momentum factor, WML (Winners Minus Losers), is constructed as the return spread between firms with high and low past twelve-month returns, excluding the most recent month.

7.2.3 Robustness checks

To strengthen the robustness of our findings, we estimate pooled panel regressions of monthly ETF returns on ETF type and sectoral characteristics, with Algorithmic ETFs serving as the reference group. This design allows us to evaluate whether performance differentials persist once common risk factors and systemic shocks are taken into account:

$$R_{it} = \alpha + \beta \cdot NonAlgo_i + \delta \cdot COVID_t + \theta \cdot (NonAlgo_i \times COVID_t) + \gamma \cdot \boldsymbol{X}_t + \varepsilon_{it}$$

where $NonAlgo_i$ is a dummy variable equal to one for non-algorithmic ETFs and zero for algorithmic ETFs, which act as the omitted reference category. The dummy $COVID_t$ equals one during the COVID period from March 2020 to May 2023 and zero otherwise. The interaction term $NonAlgo_i \times COVID_t$ captures whether the relative performance of non-algorithmic ETFs differed significantly from that of algorithmic ETFs during the pandemic. The vector X_t contains the Fama–French five factors (market, size, value, profitability, investment) to control for systematic risk exposures, ε_{it} is the idiosyncratic error term. In this framework, δ measures the performance shift of algorithmic ETFs during COVID, while θ shows whether non-algorithmic ETFs experienced an additional differential effect.

To explore heterogeneity across industries, we extend the model to incorporate industry dummies and their interactions with the COVID indicator, again treating algorithmic ETFs as the reference group. The specification is expressed as:

$$R_{it} = \alpha + \sum_{k=1}^{K} \beta_k \cdot Industry_{ik} + \delta \cdot COVID_t + \sum_{k=1}^{K} \theta_k (Industry_{ik} \times COVID_t) + \gamma \cdot X_t + \varepsilon_{it}$$

where $Industry_{ik}$ indicates whether ETF i belongs to sector $k \in \{Technologic, Industrial, Financial, Healthcare, Engergy, Sinn\}$. Algorithmic ETFs are the omitted category, so each β_k reflects the average return differential of sector k relative to algorithmic ETFs outside of COVID, while the coefficients θ_k capture whether that differential widened or narrowed during the COVID period. The inclusion of the standalone COVID dummy ensures that δ represents the shift in performance of algorithmic ETFs during the pandemic, while the interaction terms show whether industry-specific ETFs deviated from this baseline response.

Both specifications are estimated as pooled regressions with robust standard errors clustered at the ETF level to account for serial correlation. This design allows us to assess not only whether algorithmic ETFs underperform or outperform their peers under normal conditions, but also whether they exhibited superior resilience relative to conventional funds and specific industries during the COVID shock.

7.3 RESULTS AND DISCUSSION

The results from the Fama–French five-factor estimations in Table 7.3 provide the core evidence regarding the relative performance of algorithmic and industry-based ETFs. Algorithmic ETFs generate a statistically significant yet economically modest alpha of 0.08 percent per month and exhibit a market beta of 0.61, which indicates substantially lower exposure to broad market fluctuations. This pattern is consistent with Smith and Wyatt (2025), who show that AI-powered strategies often reduce systematic risk but do not translate these reductions into persistent outperformance. A similar stabilizing tendency appears in other markets where structured or institutionally reinforced mechanisms help to dampen volatility under stress (Sovbetov, 2025b). Together, these findings suggest that while algorithmic approaches

Table 7.3 Fama–French five-factor results

Portfolio	α	*MKT*	*SMB*	*HML*	*RMW*	*CMA*	*Adj.* R^2
Algorithmic	0.0008**	0.605***	−0.045	−0.081	0.053	−0.036	0.72
	(2.24)	(4.10)	(−0.87)	(−1.58)	(1.01)	(−0.65)	
Technology	0.0038*	1.207***	0.181***	−0.203***	0.046	−0.057	0.82
	(1.69)	(11.23)	(3.45)	(−3.92)	(0.76)	(−0.90)	
Industrials	0.0010	1.054***	0.096	−0.026	0.023	0.007	0.84
	(0.92)	(12.12)	(1.52)	(−0.35)	(0.54)	(0.01)	
Financials	0.0025	1.108***	0.154**	−0.104	0.065	−0.016	0.88
	(1.18)	(13.01)	(2.20)	(−1.51)	(1.27)	(−0.20)	
Healthcare	0.0018	0.953***	−0.029	−0.108	0.112**	−0.043	0.81
	(1.32)	(9.85)	(−0.33)	(−1.70)	(2.03)	(−0.77)	
Energy	0.0028	1.157***	0.209***	−0.188***	−0.064	0.103*	0.86
	(1.37)	(10.07)	(2.55)	(−2.64)	(−1.07)	(1.84)	
Sin	0.0004*	1.024***	0.074	−0.124*	0.051	−0.026	0.78
	(1.82)	(6.25)	(1.20)	(−1.95)	(1.02)	(−0.35)	

Note: This table reports results from time-series regressions of monthly portfolio excess returns on the Fama–French five factors for the period January 2013 to July 2025. The dependent variable is portfolio return in excess of the one-month US Treasury bill yield. Coefficients represent factor loadings, with t-statistics reported in parentheses. Algorithmic ETFs are included as a distinct portfolio category for comparison with industry-based ETFs. The intercept term (α) measures abnormal return unexplained by common risk factors, interpreted as Jensen's alpha. Estimates are obtained using Newey–West heteroskedasticity- and autocorrelation-consistent standard errors. Results are visually illustrated at Figures 7.1–7.5. *, **, and *** denote statistical significance at the 10%, 5%, and 1% levels, respectively.

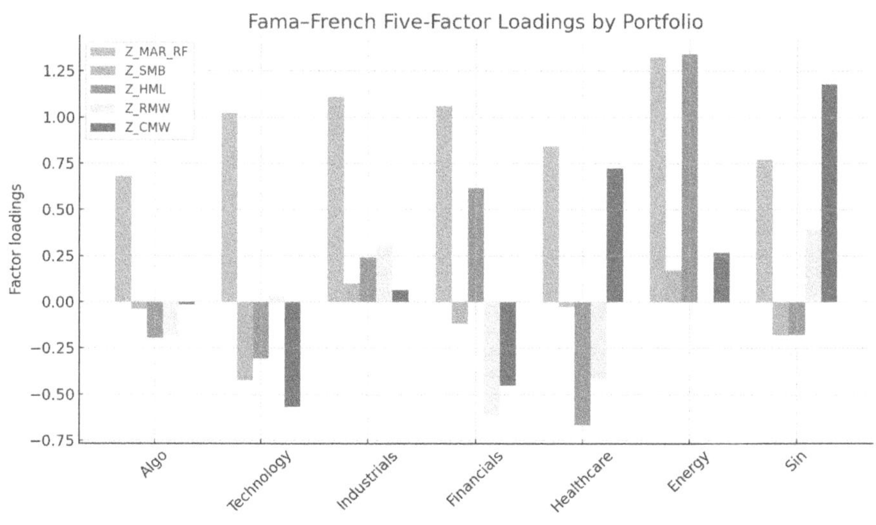

Figure 7.1 FF5 loading by portfolio

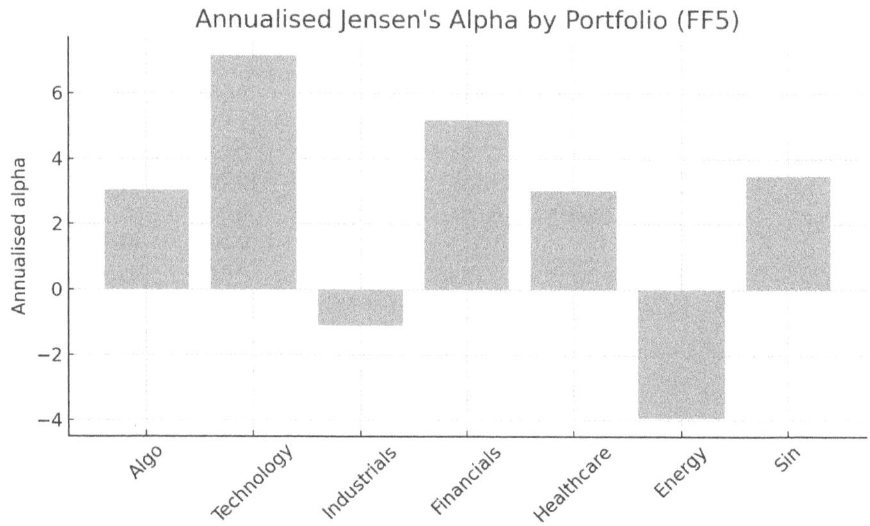

Figure 7.2 Annualised FF5 alphas.

enhance stability, they do not consistently deliver superior abnormal returns (see Figures 7.2, 7.4, and 7.5).

In contrast, technology and energy ETFs record economically larger but more volatile alphas. Technology ETFs earn an alpha of 0.38 percent per month, which is statistically significant at the ten percent level, while also exhibiting the highest market beta (1.21) and a strong positive exposure to the size factor (0.18). These characteristics are consistent with the growth-oriented and sentiment-driven nature of the technology sector, where returns

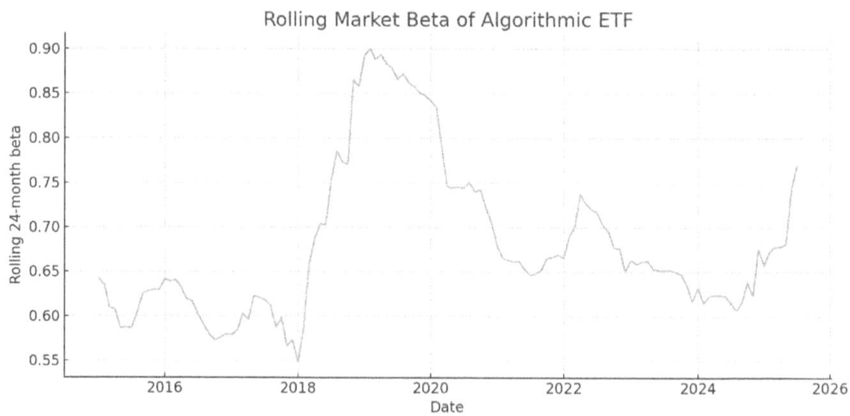

Figure 7.3 Rolling market beta of algorithmic ETFs

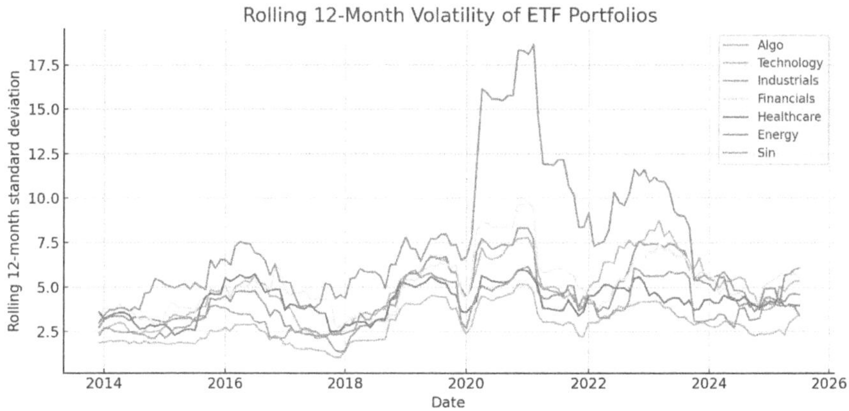

Figure 7.4 Rolling 12-month volatility of ETF portfolios

are magnified in upturns but also accompanied by higher risk. Energy ETFs also deliver a positive and economically meaningful alpha of 0.28 percent, driven partly by cyclical dynamics in global commodity markets. The significantly negative loadings on the HML factor for both technology and energy portfolios underline their growth orientation, while positive profitability and investment loadings highlight selective sensitivity to corporate fundamentals.

Healthcare ETFs display a distinctive profile, with a positive profitability loading (0.11) and a market beta below one, pointing to resilience rooted in defensive demand. Although their alpha is not statistically significant, healthcare funds' performance aligns with the narrative of defensive sectors outperforming during COVID (Blajer-Golebiewska et al., 2024). Sin industry ETFs

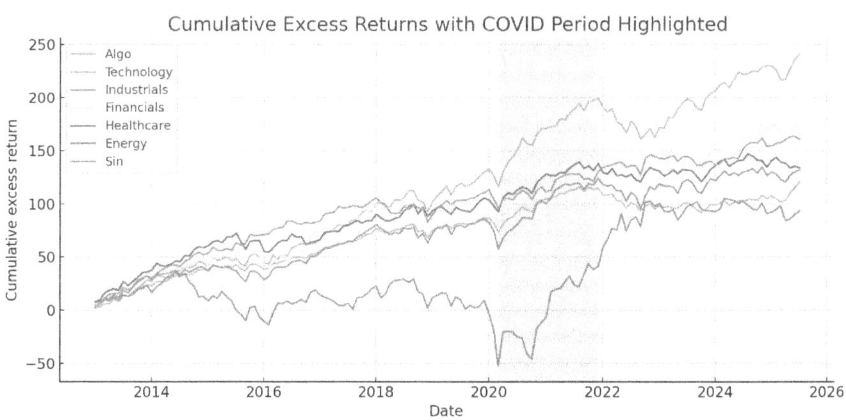

Figure 7.5 Cumulative excess returns of portfolios

show a modest but statistically significant alpha of 0.04 percent, together with relatively muted factor exposures. This finding resonates with earlier literature highlighting the abnormal returns associated with "*sin stocks*," often attributed to underpricing driven by social norms and exclusionary investment practices (Sovbetov, 2025a).

The pooled panel regressions reported in Tables 7.4 and 7.5 provide robustness checks for these time-series results. Table 7.4 compares algorithmic and non-algorithmic ETFs directly, confirming that non-algorithmic ETFs outperform algorithmic ones on average by 0.18 percent per month. This differential is both statistically and economically significant, indicating that algorithmic strategies, while delivering lower volatility, lag behind more traditional approaches in generating returns. The coefficient on the COVID dummy is strongly negative (−0.35 percent), suggesting that algorithmic ETFs themselves experienced return contractions during the pandemic, in line with widespread market distress. The interaction term between non-algorithmic ETFs and COVID is negative but insignificant, implying that non-algorithmic ETFs did not experience a systematically different shock compared to algorithmic funds once common risk factors were controlled for. Consistent with these coefficient estimates, the Wald χ^2 test rejects the joint null that non-algorithmic ETFs did not differ from algorithmic ETFs in either normal times or during COVID, confirming the statistical robustness of the observed differential.

Table 7.4 Panel regression: Algorithmic vs non-algorithmic ETFs

Variable	*Coefficient*	*t-stats.*	*p-value*
NonAlgo	0.0018**	2.44	0.015
COVID	−0.0035***	−3.82	0.000
NonAlgo × COVID	−0.0012	−1.46	0.145
MKT	1.0021***	12.57	0.000
SMB	0.0525	1.02	0.309
HML	−0.1174**	−2.14	0.033
RMW	0.0735	1.53	0.128
CMA	−0.0308	−0.66	0.511
Intercept	0.0006	0.89	0.374
Adj. R^2	0.81		
F-stats.	18.74*** (0.00)		
Wald χ^2 Test	152.84*** (0.00)		

Note: This specification is estimated as a pooled panel regression of monthly ETF excess returns from January 2013 to July 2025. Algorithmic ETFs serve as the reference category, so the coefficient on *NonAlgo* captures average return differentials between non-algorithmic and algorithmic funds, while the interaction term (*NonAlgo × COVID*) shows whether that differential changed during the COVID period. The *COVID* dummy measures the shift in algorithmic ETF returns during the pandemic. All models include Fama–French five-factor controls. Reported t-statistics are based on robust standard errors. The F-statistic refers to the joint significance of the regressors, and the Wald χ^2 test evaluates the null hypothesis: $H_0 = \beta_{NonAlgo} = \theta_{NonAlgo \times COVID} = 0$. Results are visually illustrated at Figure 7.6. *, **, and *** denote statistical significance at the 10%, 5%, and 1% levels, respectively.

Table 7.5 Panel regression: Industry differentials relative to algorithmic ETFs

Variable	*Coefficient*	*t-stats.*	*p-value*
Technology	0.0028***	3.00	0.003
Industrials	0.0005	0.60	0.549
Financial	0.0022**	2.21	0.029
Healthcare	0.0012	1.42	0.164
Energy	0.0025**	2.51	0.013
Sin	0.0015*	1.81	0.073
COVID	–0.0035***	–3.78	0.000
Technology × *COVID*	–0.0010	–1.12	0.274
Industrials × *COVID*	–0.0020**	–2.21	0.031
Financial × *COVID*	–0.0025**	–2.40	0.017
Healthcare × *COVID*	0.0018**	2.16	0.037
Energy × *COVID*	–0.0012	–1.51	0.137
Sin × COVID	–0.0003	–0.44	0.693
Controls (FF5)	Yes		
F-stats.	19.38*** (0.00)		
Wald $\chi 2$ *Test*	152.84*** (0.00)		

Note: This specification is estimated as a pooled panel regression of monthly ETF excess returns from January 2013 to July 2025. Algorithmic ETFs serve as the omitted reference group. Coefficients on industry dummies therefore represent average performance differentials between each industry ETF category and algorithmic ETFs under non-COVID conditions. The COVID dummy measures the shift in algorithmic ETF returns during the pandemic, while the interaction terms capture whether each industry responded differently relative to algorithmic ETFs. All models control for the Fama–French five factors. Reported t-statistics are based on robust standard errors. The F-statistic refers to the joint significance of the regressors, and the Wald χ^2 test evaluates the joint hypothesis that industry ETFs do not differ from algorithmic ETFs either in normal times or during COVID. Results are visually illustrated at Figure 7.6. *, **, and *** denote statistical significance at the 10%, 5%, and 1% levels, respectively.

Table 7.5 extends this analysis by benchmarking industry-specific ETFs against the algorithmic reference group. Technology, financials, and energy consistently deliver significantly higher returns than algorithmic ETFs outside of COVID, with monthly differentials of 0.28, 0.22, and 0.25 percent, respectively. This reinforces the interpretation from Table 7.3 that algorithmic ETFs underperform in high-growth and cyclical industries where active exposure to sector-specific dynamics is rewarded. Industrials and healthcare funds, by contrast, do not differ significantly from algorithmic ETFs, suggesting that in more stable or fundamentals-driven sectors, the return advantage of discretionary strategies is less evident. Sin industry ETFs record a modest return premium of 0.15 percent, significant at the ten percent level, underscoring that investor sentiment and ethical constraints may leave scope for excess returns in this niche.

The role of the COVID shock emerges clearly in the interaction terms. Industrial and financial ETFs underperform relative to algorithmic funds

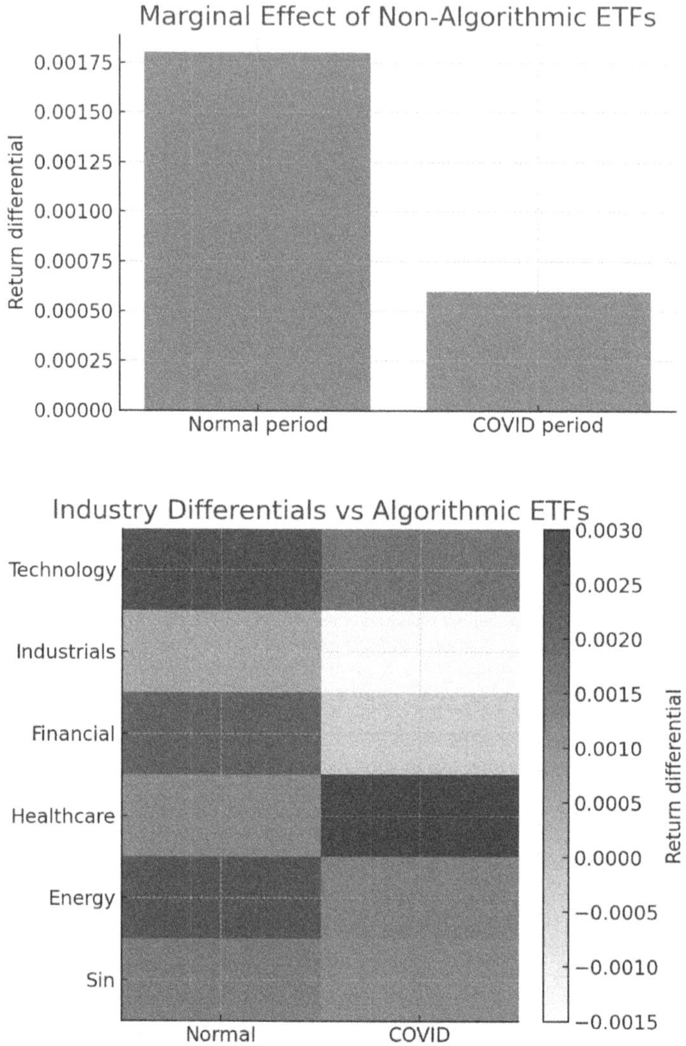

Figure 7.6 Panel marginal effects and industrial difference heatmaps

during the pandemic, consistent with supply-chain disruptions and heightened credit risks. Healthcare funds, however, gain a significant relative advantage, reflecting the sector's central role during the health crisis and supporting earlier evidence on the countercyclical nature of healthcare investments. Technology and energy ETFs show negative but insignificant interactions, indicating that their long-run outperformance was temporarily muted but not reversed during the pandemic. These dynamics confirm that the relative value of algorithmic versus discretionary strategies is contingent on the sectoral environment and on macroeconomic shocks.

Taken together, the results suggest that algorithmic ETFs provide a low-volatility, defensive alternative, but they do not dominate industry-based strategies in terms of raw or risk-adjusted returns. Their underperformance relative to technology, energy, and financial funds highlights the limits of emotionless investing in sectors where human discretion and active positioning remain critical to capturing excess returns. At the same time, algorithmic strategies show resilience in downturns, as demonstrated by their relatively muted losses in comparison with cyclical industries during COVID. These findings echo recent contributions in the literature on passive versus active management, suggesting that while automation enhances efficiency and reduces behavioural biases, it does not eliminate the sector-specific advantages of traditional discretionary investing.

7.4 CONCLUSION

This chapter set out to examine whether algorithmic ETFs outperform their non-algorithmic counterparts across industries and under systemic shocks such as COVID-19. Using a rich dataset spanning 2013 to 2025, we compared algorithmic ETFs with sector-specific portfolios in technology, industrial, finance, healthcare, energy, and sin industries. The analysis combined Fama–French five-factor time-series regressions with pooled panel estimations to isolate the performance differentials attributable to fund type, sectoral exposure, and pandemic-related disruptions.

The results demonstrate that algorithmic ETFs deliver consistently lower volatility and reduced exposure to market-wide fluctuations, underscoring their defensive nature. However, they generally underperform in terms of raw and risk-adjusted returns relative to technology, energy, and financial ETFs, which capture higher premia linked to growth, cyclical dynamics, and sector-specific risks. Healthcare emerges as a particularly important case: although healthcare ETFs are not systematically superior outside of crises, they outperform during the COVID-19 pandemic, highlighting the resilience of defensive industries in the face of systemic health shocks. Sin industry ETFs also show modest but significant outperformance relative to algorithmic ETFs, consistent with the literature on persistent risk premia in ethically controversial sectors.

These findings suggest that the value of algorithmic investing is conditional rather than universal. Algorithmic ETFs provide smoother performance profiles that may appeal to risk-averse investors and institutions seeking stability, but they do not eliminate the opportunity costs of forgoing sectoral risk-taking in high-growth industries. Non-algorithmic strategies retain an advantage where active judgment and discretionary positioning are rewarded, particularly in sectors sensitive to macroeconomic cycles or technological innovation.

The broader implication is that algorithmic investing is best understood not as a wholesale substitute for human-driven strategies but as a complementary tool within the evolving landscape of asset management. By reducing behavioural biases and managing volatility, algorithmic ETFs can enhance diversification, yet they remain bounded by the same structural and sectoral dynamics that shape financial markets more generally. As AI-led systems continue to expand their role in portfolio management, questions of transparency, accountability, and investor trust will become increasingly salient, particularly during periods of crisis when the resilience of decision-making frameworks is tested.

Future research could extend this analysis by exploring the interaction between algorithmic strategies and investor flows, examining whether the growing adoption of AI in asset management reshapes market stability, liquidity, or contagion dynamics. A deeper investigation into hybrid approaches that combine algorithmic efficiency with selective human oversight may also shed light on the optimal balance between automation and discretion in the next generation of investment management.

NOTE

1. https://mba.tuck.dartmouth.edu/pages/faculty/ken.french/data_library.html

REFERENCES

Anuar, A. A., Sulaiman, A. A., & Mohamad, M. T. (2025). Comparative analysis of AI-driven versus human-managed equity funds across market trends. *Future Business Journal*, *11*, 1–16. https://doi.org/10.1186/s43093-025-00540-8

Bahoo, S., Cucculelli, M., & Goga, X. (2024). Artificial intelligence in finance: A comprehensive review through bibliometric and content analysis. *SN Business & Economics*, *4*, 23. https://doi.org/10.1007/s43546-023-00618-x

Blajer-Golebiewska, A., Honecker, L., & Nowak, S. (2024). Investor sentiment response to COVID-19 outbreak-related news: A sectoral analysis of US firms. *North American Journal of Economics and Finance*, *71*, 102121. https://doi.org/10.1016/j.najef.2024.102121

Cao, S., Jiang, W., Wang, J., & Yang, B. (2024). From man vs. machine to man + machine: The art and AI of stock analyses. *Journal of Financial Economics*, *161*, 1–22. https://doi.org/10.1016/j.jfineco.2024.103910

Cerneviciene, J., & Kabasinskas, A. (2024). Explainable artificial intelligence (XAI) in finance: A systematic literature review. *Artificial Intelligence Review*, *57*, 216. https://doi.org/10.1007/s10462-024-10854-8

Chen, R., & Ren, J. (2022). Do AI-powered mutual funds perform better? *Finance Research Letters*, *46*, 102616. https://doi.org/10.1016/j.frl.2021.102616

D'Acunto, F., Prabhala, N., & Rossi, A. G. (2019). The promises and pitfalls of robo-advising. *The Review of Financial Studies*, *32*(5), 1983–2020. https://doi.org/10.1093/rfs/hhz014

Dammak, W., Gökgöz, H., & Jeribi, A. (2024). Analysis of gold, bitcoin, and gold-backed cryptocurrencies as safe havens during global crises: A focus on artificial intelligence companies. *Computational Economics*. https://doi.org/10.1007/s10614-024-10757-4

Duarte, R. D., & Campos, J. (2024). Looking for cognitive bias in AI-assisted decision-making. In Proceedings of the Third International Conference on Hybrid Human-Artificial Intelligence (HHAI 2024) Workshops (pp. 1–7). Malmö: CEUR-WS.

Fama, E. F., & French, K. R. (2015). A five-factor asset pricing model. *Journal of Financial Economics*, *116*(1), 1–22. https://doi.org/10.1016/j.jfineco.2014.10.010

Fischer, T., & Krauss, C. (2018). Deep learning with long short-term memory networks for financial market predictions. *European Journal of Operational Research*, *270*(2), 654–669. https://doi.org/10.1016/j.ejor.2017.11.054

Grobys, K., Kolari, J. W., & Niang, J. (2022). Man versus machine: On artificial intelligence and hedge fund performance. *Applied Economics*, *54*(40), 4632–4646. https://doi.org/10.1080/00036846.2022.2032585

Gu, S., Kelly, B., & Xiu, D. (2020). Empirical asset pricing via machine learning. *The Review of Financial Studies*, *33*(5), 2223–2273. https://doi.org/10.1093/rfs/hhaa009

Kartini, K., & Nahda, K. (2021). Behavioral biases on investment decision: A case study in Indonesia. *Journal of Asian Finance, Economics and Business*, *8*(3), 1231–1240. https://doi.org/10.13106/jafeb.2021.vol8.no3.1231

Kofman, P. (2025). Scoring the ethics of AI robo-advice: Why we need gateways and ratings. *Journal of Business Ethics*, *198*, 21–33. https://doi.org/10.1007/s10551-024-05753-5

Miguel, A. F., & Chen, Y. (2021). Do machines beat humans? Evidence from mutual fund performance persistence. *International Review of Financial Analysis*, *77*, 101913. https://doi.org/10.1016/j.irfa.2021.101913

Oechssler, J., Roider, A., & Schmitz, P. W. (2009). Cognitive abilities and behavioral biases. *Journal of Economic Behavior & Organization*, *72*(1), 147–152. https://doi.org/10.1016/j.jebo.2009.04.018

Smith, G., & Wyatt, S. (2025). The disappointing performance of AI-powered funds. *The Journal of Investing*, *34*(1), 74–83. https://doi.org/10.3905/joi.2025.1.346

Sovbetov, I. (2025a). Financial price of sin stocks across religions. *Journal of Business Ethics*. https://doi.org/10.1007/s10551-025-06072-z

Sovbetov, I. (2025b). Institutional backing and crypto volatility: A hybrid framework for DeFi stabilization. *Computational Economics*. https://doi.org/10.1007/s10614-025-11179-6

Chapter 8

Ethical AI in finance

Building fair systems

Martha Iyambo and Fanney Msimuko

8.1 INTRODUCTION

The integration of artificial intelligence (AI) into financial services has refined how institutions operate, assess risk, and engage with customers. From credit scoring and fraud detection to personalised banking and algorithmic trading, AI has become deeply embedded in the global financial ecosystem (Adeyelu et al., 2024; Talreja, 2022). AI enhances efficiency, decision accuracy, and customer experience, however, the increased adoption has also introduced ethical, social, and regulatory challenges, particularly relating to fairness, accountability, and transparency (Bailey, 2019; Talreja, 2022).

Given that these systems often learn from historical financial data that may reflect existing social and economic inequalities, they risk perpetuating and amplifying bias. For example, biased training data or the overemphasis of certain demographic or geographic factors can lead to discriminatory lending and exclusionary financial practices (Adeyelu et al., 2024; Bailey, 2019). Such algorithmic bias not only challenges institutional ethics but can also erode consumer trust and expose financial institutions to regulatory penalties, as illustrated by the 2023 U.S. Equal Employment Opportunity Commission case against iTutorGroup, in which AI-based hiring discrimination resulted in significant sanctions (Bailey, 2019).

At the same time, ethical AI has become central to trust and integrity in financial decision-making (Talreja, 2022). Ethical AI frameworks emphasise the need for fairness audits, explainable AI mechanisms, and strong human oversight to ensure that automation enhances, rather than replaces, responsible judgement. Yet the implementation of these frameworks varies widely across jurisdictions, reflecting differing regulatory priorities, technological capacities, and institutional readiness (Adeyelu et al., 2024; Talreja, 2022).

8.1.1 The global divide

The adoption and governance of AI in finance must also be understood through the lens of the Global North and Global South divide. The Global North, characterised by advanced infrastructure, high R&D investment,

 DOI: 10.1201/9781003656463-8

and mature regulatory systems, has emerged as a leader in AI deployment (Invogue Solutions, 2024; Kowalski, 2020). Financial institutions in these regions make extensive use of AI for fraud detection, risk management, and regulatory reporting, supported by strong talent pipelines and data availability (Talreja, 2022). By contrast, Global South faces significant barriers, including limited internet connectivity, poor data quality, weaker infrastructure, and skill shortages (Invogue Solutions, 2024; Yu et al., 2023). These disparities create what the World Economic Forum describes as an "AI divide", where the benefits of AI remain concentrated in the Global North while the Global South struggles with implementation (Yu et al., 2023). Moreover, the historical legacies of colonialism and structural inequality continue to shape resource allocation and technological access in the Global South, exacerbating vulnerability to digital dependency and "digital colonialism" (Angermann, 2022; Kowalski, 2020).

8.1.2 Problem statement and research question

While AI adoption in financial services promises efficiency and inclusion, the ethical and governance challenges it generates vary significantly between the Global North and Global South. In advanced economies, concerns center on algorithmic bias, transparency, and regulatory compliance within already mature systems (Talreja, 2022). In developing economies, however, limitations such as weak governance and data scarcity amplify risks of exclusion, bias, and exploitation (Yu et al., 2023). Despite these differences, comparative research on how ethical challenges of AI adoption in finance vary between the Global North and Global South remains limited.

This chapter addresses that gap by investigating how institutions operating under the different regions approach fairness, accountability, and transparency in AI governance. It also explores how regulatory frameworks in the Global South, often modelled on those of the Global North, may inadvertently reproduce existing biases embedded in Northern-designed AI systems. Understanding these dynamics is essential for developing ethical governance strategies that are equitable, context-sensitive, and globally inclusive.

Accordingly, the chapter is guided by the following question: How do the ethical challenges associated with AI adoption in financial services differ between the Global North and Global South, and what governance approaches can promote equitable, context-appropriate AI deployment across regions?

8.1.3 Research objectives

This chapter examines the ethical implications of AI adoption in financial services across the Global North and Global South. It aims to identify region-specific opportunities and challenges related to fairness, accountability, transparency, and data privacy, with a focus on AI applications in financial services such as credit scoring, loan approvals, and fraud detection. Through comparative analysis, the research evaluates how differing regulatory frameworks, governance capacities, and infrastructural conditions influence the ethical use of AI in each region. It further investigates how the replication of Global North regulatory strategies within the Global South may reinforce biases embedded in Northern-designed AI systems. Ultimately, the study aims to propose policy and governance recommendations that advance fairness, inclusivity, and ethical integrity in global AI-driven financial innovation.

8.2 ANALYTICAL FRAMEWORK

To support the comparison of AI ethics in financial services across the Global North and Global South, this chapter adopts a five-pillar analytical framework grounded in the ethical AI literature and philosophical perspectives. The framework operationalises widely recognised ethical AI principles, fairness, transparency, accountability, privacy, and contextual alignment, to assess how ethical risks emerge and how regulatory and institutional responses vary across the Global North and Global South.

8.2.1 Fairness and bias

The first pillar examines whether AI-driven financial systems produce equitable outcomes across demographic groups. Ethical AI literature emphasises fairness as a core principle, requiring the mitigation of embedded social biases, diverse and representative datasets, and continuous fairness auditing. Societal biases can be encoded and amplified through AI models when engineering teams lack diversity or when datasets reflect structural inequalities. Philosophical frameworks emphasise that fairness is not merely technical but also moral (Adeyelu et al., 2024).

In practice, this pillar assesses several factors, including whether historical biases are embedded in the training data, how consistently models perform across different demographic subgroups, the extent to which institutions employ fairness metrics and conduct algorithmic audits and the organisational capacity to identify, monitor, and remedy discriminatory outcomes (Talreja, 2022).

8.2.2 Accountability and human oversight

Accountability is the ethical principle that ensures responsibility for AI-generated decisions remains traceable (Adeyelu et al., 2024). This aspect examines organisational and regulatory mechanisms for oversight, including ethics committees, hybrid AI models, governance structures, and clear delineation of roles (Talreja, 2022). The Estonian case cited in Adeyelu et al. (2024) demonstrates the practical complexities of translating ethical principles into actionable oversight throughout the AI lifecycle.

In Talreja (2022), evaluation of this pillar considers several institutional and regulatory factors, including whether formal governance bodies exist to oversee AI development and deployment, the extent to which liability for harmful decisions is clearly defined, and the presence of structured human-review mechanisms capable of intervening in automated outputs. It also assesses the broader capacity of regulatory authorities to supervise AI systems effectively, particularly in terms of technical expertise, monitoring processes, and enforcement capabilities.

8.2.3 Transparency and explainability

Transparency and explainability are essential for building trust, ensuring contestability, and maintaining compliance with legal requirements (Adeyelu et al., 2024). This pillar assesses the interpretability of AI decision processes, the provision of meaningful explanations to users, and the ability of institutions to audit or challenge model outputs. Both ethical guidelines in Adeyelu et al. (2024) and philosophical arguments in Kakembo and Annet (2025) recognise transparency as indispensable for respecting individual autonomy. Kantian ethics, for instance, demands that decision rules be comprehensible and subject to ethical justification.

In the financial sector, transparency includes several interrelated components, such as technical explainability of credit, clear customer-facing disclosures about how automated decisions are generated and institutional openness regarding data usage and underlying assumptions (Talreja, 2022). It also requires mechanisms through which individuals can meaningfully challenge AI-driven decisions, ensuring that automated assessments do not become opaque or unaccountable forms of financial governance (Kakembo & Annet, 2025).

8.2.4 Data governance and privacy

Data governance and privacy form a key pillar because AI systems depend on extensive personal and behavioural data (Adeyelu et al., 2024). As Kakembo and Annet (2025) emphasise, financial AI raises profound ethical challenges regarding data minimisation, consent, and data security. Privacy is also closely linked to fairness, because biased datasets derived from historical inequalities can produce discriminatory outcomes (Kakembo & Annet, 2025). In Adeyelu et al. (2024), ethical guidelines highlight data protection as a prerequisite for trust, while applied literature stresses compliance with frameworks such as the General Data Protection Regulation (GDPR) and California Consumer Privacy Act (CCPA) (Talreja, 2022).

This pillar evaluates the integrity of data governance and privacy practices by examining the effectiveness of consent mechanisms and informed data-use procedures, and institutional adherence to data protection principles and controls as required in ethical and regulatory frameworks (Kakembo &

Annet, 2025; Talreja, 2022). It also considers how financial institutions manage cross-border data flows, as well as the degree of dependence on foreign AI vendors, which can shape data sovereignty, regulatory compliance, and institutional control over AI systems.

8.2.5 Contextual appropriateness (socio-technical fit)

The final pillar assesses whether AI systems align with local socio-economic, cultural, and infrastructural conditions. Ethical AI literature stresses that principles such as fairness, transparency, and privacy must be embedded throughout the AI lifecycle and adapted to specific contexts (Adeyelu et al., 2024). Misalignment, such as Northern models applied to Southern financial behaviours, can lead to exclusion, misclassification, or ethical colonialism.

This pillar assesses the contextual appropriateness of AI systems by examining whether the datasets used are suitable for local populations, whether models reflect relevant cultural and linguistic nuances, and the institutional capacity to implement and sustain ethical guidelines in practice. It further considers socio-technical constraints, such as the prominence of informal economies in many regions of the Global South and evaluates the degree of dependency on externally developed AI systems, which may embed assumptions or design choices that do not align with local financial behaviours or regulatory realities (Talreja, 2022).

8.3 AI IN FINANCIAL SERVICES: GLOBAL NORTH ANALYSIS

Financial institutions in the Global North have integrated AI across a wide range of operations to enhance efficiency, decision-making, and customer engagement. This reflects both the maturity of financial markets in these regions and the availability of advanced technological infrastructure. From customer-facing applications such as virtual assistants and chatbots to back-office functions like fraud detection, credit scoring, and regulatory compliance, AI has become embedded in core banking operations. As leading banks experiment with generative AI, explainable AI frameworks, and fairness auditing tools, the Global North illustrates how AI can drive both operational transformation and ethical innovation in financial services.

8.3.1 Key applications of AI in Global North financial services

8.3.1.1 Customer support and virtual assistants

Financial institutions in the Global North increasingly deploy virtual AI-powered assistants to streamline service delivery and enhance customer engagement. Bank of America's Erica, for instance, has processed over two billion interactions, enabling customers to manage transactions, payments, and personalised financial insights, while similar tools such as Wells Fargo's Fargo and NatWest's Cora demonstrate large-scale adoption and measurable gains in customer satisfaction (UXDA|Financial UX Design, 2025).

These systems also raise ethical concerns central to AI governance in finance. Studies highlight risks related to transparency and informed consent, as customers may be unaware that interactions are automated (Kakembo & Annet, 2025). Bank of America's explicit disclosure strategy illustrates how transparency can mitigate these concerns and support trust. Privacy risks further arise from the extensive processing of behavioural and transactional data, underscoring the importance of data minimisation and respect for individual autonomy (Kakembo & Annet, 2025)

8.3.1.2 Fraud detection and anti-money laundering (AML)

AI is widely used in fraud detection and AML compliance to analyse large volumes of transactional data and identify anomalous behaviour (Space Technologies, 2025). Systems such as JPMorgan's COiN platform and HSBC's deep-learning models enable real-time monitoring and have significantly reduced investigative workloads, with COiN reportedly cutting fraud analysis time by over 90% (Kakembo & Annet, 2025).

However, these gains raise ethical concerns related to data minimisation, proportionality, and fairness. Fraud detection systems rely on extensive behavioural and financial data, which can conflict with privacy principles and increase the risk of false positives (Kakembo & Annet, 2025). When trained on historically biased datasets, deep-learning models may disproportionately flag certain demographic groups as higher-risk, producing discriminatory outcomes. Transparency is further limited by the "black-box" nature of many fraud models, constraining customers' and regulators' ability to understand or challenge erroneous classifications.

8.3.1.3 Credit scoring and loan approvals

Credit scoring in the Global North increasingly relies on machine-learning models that incorporate non-traditional data sources. Platforms such as Zest AI and Upstart use variables including employment history, education, and spending behaviour to generate more granular assessments of creditworthiness. Zest AI reports increased mortgage approvals for Black and Hispanic borrowers while reducing default risk, indicating the potential for fairer credit allocation (Kakembo & Annet, 2025). Upstart similarly reported higher approval rates and lower average Annual Percentage Rates (APRs) in submissions to the Consumer Financial Protection Bureau (CFPB).

Despite these advances, the inclusion of educational or socioeconomic variables risks encoding structural inequalities if not subject to rigorous fairness testing (Kakembo & Annet, 2025). Model opacity also challenges explainability, raising concerns about borrowers' ability to understand automated decisions, a core requirement of autonomy and transparency. Ethical scholarship therefore emphasises the need for non-discrimination, privacy protection, and clear accountability mechanisms in AI-driven credit systems (Kakembo & Annet, 2025; Talreja, 2022).

8.3.2 Ethical challenges

While the preceding examples demonstrate the efficiency and scalability of AI in financial services, their deployment also exposes a set of ethical challenges that must be addressed to maintain fairness, accountability, and public trust.

8.3.2.1 Algorithmic bias and fairness

A persistent concern is the risk that AI systems reproduce historical inequalities embedded within financial datasets. Even when model accuracy improves, differential error rates across demographic groups can lead to disproportionate harm for marginalised populations (Talreja, 2022; Thiruma Valavana, 2024). The adoption of fairness-auditing tools and bias-mitigation techniques has expanded in the Global North, yet these interventions often function as technical remedies for essentially social and structural inequities. Consequently, fairness remains as much an organisational and governance issue as a computational one.

8.3.2.2 Accountability

As AI systems take on greater decision-making responsibilities, questions arise regarding who is responsible for errors or harmful automated decisions. The diffusion of responsibility across data scientists, product teams, and executives complicates liability (Talreja, 2022). While some institutions have established ethics committees and oversight structures (Smit, 2025), accountability gaps persist, particularly where high-risk systems operate with limited human intervention. Clearer governance architectures are therefore required to ensure that responsibility remains traceable throughout the AI lifecycle.

8.3.2.3 Transparency

A major ethical obstacle arises from the "black-box" nature of advanced AI models, particularly deep learning and generative AI. Customers, auditors, and regulators often cannot access intelligible explanations for decisions that shape credit access or trigger fraud alerts (Tahir, 2025; UXDA|Financial UX Design, 2025). While the adoption of explainable AI (XAI) frameworks is expanding, significant technical and institutional limitations remain. The challenge is not only making models interpretable but ensuring that explanations are actionable, comprehensible, and subject to accountability.

8.3.2.4 Data privacy

Transparency challenges intersect with data privacy concerns. AI systems rely on vast amounts of personal and financial data, making compliance with frameworks such as the GDPR in Europe and the CCPA in the U.S. increasingly demanding (Tahir, 2025; Talreja, 2022). Data breaches or misuse can have severe reputational and legal consequences. U.S. regulators, including the Office of the Comptroller of the Currency (OCC) and Federal Reserve, have intensified oversight of generative AI applications in banking, emphasising the need for robust governance and data protection (UXDA| Financial UX Design, 2025).

8.3.2.5 Balancing innovation with regulation

Financial institutions must balance the pursuit of AI-driven innovation with adherence to evolving legal standards. The EU AI Act designates credit scoring as a high-risk activity, requiring rigorous fairness and transparency mechanisms (Smit, 2025). Similarly, U.S. legislation such as the Fair Credit Reporting Act (FCRA) and Equal Credit Opportunity Act (ECOA) prohibits discriminatory lending practices (Thiruma Valavana, 2024). Maintaining this equilibrium between innovation and compliance is essential to sustaining ethical and trustworthy AI adoption. These ethical challenges have prompted regulators and financial institutions across the Global North to design comprehensive governance frameworks.

8.4 AI ETHICS IN BANKING IN THE GLOBAL SOUTH

The use of AI in banking across the global South has increased over the past few years. Though AI is not a new phenomenon, recent developments concerning data analytics and machine learning have significantly contributed to AI's penetration in the banking sector (Ganesan & Meena, 2024). The banking and finance industry's expenditure on AI is projected to rise to $97 billion by 2027 from $35 billion in 2023, representing a compound annual growth rate of 29% (statista, n.d.). The boom of AI in banking has also been driven by the growing emphasis on financial inclusion and operational efficiency. Banks and other financial institutions are increasingly implementing AI use for key functions such as customer service automation and compliance monitoring.

AI has assisted in extending banking services to previously unbanked populations, reducing costs, and enhancing risk management. However, the lack of regulation raises critical ethical and governance questions, particularly when systems and datasets developed in the global North are transplanted into vastly different socio-economic and regulatory environments in the South. In addition to the adoption of these AI systems, the conversations around ethics in AI are very much Northern-centered, which has led to the emergence of epistemic injustice. In the context of banking and finance, this injustice occurs when certain demographics are constantly misrepresented or undervalued in financial decision-making processes (Ganesan & Meena, 2024).

8.4.1 The use of AI in global South financial services

8.4.1.1 AI-driven credit scoring

AI has the capability to process complex datasets far more efficiently than human beings, making it more efficient and accurate when it comes to assessing creditworthiness, as it can detect patterns that cannot be easily spotted through traditional methods (World Bank Group, 2024). In many countries across Africa, Asia, and Latin America, banks and financial institutions are using machine learning models to evaluate creditworthiness based on alternative data such as mobile phone usage, social media behaviour, and transaction histories (World Bank Group, 2024). These alternative data sources widen the net for people who may lack traditional data such as loan histories or credit card usage.

While this expands access to credit, it also introduces risks of murky decision-making and algorithmic discrimination, mainly against marginalised groups whose alternative data may be unconventional according to global North standards (World Bank & IFC, 2022). Additionally, AI credit risk assessment algorithms may skip over crucial context-specific ethical considerations that human beings would consider (Martin, 2019). This raises concerns on whether AI algorithms use appropriate factors when conducting credit risk assessments in the global South.

8.4.1.2 Fraud detection and anti-money laundering (AML)

AI systems are widely used to identify suspicious transactions and prevent fraud and money laundering. According to (Rosaline & Emiliya, 2024), algorithms monitor and analyse user behaviour and transaction patterns in real-time, which enables swift detection of suspicious or fraudulent transactions (Kesireddy, 2025). This significantly reduces fraud-related financial losses, protecting both clients and institutions. AI can also reduce false positives through natural language processing (NLP) and deep learning, which help understand context behind user behaviour (Williams et al., 2025). An example of this is Absa Bank, an African bank that utilises AI to improve detection capabilities. The use of AI has reportedly outperformed traditional rules-based systems, reduced false positives by 77%, and revealed risk patterns that were previously unidentified (FinTech Global, 2025).

However, majority of these models are developed in the North and often fail to account for informal financial behaviours common in the South, such as Rotating Savings and Credit Associations (ROSCAs), popular across the global South. ROSCAs are informal financial cooperative schemes where individuals collectively save and borrow money at intervals. These schemes have built financial resilience in low-income communities, where cultural and socioeconomic barriers keep most of the population from accessing formal banking services (Zambrano et al., 2023). This is one of many examples of informal financial systems in the region, that AI algorithms trained on the financial behaviours of populations in the global North cannot pick up on. This can lead to higher false positives and customer exclusion when applied to the South. The ethical challenge lies in balancing regulatory compliance with financial inclusion, which can only be achieved if the behavioural context in the global South is given due consideration.

8.4.1.3 Chatbots and customer service automation

Automated customer interaction tools have become popular for low-cost service delivery. These AI tools utilise NLP to interpret human language and understand human requests, enabling them to provide personalised assistance to customers (Bragas et al., 2025). The high customer satisfaction ratings demonstrate a positive impact of AI in banking and finance on both individuals and institutions. Yet, it raises issues around data privacy, consent, and the linguistic biases intrinsic to NLP systems predominantly trained on English-language data. Linguistic and cultural biases mainly affect the global South, since AI has been mostly trained on the views, values and languages of advanced economies in the global North (Unger & McLean, 2025).

8.4.1.4 Risk management and market forecasting

Banks in emerging markets increasingly use predictive analytics to manage liquidity and assess market risks. On the market forecasting front, for instance, South African company Xineoh helps financial institutions increase their profits and customer satisfaction ratings by utilising AI to predict customer behaviour (*Home* | Xineoh – Predicting Consumer Behavior with AI, n.d.).

However, there is heavy reliance on imported AI systems, developed by vendors in the global North, which creates dependencies when applied in the Southern context. Firstly, AI risk classification based on factors developed in the global North, which may lead to the exclusion of a significant number of the low-income population in the South (Isreal et al., 2025). Northern benchmarks may consider individuals who make up a large percentage of the global South populace such as informal workers and smallholder farmers as too risky because of their unusual income patterns or lack of formal documentation (Isreal et al., 2025).

Secondly, market forecasts based on more stable economies and predictable customer behaviour prevalent in the North may not accurately predict the realities in many Southern economies. This can lead to mispriced financial products and inaccurate risk assessments.

Importantly, utilising AI tools developed in the global North makes Southern institutions data users instead of data owners, because they have limited control over data and model design (Salami, 2024). This reinforces unequal power dynamics and perpetuates algorithmic dependency on the North, because AI is imported from the region (Birhane, 2020).

8.4.2 Ethical and contextual challenges

The ethical issues arising from applying AI built for the global North in the global South are multifaceted. The preceding paragraphs have highlighted the key ethical concerns and contextual challenges. The first is algorithmic bias, as many AI models reflect the socio-economic realities of the global North, which results in structural biases when applied in Southern contexts. The proprietary and opaque nature of algorithmic systems enables structural discrimination based off existing discriminatory behaviours to hide behind the ideological cover of objectivity, precision, accuracy and technological rationality (Garcia et al., 2024; Wang, 2025). The decision-making processes are rendered inscrutable, defended by claims of commercial confidentiality and technical complexity. Yet, these AI systems are increasingly wielding great biopolitical power, and their decisions can materially shape individuals' access to financial services such as credit, in turn negatively affecting their livelihoods. This decision-making not only reproduces biases, it transforms bias from being an identifiable human act into a dispersed, algorithmic condition, making it hard to detect and even harder to contest (Garcia et al., 2024).

Secondly, data privacy and sovereignty are a serious concern, as weak or uneven data protection regimes in parts of the global South make citizens vulnerable to exploitation and surveillance. This results in AI being used against populations in the global South, for instance concerning facial recognition, which has a tendency of misidentifying people of colour (Monasterio Astobiza et al., 2022). The dominance of Northern technology providers also raises concerns about cross-border data flows and digital sovereignty. Major global players in the global North, such as the United States, China, and the European Union (EU) are increasingly prioritising AI sovereignty and asserting dominance in relation to AI infrastructure and governance, as they want to regulate AI development in line with their national security interests, economic goals and values (Owuor, 2025).

Additionally, there are transparency and accountability concerns. It is important to always consider ethical standards such as transparency, accountability, fairness, privacy, and inclusivity in AI deployment, however, this is not the case especially in the global South (Salman & Chaya, 2025). This is because the limited infrastructure and regulatory oversight in the South make it difficult to audit or explain AI decision-making processes. This lack of transparency and accountability erodes public trust and makes consumer protection difficult to achieve. Given that AI utilises large amounts of personal data, without solid data governance, data subjects in the South are at a higher risk of data misuse, breaches as well as unauthorised access (Almustafa et al., 2023).

Lastly, there are regulatory and governance concerns where AI developed in the North is applied in the South, because majority of Southern jurisdictions lack comprehensive AI regulations. This leads to oversight of AI use being designated to fragmented financial or data protection authorities with limited resources or expertise to properly regulate and ensure the ethical use of AI. Importantly, it leads to epistemic injustice which can in turn lead to digital colonisation (Kiemde & Kora, 2022), as there is little to no regard paid to the ethical values of the global South in the development of AI regulations and governance (Yilma, 2025)

8.5 REGULATORY FRAMEWORKS AND STRATEGIES FOR MITIGATING ETHICAL CHALLENGES

8.5.1 Comparing regulatory trajectories

8.5.1.1 Global North regulatory developments

Across major financial markets, regulatory responses to AI vary in scope and approach. In the EU, the AI Act represents a great initiative that establishes a risk-based regulatory model, classifying AI systems into four categories: prohibited, high-risk, limited-risk, and minimal-risk (Abdullah, 2025). Applications such as credit scoring and fraud detection are considered high-risk, necessitating rigorous compliance obligations including human oversight, algorithmic transparency, and fairness testing. The AI Act aligns with broader EU frameworks such as the GDPR, ensuring that data privacy, consumer protection, and ethical principles are integrated across all AI applications in finance (Abdullah, 2025; Massey & Massey, 2025). Complementing this, the OECD AI Principles, updated in 2024, provide an international benchmark for trustworthy AI emphasising inclusiveness, transparency, robustness, and human rights protection (Crisanto et al., 2024).

By contrast, the United States employs a decentralised regulatory approach, relying on sector-specific agencies like the Securities and Exchange Commission (SEC) and the Consumer Financial Protection Bureau (CFPB) to oversee AI compliance (Abdullah, 2025). Although there is no overarching federal AI law, several initiatives have emerged, including President Biden's Executive Order 14110 on Safe, Secure, and Trustworthy AI, and state-level regulations such as California's AI Bill and the California Privacy Protection Agency's Automated Decision-Making Technology (ADMT) framework (Abdullah, 2025; Lumenova, 2025). These efforts collectively target bias mitigation, model explainability, and data security. Additionally, the NIST AI Risk Management Framework promotes dynamic compliance through continuous model validation and risk monitoring (Lumenova, 2025).

The United Kingdom, while diverging from the EU's legislative model, has adopted a principles-based regulatory framework emphasising proportionality and innovation. The Financial Conduct Authority (FCA) provides non-binding guidance focusing on fairness, transparency, and accountability in AI deployment (Abdullah, 2025). This approach allows flexibility while encouraging institutions to align with global ethical norms. The U.K. government has also signalled future movement towards binding regulations for advanced AI systems, potentially harmonising with the EU's approach.

In the Asia-Pacific (APAC) region, regulatory diversity reflects varying levels of economic maturity and technological adoption. Jurisdictions such as China and South Korea have introduced binding AI-specific legislation, including China's Algorithmic Recommendation Management Provisions and South Korea's Act on Fostering the AI Industry, both emphasising data transparency and accountability (Abdullah, 2025). Meanwhile, countries like Singapore and Japan promote voluntary governance frameworks, such as Singapore's FEAT Principles (Fairness, Ethics, Accountability, and Transparency) and Japan's AI Governance Guidelines, which encourage responsible innovation while maintaining flexibility (Abdullah, 2025). Public-private collaboration initiatives, such as the Monetary Authority of Singapore's (MAS) Veritas Initiative and Hong Kong Monetary Authority's GenAI Sandbox, exemplify proactive approaches to testing and validating AI systems within supervised environments (Crisanto et al., 2024).

8.5.1.2 Global South regulatory developments

The global South finds itself struggling to find the balance between innovation and imitation. There is a tendency of lawmakers in the global South to draw inspiration from developed countries in the North when developing regulatory frameworks. This often goes beyond inspiration to actually copying these frameworks and "best practices," which are contextually misaligned with the Global South (LaForge, 2024). Such mimicry risks producing formal compliance without substantive ethical governance, hence the need for the development of AI regulatory frameworks that focus on the global South.

While the Northern frameworks are sophisticated, they apply to countries with advanced digital infrastructure, stronger enforcement mechanisms, and more efficient legal systems. Therefore, simply importing these frameworks into the South without adapting them to local conditions leads to regulatory disconnect and consequently a gap between policy intent and practical implementation, leaving Southern ethical issues unaddressed in real-world banking operations.

However, this is not to say that the global South has not made strides in AI regulation. For instance, the 2024 African Union AI Strategy adopted alongside the Digital Compact for Africa, demonstrates Africa's determination to pursue an Africa-centered and development-oriented vision for AI, grounded in ethical, responsible, and equitable AI use (Centre for Intellectual Property and Information Technology Law, 2024). The Strategy was developed on pre-existing continental digital governance instruments, such as the AU Data Policy Framework (*AU Data Policy Framework | African Union*, 2022), Resolution 473, and the Malabo Convention on Cyber Security and Personal Data Protection (Macdonald, 2024). It represents a pivotal move towards leveraging AI as a driver of inclusive growth across the continent. Essentially, the Strategy is a coordinated framework to guide national adoption of AI technologies in support of broader socio-economic transformation goals. Collectively, these initiatives align closely with the African Union's 2030 Digital Transformation Strategy (*The Digital Transformation Strategy for Africa (2020-2030) | African Union*, 2020) and Agenda 2063 (*Agenda 2063: The Africa We Want. | African Union*, n.d.), reaffirming a continental commitment to technological sovereignty and human-centered innovation (Global Center on AI Governance, 2024).

Another Southern regional effort is the Inter-American Framework on Data Governance and Artificial Intelligence (MIGDIA), coordinated by the Organization of American States (OAS, 2023), which provides model principles for ethical AI adoption. MIGDIA promotes transparency, human rights protection, and cross-border cooperation, showing an important step towards regional policy harmonisation (*Inter-American Framework on Data Governance and (MIGDIA)*, 2023). It has already yielded positive results, such as 104 Inter-American data governance and Artificial Intelligence guidelines developed and agreed (*Inter-American Framework on Data Governance and (MIGDIA*, 2023).

Additionally, the Association of Southeast Asian Nations (ASEAN) launched a Guide on AI Governance and Ethics in 2024 and an Expanded ASEAN Guide on AI Governance and Ethics in 2025, focused on Generative AI. The guide sets out recommendations in AI governance for all member countries, illustrating collaboration for a trusted Generative AI ecosystem in the region (ASEAN Secretariat, n.d.).

On a national level, different countries in the global South have made efforts to regulate AI use. For example, 2023 Peru's Law 31814, and Supreme Decree No. 115-2025-PCM to come into force in 2026, this includes risk-based security standards; public interest; ethical principles; privacy obligations; profiling and automated decision-making rules (Kaiteki Regulación, n.d.).

In South Asia, Pakistan approved its National AI Policy 2025 to utilise the potential of AI and associated technologies for national growth. The Policy emphasises on capacity building, innovation, and creation of new employment opportunities. Additionally, the Ministry of IT aims to provide training to one million individuals in AI over the next three years (Pakistan Approves 1st National AI Policy, 2025).

Similarly, in Africa, Kenya launched its National AI Strategy 2025–2030, in alignment with the country's digital transformation agenda. Key pillars of the Strategy include ethical AI deployment, improving digital infrastructure, research and innovation, and developing a governance and regulatory framework and aims at creating an AI council or task force, AI risk and safety institute, regulatory audits, and regulatory sandboxes (Ministry of ICT and Digital Economy [MICDE], 2025).

In Latin America, Brazil's draft AI Bill (*PL 2338/2023*) incorporates provisions on transparency, human oversight, and algorithmic auditability. In 2024, Chile launched its National AI Policy and action plan, as well as an AI bill aimed at regulating and promoting the ethical and responsible development of AI (UNESCO, 2024). Colombia's National AI Policy focuses on ethics and governance, data and infrastructure, research, development and innovation; capabilities and digital talent; risk mitigation and safe and secure AI adoption and AI use (White & Case LLP, 2025).

8.5.2 Towards contextual AI ethics in the global South

The emerging Southern frameworks reflect a shift from theoretical commitments to actual institutionalisation of AI governance. Yet this process is uneven. The legal formalisation process outpaces the development of infrastructure, regulatory capacity, technical expertise, and independent oversight mechanisms. Many Southern countries still depend on imported technologies, foreign cloud infrastructure, and donor-supported capacity building, raising concerns about digital dependency and technological sovereignty.

While these Southern frameworks are important steps towards ethical and accountable AI, their success ultimately depends on whether they can develop context-specific, locally embedded approaches, rather than replicating the regulatory logics of the Global North.

Rather than copying Northern models, such as Chile's National AI Policy developed based on the EU AI Act (Laboris, 2025), the global South has an opportunity to craft context-specific approaches to AI regulation, taking into consideration the ethics that apply to different regions. Such frameworks need to focus on inclusivity, accessibility, and social justice, emphasising the local realities of informal economies, linguistic diversity, and infrastructural limitations (Tony Blair Institute for Global Change, 2025). Developing regulatory capacity, fostering regional cooperation, and encouraging homegrown AI innovation are essential steps towards ethical sovereignty (Farhad, 2025).

Grounding AI ethics in local values and socio-economic priorities will enable the global South to move beyond regulatory imitation towards a more equitable and sustainable model of AI governance, one that not only mitigates harm but also actively advances financial inclusion and social development (Farhad, 2025).

8.5.3 Strategic approaches to ethical risk mitigation

Regulators and financial institutions are implementing targeted strategies to embed ethics within AI governance frameworks. A primary approach involves establishing internal ethical codes and standards that define benchmarks for fairness, accountability, and transparency, ensuring alignment between institutional values and regulatory mandates (Burgt, 2019). Regular bias auditing and the use of fairness metrics further enable institutions to identify and mitigate discriminatory outcomes early in the AI lifecycle (Burgt, 2019; Massey & Massey, 2025).

Given AI's adaptive nature, organisations are developing dynamic compliance frameworks, which incorporate continuous monitoring and reassessment to ensure models remain fair, accurate, and aligned with legal standards over time (Massey & Massey, 2025). Transparency is further strengthened through public disclosure of AI governance policies and decision-making practices, reinforcing institutional accountability and customer trust (Burgt, 2019).

Finally, strategic reliance on public-private partnerships demonstrates how cooperation between regulators and industry stakeholders can promote responsible experimentation within controlled environments (Crisanto et al., 2024). Such partnerships help establish best practices that balance innovation with ethical safeguards.

8.6 CONCLUSION

The current global AI regulatory landscape reveals a much-needed shift towards ethical and collaborative AI governance in financial services. The EU AI Act remains the most comprehensive framework to date, yet parallel developments in the U.S., U.K., and APAC demonstrate an emerging alignment around ethical priorities encompassing fairness, transparency, accountability, and human oversight. This shift reflects a move from reactive compliance to proactive, value-based governance aimed at promoting responsible innovation.

However, global convergence must not be mistaken for uniformity. The Global South continues to face capacity gaps, infrastructural limitations, and data constraints that challenge the direct adoption of Northern regulatory frameworks. Without contextual adaptation, these frameworks risk reproducing structural inequalities and embedding the very biases they aim to mitigate. Similarly, though ethical AI use is a global challenge, majority of ethical challenges faced in the South stem from the application of Northern-trained AI systems. This highlights the urgent need for contextual and ethical AI adoption in the South.

The effectiveness of AI governance will ultimately depend on maintaining adaptability and inclusivity, ensuring that innovation in AI-driven finance advances not only efficiency and trust but also global equity and ethical integrity.

REFERENCES

Abdullah, I. N. (2025, February 12). An Overview of AI Regulations in Financial Services Around the World. *Fintech Singapore*. https://fintechnews.sg/107530/ai/ai-regulations-asia-financial-services/

Adeyelu, O. O., Ugochukwu, C. E., & Shonibare, M. (2024, April 17). Ethical Implications of AI in Financial Decision – Making: A Review with Real World Applications. *ResearchGate; Fair East Publishers*. https://doi.org/10.51594/ijarss.v6i4.1033

African Union. (n.d.). *Agenda 2063: The Africa we want*. African Union Commission. https://au.int/en/agenda2063/overview

African Union. (2020). *Digital transformation strategy for Africa (2020–2030)*. African Union Commission. https://au.int/sites/default/files/documents/38507-doc-dts-english.pdf

Almustafa, E., Assaf, A., & Allahham, M. (2023). Implementation of artificial intelligence for financial process innovation of commercial banks. *Revista de Gestão Social e Ambiental*, 17, e04119. https://doi.org/10.24857/rgsa.v17n9-004

Angermann, M. (2022, August 2). Global South and Global North: What Are They & What's the Conflict? *Utopia*. https://utopia.org/guide/global-south-and-global-north-what-are-they-whats-the-conflict/

ASEAN Secretariat. (n.d.). Expanded ASEAN guide on AI governance and ethics—generative AI. https://asean.org/book/expanded-asean-guide-on-ai-governance-and-ethics-generative-ai/

Bailey, K. (2019). The Ethics of AI in Finance: How to Detect and Prevent Bias. *Corporate Finance Institute*. https://corporatefinanceinstitute.com/resources/data-science/ai-ethics-in-finance-detect-prevent-bias/

Birhane, A. (2020). Algorithmic colonization of Africa. *SCRIPTed: A Journal of Law, Technology & Society*, 17(2). https://doi.org/10.2966/scrip.170220.389

Bragas, C., Villaneza, J., & Mina, M. (2025). AI in the Banking sector: a friend or a foe? *International Journal of Research Publication and Reviews*, 6(4), 3919–3936. ResearchGate | Find and share research

Burgt, J. (2019) General principles for the use of Artificial Intelligence in the financial sector. https://www.dnb.nl/media/voffsric/general-principles-for-the-use-of-artificial-intelligence-in-the-financial-sector.pdf

Centre for Intellectual Property and Information Technology Law. (2024, December 20). An in-depth analysis of the AU -- AI continental strategy and implications on AI governance in the continent. https://cipit.strathmore.edu/an-in-depth-analysis-of-the-au-ai-continental-strategy-and-implications-on-ai-governance-in-the-continent/

Crisanto, J. C., Leuterio, C. B., Prenio, J., & Yong, J. (2024, December 12). Regulating AI in the financial sector: Recent developments and main challenges. *BIS* https://www.bis.org/fsi/publ/insights63.htm

Farhad, S. (2025). Passengers in flight: AI governance capacity in the global South. *Digital Society*, 4(2). https://doi.org/10.1007/s44206-025-00195-6

FinTech Global. (2025, July 14). How South African banks lead AML innovation with AI. *FinTech Global*. https://fintech.global/2025/07/14/how-south-african-banks-lead-aml-innovation-with-ai/

Ganesan, P., & Meena, R. (2024). The Ethics of AI in Banking A Philosophical Perspective (1). ResearchGate | Find and share research

Garcia, A. C. B., Garcia, M. G. P., & Rigobon, R. (2024). Algorithmic discrimination in the credit domain: What do we know about it? *AI & SOCIETY*, 39(4), 2059–2098. https://doi.org/10.1007/s00146-023-01676-3

Global Center on AI Governance. (2024). Africa now has a continental AI strategy: What next?. https://www.globalcenter.ai/research/africa-now-has-a-continental-ai-strategy-what-next

Invogue Solutions. (2024, May 9). Bridging the gap: Artificial intelligence comparisons between global South and North – challenges and solutions. https://invoguesolutions.com/ai-gap-global-south-north-solutions/

Isreal, O., Torres, A., David, O., Banks, B., & Gatete, O. (2025). Bias, Ethics, and Social Implications of Machine Learning in Credit Scoring for Low-Income Populations. ResearchGate | Find and share research

Kakembo, A., & Annet, U. IV (2025). The ethics of AI: Philosophical perspectives. *Research Invention Journal of Research in Education*, 5(2), 65–71. https://doi.org/10.59298/RIJRE/2025/526571

Kaiteki Regulación. (n.d.). Peru approves its first artificial intelligence regulation. https://www.kaitekiregulacion.pe/en/peru-aprueba-su-primer-reglamento-de-inteligencia-artificial/?utm_source=chatgpt.com

Kesireddy, S. (2025). Intelligent claims processing in insurance: AI-augmented ETL for faster decisioning. *European Journal of Computer Science and Information Technology*, *13*, 37–57. https://doi.org/10.37745/ejcsit.2013/vol13n443757

Kiemde, S. M. A., & Kora, A. D. (2022). Towards an ethics of AI in Africa: Rule of education. *AI and Ethics*, 2(1), 35–40. https://doi.org/10.1007/s43681-021-00106-8

Kowalski, A. (2020, June). (PDF) Global South-Global North Differences. *ResearchGate*. https://doi.org/10.1007/978-3-319-69625-6_68-1

Laboris, I. (2025, August 29). *Kliemt.blog*. https://kliemt.blog/2025/08/29/chiles-ai-bill-a-pioneering-policy-facing-local-limits/

LaForge, G. (2024, September 5). The dangers of imposing global North approaches to AI governance on the global South. TechPolicy.Press. https://techpolicy.press/the-dangers-of-imposing-global-north-approaches-to-ai-governance-on-the-global-south

Lumenova. (2025, August 15). Understand Your AI: Compliance & Regulatory Insights for AI in Banking. https://www.lumenova.ai/blog/understand-your-ai-banking/

Macdonald, A. (2024, July 25). African Union adopts AI strategy to streamline continental digital transformation efforts | *Biometric Update*. https://www.biometricupdate.com/202407/african-union-adopts-ai-strategy-to-streamline-continental-digital-transformation-efforts

Massey, B., & Massey, S. (2025). The State of AI Regulation in Financial Services. *Anordea Insights*. https://www.anordea.com/wp-content/uploads/2025/06/The-State-Of-AI-Regulation-In-Financial-Services.pdf

Ministry of ICT and Digital Economy [MICDE]. (2025). Kenya's artificial intelligence (AI) strategy 2025–2030 launched at the KICC, Nairobi https://ict.go.ke/kenyas-artificial-intelligence-ai-strategy-2025-2030-launched-kicc-nairobi?utm_source=chatgpt.com

Monasterio Astobiza, A., Ausín, T., Liedo, B., Toboso, M., Aparicio, M., & López, D. (2022). Ethical governance of AI in the global South: A human rights approach to responsible use of AI. *Proceedings*, 81(1), 136. https://doi.org/10.3390/proceedings2022081136

OAS. (2023). Inter-American framework on data governance and artificial intelligence (MIGDIA). https://www.oas.org/ext/en/democracy/inter-american-framework-on-data-governance-and-artificial-intelligence-migdia

Owuor, B. (2025). AI Sovereignty, and Strategy: Navigating the Geopolitical Landscape for African States. ResearchGate | Find and share research

Pakistan approves 1st national AI policy, moves to create "complete AI ecosystem." (2025). https://www.aa.com.tr/en/asia-pacific/pakistan-approves-1st-national-ai-policy-moves-to-create-complete-ai-ecosystem/3646619

Rosaline, S. L., & Emiliya, I. (2024). Role of AI in banking sector. *International Journal of Cultural Studies and Social Sciences*, *20*(2), Article 11. https://www.researchgate.net/publication/385142661_Role_of_AI_in_Banking_sector

Salami, A. O. (2024). Artificial intelligence, digital colonialism, and the implications for Africa's future development. *Data & Policy*, 6, e67. https://doi.org/10.1017/dap.2024.75

Salman, S., & Dr. Chaya R. (2025). Humanising the machine: Conceptual reflections on responsible AI in Banking. *International Research Journal of Humanities and Interdisciplinary Studies*, 6(6), 18–25. https://irjhis.com/review.aspx?paper=IRJHIS2506003

Smit, J. (2025). Ethical AI in Banking: A sectoral literature review with case-based interventions. *Open Journal of Business and Management*, 13(04), 2420–2430. https://doi.org/10.4236/ojbm.2025.134125

Space Technologies. (2025). AI use cases banking: 15 applications + real examples. https://www.spaceo.ai/blog/ai-use-cases-in-banking/

statista. (n.d.). Estimated value of the financial sector's artificial intelligence (AI) spending worldwide from 2017 to 2025, with forecasts from 2026 to 2028. (n.d.). *Statista*. https://www.statista.com/statistics/1446037/financial-sector-estimated-ai-spending-forecast/

Tahir, F. (2025, February 21). Microsoft Dynamics and NetSuite Partner & Dynamics CRM Consultants in San Diego. *AlphaBOLD*. https://www.alphabold.com/ai-for-banking-benefits-risks-use-cases/

Talreja, V. (2022) Ethical AI in Banking and Financial: Balancing Innovation with Responsibility. *Apexon.com* https://www.apexon.com/blog/ethical-ai-in-banking-and-finance-balancing-innovation-with-responsibility/

Thiruma Valavana (2024). Usage of AI in Banking – Ethical challenges of bias, fairness, transparency, and accountability. *ResearchGate*, XI(8), 26–31. ResearchGate | Find and share research

Tony Blair Institute for Global Change. (2025, February 6). How leaders in the global South can devise AI regulation that enables innovation. https://institute.global/insights/tech-and-digitalisation/how-leaders-in-the-global-south-can-devise-ai-regulation-that-enables-innovation

UNESCO. (2024) Chile launches a national AI policy and introduces an AI bill. https://www.unesco.org/en/articles/chile-launches-national-ai-policy-and-introduces-ai-bill-following-unescos-recommendations-0

Unger, N., & McLean, M. (2025). An Open Door: AI Innovation in the Global South amid Geostrategic Competition. *Csis.org*. https://www.csis.org/analysis/open-door-ai-innovation-global-south-amid-geostrategic-competition

UXDA | Financial UX Design. (2025, June 30). *Inside the AI Revolution in Digital Banking UX: Case Studies, Data, and Strategic Takeaways*. Medium; UX Planet. https://uxplanet.org/inside-the-ai-revolution-in-digital-banking-ux-case-studies-data-and-strategic-takeaways-349ac7aeabd6

Wang, S. (2025, January 28). Bias in Code: Algorithm Discrimination in Financial Systems - Robert F. Kennedy Human Rights. *Robert F. Kennedy Human Rights*. https://rfkhumanrights.org/our-voices/bias-in-code-algorithm-discrimination-in-financial-systems/

White & Case LLP (2025, June 26). AI watch: Global regulatory tracker – Colombia. https://www.whitecase.com/insight-our-thinking/ai-watch-global-regulatory-tracker-colombia

Williams, A., John, A., & Ruth, A. (2025). *The ethical implications of implementing AI-based fraud detection systems in financial institutions*. ResearchGate. https://www.researchgate.net/publication/390767992

World Bank Group. (2024). *The use of alternative data in credit risk assessment: Opportunities, risks, and challenges*. World Bank Group. https://documents1.

worldbank.org/curated/en/099031325132018527/pdf/P179614-3e01b947-cbae-41e4-85dd-2905b6187932.pdf

World Bank & International Finance Corporation. (2022). *Regulation and supervision of fintech: Considerations for EMDE policymakers* (Fintech and the Future of Finance Flagship Technical Note). World Bank Group. https://documents1.worldbank.org/curated/en/099735204212215248/pdf/P173006033b45702d09522066cbc8338dcb.pdf

Xineoh (2026). Predicting Consumer Behavior with AI. (n.d.). *Xineoh.com*. Retrieved from https://xineoh.com/

Yilma, K. (2025). Ethics of AI in Africa: Interrogating the role of ubuntu and AI governance initiatives. *Ethics and Information Technology*, 27(2). https://doi.org/10.1007/s10676-025-09834-5

Yu, D., Rosenfeld, H., & Gupta, A. (2023, January 16). The "AI divide" between the Global North and Global South. *World Economic Forum*. https://www.weforum.org/stories/2023/01/davos23-ai-divide-global-north-global-south/

Zambrano, A. F., Giraldo, L. F., Perdomo, M. T., Hernández, I. D., & Godoy, J. M. (2023). Rotating savings and credit associations: A scoping review. *World Development Sustainability*, 3, 100081. https://doi.org/10.1016/j.wds.2023.100081

Chapter 9

Decision intelligence and risk management in AI-Driven investments

Building resilient financial systems

Venkatesh Ankarla Sri Ramuloo

9.1 INTRODUCTION

Over the past decade, decision-making research has increasingly shifted toward an engineering-oriented perspective that emphasizes the structured design and practical implementation of decision processes. Within this framework, decision intelligence (DI) refers to a discipline focused on developing decision models that support human and organizational objectives (Hassan, 2025; Yeomans & Wilson, 2021). It integrates diverse decision-making aspects, including psychology, ethics, philosophy, social choice, economics, decision analysis, methodology, modeling, theory, and computing, with the support of information systems, software, and databases. DI has emerged in response to the demand from investors, risk managers, and business executives for more accurate statistical information and intuitive modeling for easier decision-making (Sohail et al., 2023; Tanim & Ahmad, 2025).

In practice, this discipline brings structure to decision-making by combining a range of methods, including artificial intelligence (AI), traditional business intelligence, and data science, alongside qualitative techniques such as storytelling. Together, these elements support a coherent progression from data collection and analysis to informed decision-making (Chen & Chen, 2023; Zhang et al., 2023). The integration of AI and DI is transforming risk management and shaping the future of financial decision-making (Choi et al., 2025; Faheem, 2021). AI Application Programming Interfaces (APIs) enable the analysis of vast and diverse datasets, supporting business decisions and mitigating corporate risks; DI systems provide decision-makers with actionable insights and foresight based on AI-driven risk assessments. Together, AI and DI chart the course toward a data-driven and risk-aware future.

The term AI refers to the technologies that are sufficiently strong to perform the tasks traditionally performed by human intellect, including image recognition, speech recognition, pattern recognition, and prediction (O'Halloran & Nowaczyk, 2019; Unger et al., 2019). Machine learning (ML) is a subfield of AI that uses data and algorithms to represent outputs to make faster, better, and less expensive decisions and predictions than before. The

 DOI: 10.1201/9781003656463-9

latest algorithms are based on increasingly more advanced methods, such as gradient-boosted models, which can gradually decrease the error levels to those achieved by deep-learning neural networks capable of analyzing and synthesizing human-like audio, images, and text. Utilizing AI models in the decision-making process is a qualitative decision: they are determined based on analysis and risk, not only gut decision-making, experience, and intuition. ML models are very useful in risk management and have excellent uses in the financial landscape, where the most important aspect of risk management is the use of previous information (Goutte, 2018; Zoey et al., 2024).

Risk management is the prioritization, assessment, and mitigation of risks. Risks are the possible events that may have a negative effect on an individual, project, or organization. Risk managers make sure that their institutions meet all government and industry regulations, develop standards to prevent negative future consequences, mitigate risks when they occur, and minimize the impact of risk on their companies. Risk management is typically defined in terms of financial risks, but it can apply to many other areas as well, including health-risk management, environmental risk management, and the like (Galaz et al., 2021; Sarioguz, 2024).

In response to the diverse and evolving nature of risks described above, risk management research has adopted a range of analytical frameworks to support prioritization, assessment, and mitigation activities. Commonly used approaches include the Delphi method, the nominal group technique, structured subjective expert judgment, and the SWOT (Strengths, Weaknesses, Opportunities, and Threats) framework, all of which facilitate systematic evaluation through expert knowledge and strategic analysis. When applied either independently or in combination, these technologies strengthen risk management processes by enabling more adaptive, data-driven, and timely decision-making. For instance, AI-enabled dynamic risk assessment allows investment and trading organizations to respond more effectively to emerging financial risks by operationalizing DI, resulting in decisions that are often more robust than those derived from traditional credit and non-credit risk assessment models (Assaf et al., 2021; Goutte, 2018).

DI establishes a cohesive framework for considering all possible decisions, suggested or implied, thus allowing an AI system to better model possible corrective actions and, ultimately, situations (Chen & Chen, 2023; Zhang et al., 2023). DI helps convert data into decisions, focusing on the logic behind decisions and framing the ultimate questions to be answered. The creation of a DI framework involves a detailed perspective that addresses real-world components, encompassing all variables, actions taken or not taken, and known or unknown objectives, whether explicit or implicit. This perspective considers all contributing decision points to the data and the timeframe of the data, where a decision question is integrated into forecasting. Coupling the DI framework with AI brings many benefits. Although AI has become an essential element of risk-management strategies, executing AI pilots effectively remains a significant challenge for most organizations.

A structured approach, such as DI, can help companies convert their exploratory AI initiatives into pragmatic, end-to-end solutions for risk management. Applying AI techniques to risk management processes can substantially improve the accuracy and effectiveness of future risk assessments, leading to distinct strategic advantages. Risks are rarely static or predictable, and failure to predict future threats faster than competitors may necessitate an organization's wholesale blocking of their success. Risks have the ability to rapidly evolve over time as a result of decisions made or not made. Factors such as unforeseen volume growth, unanticipated project change requests, emerging regulatory requirements, limitations in the current systems landscape, changing business priorities, and increased operational overhead paint only a few of the hundreds of varying real-world scenarios responsible for risk evolutions (Tanim & Ahmad, 2025; Yeomans & Wilson, 2021).

Advanced analytical technologies play an increasingly important role in strengthening investment decision-making and risk management by enabling organizations to interpret and act on large volumes of digitally generated data. These capabilities help address the complexity and scale associated with data-rich environments, supporting more timely and informed risk-related judgments. When such analytical approaches are combined with decision-oriented frameworks, they offer a broader and more integrated perspective on risk management, linking data analysis with structured reasoning. This integration also provides a useful reference point for future research and practice, particularly in understanding how complementary analytical and decision-support capabilities can be leveraged together (Choi et al., 2025; Zoey et al., 2024).

AI enables organizations to continuously monitor their business processes and automatically refine their models, both in predictive and prescriptive analytics, to support managerial decision-making, provided sufficient data is available (Faheem, 2021; Singh et al., 2023). Organizational decision-making is inherently subject to uncertainty, making effective risk management critical to the success of strategic initiatives. As risk environments continue to evolve, organizations increasingly rely on advanced analytical and communication technologies to support timely and informed risk assessments. These developments enable more robust risk management frameworks while also introducing ethical challenges related to algorithmic bias, data privacy, and regulatory compliance, including compliance with data protection regulations such as the General Data Protection Regulation (GDPR) (Sarioguz, 2024; Zoey et al., 2024). Nevertheless, these technological innovations also raise ethical concerns related to algorithmic bias, data privacy, and compliance with GDPR regulations.

9.2 DECISION-MAKING PROCESSES ENHANCED BY AI

The field of DI explores decision-making blind spots and methods to enhance decision quality (Kahneman et al., 1982; Yeomans & Wilson, 2021). Humans experience weaknesses, particularly in judgment, decision-making, and reasoning, when selecting future courses of action. Since decisions link causes to effects, improving decision quality entails connecting them more effectively. Impact is the ultimate factor for decision quality: better decisions lead to better outcomes and effects. Given the ubiquity of decisions, their significance to life, and their repeated occurrence, it is surprising that there is so little knowledge or discussion about how to make better decisions (Choi et al., 2025; Shiller, 2003).

Although financial decisions are made by many people with diverse backgrounds and aims, financial risk is a universal concern. Financial risk management (FRM) involves assessing, analyzing, and mitigating the risks that financial institutions face. The world of finance is highly dynamic; when the financial markets are extremely volatile, FRM becomes more vital. During such times, preparing for any unexpected financial changes is necessary. Therefore, employing data and algorithms to predict and understand financial risks is essential. By using automated decision-making, AI applications can enhance business operations and improve human decision quality (Choi et al., 2025; Tanim & Ahmad, 2025). Additionally, collaboration tools aid humans by presenting decisions with accompanying evidence, enabling superior human judgment.

9.2.1 Automated decision systems

The system leverages automation to implement established rules, sophisticated methodologies, and cutting-edge technologies to generate, evaluate, and make financial decisions. The rules account for all possible scenarios and the set objectives. Expert systems combine domain knowledge supplied by human experts with a rule engine. Typically, domain knowledge is represented in a large set of if-then rules that are evaluated against the dataset to arrive at a decision. Automated detection of potential financial risks and fraud may trigger an alert for investigation, automatically request additional information, or proceed in other appropriate ways (Chen & Chen, 2023; Faheem, 2021).

Enterprise intelligence tools extensively utilize business rules to establish policies and mitigate the often hidden financial and operational risks that are inherent to day-to-day business. Organizations need to identify and monitor customers and employees engaged in unethical behavior, such as fraud or money laundering. Business rules can be combined with other deliverables, such as predictive models, clustering, speech technologies, and natural language processing (NLP), to detect potential workforce and customer risks and to automate risk assessment (Singh et al., 2023; Zoey et al., 2024).

9.2.2 Human-AI collaboration

AI technology is capable of working in tandem with humans, enhancing their decision-making system and expanding their abilities. This becomes particularly relevant in the domain of financial risk control, where AI tools can be used to complement formal models due to their lower modeling cost and their capability to process pulsing, unstructured data across various sources. Collaborative models mitigate the threat of full automation and represent an initial step toward facilities founded on the human-in-the-loop AI paradigm, which is just starting to emerge in practice (Hassan, 2025; Yeomans & Wilson, 2021).

Humans can intervene during the model's functioning. For example, a user can utilize a conversational interface to explore the reasoning behind the system's predictions or receive an assessment of how the model handles uncertainty. The system can also suggest that a user with risk-control expertise approach the problem from a different perspective using alternative metrics generated after an iterative explainability process. Thus, the user can guide the model toward what is truly essential for the organization, leveraging domain expertise to improve the initial approach (Choi et al., 2025; Tanim & Ahmad, 2025). Internal data, such as financial institutions' assets and liabilities, financial statements, income statements, credit authorization data, and additional assessments, provide the classic basis for risk control. External data, including market data, economic and industry data, forex rates, short-selling data, merger and acquisition information, and related news, is fundamental but scarcely used, as incorporating them requires NLP techniques. Combining internal and/or external data with alternative datasets like Twitter or Google Trends further enhances awareness (Singh et al., 2023; Zoey et al., 2024).

9.2.3 Harnessing AI's power: Pattern recognition meets strategic decision-making

The use of advanced analytical tools in strategic decision-making has strengthened risk management practices in sustainable investment. These tools process information from multiple sources, compare it with historical trends, and generate insights that support informed investment judgments. By improving efficiency, consistency, and analytical depth, they help investors manage risk more effectively. Prior research notes benefits such as faster analysis, improved handling of large datasets, enhanced decision quality, and the potential for stronger risk-adjusted returns (O'Halloran & Nowaczyk, 2019; Unger et al., 2019).

AI helps reduce costs by performing functions traditionally carried out by security guards or analysts, such as facility protection. It enables decisions to be made faster by structuring large datasets that a human cannot process. AI systems can perform fast evaluations to mitigate risks. In the financial sector, AI can analyze vast amounts of data, including textual, numerical, and historical data, to facilitate predictions (Assaf et al., 2021; Zhang et al., 2023). AI techniques applied to a vast volume of data can aid in making informed investment decisions, thereby enhancing portfolio strategy. Complex investment decisions such as stock selection, timing, and allocation can be facilitated by AI algorithms (Assaf et al., 2021; Zhang et al., 2023).

9.2.4 Traditional vs. AI-Enhanced Decision-Making

Observing the decision-making process of risk management in sustainable investments a little closer may be both valuable and reflective of how AI methods may assist in achieving such a goal. The traditional decision-making strategies work within a given paradigm. That framework contains a cycle of activities, defining the goal, identifying and evaluating potential risks, assigning priorities, creating a risk management plan, implementing the plan, and monitoring and reviewing the progress toward the goal. New risks are identified or conditions modified, and decisions are taken in relation to current conditions to repeat the process. AI-enhanced decision-making systems are more adaptive and flexible and can change throughout the process.

Traditional decision-making approaches can be strengthened through two distinct improvements. First, AI can expand risk identification and selection. The most advanced predictive analytics or ML models utilize data to identify risks in their operating environment and in similar environments, and continually update them. Second, the process of plan creation can happen with the help of AI. By mapping the potential effects of any given risk, these models also determine what might change the likelihood or magnitude of a risk, following the links in both directions. Continuing research indicates that whole networks of risks evolve. This kind of understanding can be used as a deep background to plan development, offering new opportunities to minimize risk, as well as identifying new spheres of priority (Goutte, 2018; Sarioguz, 2024).

The analysis reveals that these benefits are not automatic. AI-powered risk management tools can lead to poor decisions (Tanim & Ahmad, 2025; Yeomans & Wilson, 2021). Success requires understanding how AI-enhanced decision-making strategies augment traditional frameworks. Smart decision-makers deploy AI as a source of additional insight, not as an autonomous creator of investment plans. In doing so, they avoid learned helplessness, gaming the system, and other cognitive pitfalls that weaken risk management. A continually evolving framework, AI-enhanced planning operates alongside a traditional, rule-based framework and a third, risk-detection framework that depends heavily on predictive analytics, as summarized in Table 9.1.

9.2.5 Integrating AI into strategic frameworks

9.2.5.1 Strategic decision-making frameworks

Traditional decision-making frameworks remain relevant when incorporating AI. Despite the enthusiasm for AI-driven techniques such as ML, their limitations and challenges must be addressed. Also, the integration of AI models for decision support requires a clear understanding of their contributions and a set of guidelines to leverage their capabilities effectively (Hassan, 2025; Yeomans & Wilson, 2021). The comparison of both AI-based and traditional approaches for an investment risk model highlights that different underlying

Table 9.1 Comparison of traditional and AI-enhanced decision-making in risk management

Aspect	*Traditional decision-making*	*AI-enhanced decision-making*
Core Process	Cyclical, linear process: Define goal -> Identify risks -> Create plan -> Implement -> Monitor	Adaptive, dynamic, and iterative process that can change in real-time
Risk Identification	Relies on historical data, expert judgment, and structured workshops (e.g., SWOT, Delphi method)	Uses ML models to continuously scan vast internal/external datasets to identify emerging and complex risks
Flexibility	Modifiable but often slow to adapt to new, unforeseen market conditions	Highly flexible and can update risk models and strategies based on real-time data feeds
Primary Strength	Well-established, understandable, and strong in evaluation, classification, and human oversight	Superior in prediction, forecasting, pattern recognition, and processing unstructured data (e.g., news, social media)
Human Role	Human intelligence is the central driver of the entire process	Human acts as a supervisor, guide, and final decision-maker, leveraging AI as a powerful analytical tool

tasks must be addressed. AI processes vast amounts of data for prediction and forecasting of risk events, whereas traditional risk management encompasses the evaluation of consequences, risk classification, decision-making, and risk treatment. The resulting performance differences suggest that the best of both worlds should be combined to create an advanced framework for interpreting investment risk and providing decision support. It is essential to integrate AI's predictive and forecasting strengths with traditional methods for evaluation, classification, decision-making, and risk mitigation (Assaf et al., 2021; Zhang et al., 2023).

An investment strategy should consider the risks being hedged not only in isolation but also against a backdrop of the whole investment community by incorporating all drivers of risk prevalent in the investment universe. The next decade in this research field will continue to see a growing number of fund managers inspired to pursue sustainability goals in addition to their primary objective of generating returns. For forecasting, additional, deeper layer architectures beyond LSTMs, such as attention-based models, can be particularly useful in working with longer time series and extracting more complex relations within the data (Choi et al., 2025). It is worth noting that more advanced Google models, such as BERT, RoBERTa, DistilBERT, ALBERT, or XLNet, can be considered in order to perform more sophisticated detection and forecasting of relationships. On the technology side, information extraction from news and social media is becoming more automated through the help of AI and NLP. Nevertheless, the final analysis still heavily depends on financial analysts capable of linking the information provided with specific companies and sectors. In this way, the role of Large Language Model (LLM) is not seen as a replacement capable of automating the whole investment process but rather as a valuable assistant and helpful decision-making support tool (Faheem, 2021; Zoey et al., 2024).

9.2.6 AI models for risk assessment

Risks in financial portfolios are gauged by applying AI models. These incorporate historical and recent data to detect and confirm risk signals, filtering out misleading indications. The subsequent evaluation assigns a risk level for each signal, presenting only high-risk situations to the risk management team. This approach yields more complete and timely risk information, clarifying the interconnections within the portfolio. It permits the exploration of "what if" scenarios, such as changes in interest rates and currency, and the adjustment of portfolio structures to reduce risk (Goutte, 2018; Tanim & Ahmad, 2025). In another mode, Assaf et al. (2021) developed an integrated financial risk assessment model employing feature selection and data processing techniques, combined with an Extreme Gradient Boosting (XGBoost) classifier, to assess the financial risk levels of financial institutions.

The availability of vast amounts of data and the ongoing development of economy-related models continually grant companies increased opportunities to grow, improve their financial situation, and enhance shareholder value. However, these options also carry considerable risks, especially when the underlying macroeconomic situations are volatile. Strategic decisions must account for such risks by assessing the probability of potential negative outcomes and establishing concrete actions to mitigate them. AI-based models can aid in the diversity of risk early warning and strategic decision-making processes (Assaf et al., 2021; O'Halloran & Nowaczyk, 2019). The prior logical consideration illustrates where AI can assist strategic decision-making. Financial risk test results serve as input for strategic decisions, incorporating the model suggestions. When conditions differ, the final decision is made by business experts; human intelligence retains the ultimate authority, particularly in cross-domain areas such as strategy setting. If the probability of an adverse event is low despite a poor financial situation, the general risk-warning level remains set for business controllers. In contrast, when a poor financial situation coincides with a high probability of a negative event, the risk-warning level is heightened, and specific actions are recommended, thereby contributing to comprehensive risk management (Zhang et al., 2023).

9.3 MITIGATING RISK: BEHAVIORAL, SYSTEMATIC, AND UNSYSTEMATIC CHALLENGES

9.3.1 Behavioral risks

Behavioral finance is a subcategory of economics that seeks to explain the implications of psychology for pursuing a portfolio of investment assets

(Kahneman et al., 1982; Shiller, 2003). It challenges the classical assumption that investors act rationally, consistently pursuing their best interests, arguing instead that investors often behave irrationally due to psychological biases. Factors such as over-optimism, untreated mental illness, and even the lunar cycle can significantly impact an investor's ability to make informed decisions about risk. With these factors in mind, what are some of the psychological biases that cause an investor to behave irrationally? How can an investor mitigate those biases, acting rationally to suppress the associated behavioral risk? A well-structured risk-mitigation strategy for behavioral finance must address the underlying human psychology. Carefully tuned neural networks can provide a powerful way to analyze investor sentiment and detect anomalies in investment behavior, thereby helping to quantify the behavioral risk faced by an individual client. Predictive analytics can then forecast shifts in behavior, enabling a bank to position its risk profile appropriately (Chen & Chen, 2023; Choi et al., 2025).

9.3.2 Systematic risks

Systematic risks affect the entire financial market. They include unexpected events such as natural disasters or economic recessions. Systematic risks are sometimes referred to as "market risks" because they are unavoidable. Changes in interest rates and exchange rates, or fluctuations in the market, can disrupt the entire financial system. These risks affect the whole system and cannot be diversified (Galaz et al., 2021; O'Halloran & Nowaczyk, 2019).

9.3.2.1 Market volatility

Market volatility is generally referred to as fluctuations in the performance of financial markets that can subsequently affect the behavior and price of securities, industries, or entire economies. The financial market exhibits volatility when prices move up or down rapidly over a short period, resulting in significant price changes that could negatively impact the investor's portfolio and decision-making processes. Market volatility can be caused by various factors, including shifts in interest rates, natural disasters, corporate reforms, announcements of financial earnings (whether better or worse than expected), production costs, government policies, wars and political unrest, inflation, and recession. The markets typically experience volatility during production hikes, higher inflation, war, and recession. A volatile market may influence investor behavior and the decision-making process, as it can determine the price movement of financial instruments (Tanim & Ahmad, 2025; Zhang et al., 2023).

High volatility in the financial market can result in rapid price rises, making it difficult for investors to instantly sell their shares for various reasons, thereby increasing investors' risk. A volatile market also adversely affects trade performance, productivity, and economic growth as a result of the fluctuations in financial market conditions. These fluctuations can make it challenging for investors to predict future price directions, possibly leading to losses during investment. They may require substantial amounts of money to remain in the market despite poor performance during uncertain conditions of turmoil, conflict, and recession in the market. Unpredictable and rapid price movements in the market, therefore, may result in diminished investor confidence. An investment strategy commonly employed to mitigate the adverse effects of a turbulent market is the buy-and-hold approach, whereby an investor makes strategic decisions to retain investments under any market condition (Hassan, 2025; Sohail et al., 2023).

9.3.2.2 Economic indicators

Other types of systematic risks include economic indicators. Economic indicators are the statistics that give us an insight into the economic performance of the country and help investors to make out of all the available economic data and make predictions in the market. These indicators reflect the prevailing performance of the economy and the sector, classifying the economy as either in a growth or shrinkage stage, which affects the markets (Faheem, 2021; Galaz et al., 2021). These economic indicators cover a broad range of statistics, which include inflation rate, employment level, disposable income, business cycles, credit prospects, monetary prospects, interest rate prospects, and government programs within the financial sector. The environment can significantly influence investment-related decisions and can predetermine the level of risk because the economy determines the impact of business. Industry performance, existing stock markets, occupation, interest rates, inflation rates, economic prosperity, and government policies are the indicators that provide valuable information to investors (Sarioguz, 2024; Zoey et al., 2024).

9.3.2.3 Global events

Besides market volatility and economic factors, another important systematic risk of financial investment is global events. Systematic risks are those risks that affect the market as a whole. The long-term dislocation and destruction of investors' purposes due to global events, such as political instability, natural calamities, and health emergencies. As an example, the COVID-19 crisis affected the economy on a grand scale (Galaz et al., 2021; O'Halloran & Nowaczyk, 2019).

One of the factors that may push the market prices downwards is political instability, such as wars, political turmoil, and riots. Natural catastrophes, including floods, droughts, and earthquakes, would disrupt production and supply chains, thereby destroying the economy. Correspondingly, a health crisis can undermine investor confidence and subsequently result in loss of jobs and income. When an event occurs, human beings often panic, fear, and make incorrect judgments that lead to significant losses or missed opportunities.

Considering these factors, it is important to manage systematic risks in order to protect investments (Hassan, 2025; Tanim & Ahmad, 2025).

Forecasting is the most effective method of preparing against any sudden attack on the market economy. The forecasting process reduces uncertainty in the economy and the stock market. The use of artificial intelligence to predict the economy and the stock market is being explored by many people currently. Approaches based on ML utilize the last two decades of data. The Indian market also experienced various shocks during this period, such as the terrorist attack in Mumbai, the 2008 economic crisis, and the 2011 global super cyclone (Goutte, 2018; Zhang et al., 2023).

9.3.3 Unsystematic risks

Unsystematic risk refers to the risk associated with a particular company or specific sector. It arises due to the company's failure to adapt its prices or operations in response to market changes and can be caused by various factors, such as the cost of attracting capital, debt financing, operational and investment decisions made during economic booms and recessions, and reputation distress. Additionally, the excessive diversification and concentration of assets in a particular sector make a portfolio susceptible to sectoral events. Industry or cyclical risk plays a significant role in the bank and non-lending financial investment sectors. For example, the FSCS covered financial service companies collapsed in 2008, and since then, the Financial System has gradually gained strength. However, not all sectors will remain stable, and therefore, various companies and funds in the investment arena have been employing strategies such as portfolio diversification to minimize their exposure to company risk. Previous research has indicated that diversification in a portfolio protects the investors from the extreme systematic risk associated with asset classes (Assaf et al., 2021; Unger et al., 2019). Although it does not reduce the systematic risk associated with the asset class, investors can mitigate the risks associated with different companies. Additionally, asset price valuation plays a significant role in determining risk. Uncertain investor perceptions create negative sentiment towards valuation, resulting in a temporary deviation of asset prices from their intrinsic value. Researchers have identified a risk factor associated with the price-to-book ratio, indicating that investors face a higher unsystematic risk when investing in assets with a low price-to-book ratio.

Mitigating service disruptions is essential for effective disaster recovery. The Archive Recovery Facility provides a resilient, disaster-tolerant architecture that automates provisioning and enables recoverability at the volume level. Its primary repository is cloud-based, supporting business continuity. The facility allows seamless switching of production and archive volumes between sites, enhancing system reliability. Service interruptions are minimized by distributing the active archive environment across multiple data centers. Recent research has evaluated this facility as an online solution for archiving, restoring, and classifying diverse types of content, complementing other forensic analysis techniques. Results indicate that archiving to Amazon S3 is both faster and more cost-effective compared to commercial archiving services (Sarioguz, 2024; Zoey et al., 2024).

9.3.4 AI application on risk-reduction techniques in financial investment

AI can have a significant impact on risk-reduction techniques in financial investment. First, behavioral risks can be mitigated by applying digital data processing to account for human cognitive and emotional bias, as well as market mood swings. Moreover, systematic risks may be lessened to some degree through the use of predictive analytics to consult related economic indicators. Lastly, data processing and ML algorithms can also help investors screen out some of the non-systematic risks by performing company benchmarking, industry trend analysis, and risk assessment of regulatory changes (Chen & Chen, 2023; Tanim & Ahmad, 2025). The key technologies are predictive analytics and machine-learning algorithms, which are trained to identify the three main categories of risk in a financial context. Table 9.2 summarizes the various ways in which AI can be deployed to mitigate these risks.

9.3.4.1 *AI-Driven behavioral analytics*

The financial stock market plays a prominent role in the economy, contributing to both corporate growth and national economic development. This stock market falls under the risk category, as the investor risks losses in future prices. Varieties of behavioral mistakes are committed by the investor at the time of investment. The investors are mostly affected by behavioral bias while deciding their investment pattern. Many researchers suggest that

Table 9.2 Strategies to address different risk categories

Risk Type	*Description*	*AI mitigation strategies & technologies*
Behavioral Risk	Risk arising from investors' cognitive and emotional biases (e.g., overconfidence, herd mentality)	Sentiment Analysis (NLP) on news/social media, Behavioral Analytics to detect anomalous investment patterns, Personalized AI advisors to counter bias
Systematic Risk	Market-wide, unavoidable risk (e.g., recession, interest rate changes, geopolitical events)	Predictive analytics on economic indicators, market volatility prediction models (LSTM, NARX), AI-driven macroeconomic forecasting
Unsystematic Risk	Company or industry-specific risk (e.g., management scandal, product failure, supply chain issue)	Company-specific risk assessment using financial data analysis, event-driven risk management with NLP to analyze news impact, ML models for fraud detection, and early warning signals

behavioral bias has an impact on the investor's irrational decision-making. The examination reveals the association between cognitive biases, emotional biases, and social biases in investment decision-making. The study focuses on the impact of social, emotional, and cognitive bias on an individual investor's fear and greed factors. Investors are also influenced by various sources of information, but primarily rely on social media during the investment process (Choi et al., 2025; Shiller, 2003).

Behavioral risk arises from cognitive and emotional biases that influence human behavior, potentially leading to suboptimal decisions in various aspects of life, particularly in investment. Although AI-powered analytics may never fully address emotional biases, personal analytics and the security master approach to risk assessment offer means of pinpointing biases and establishing protective mechanisms accordingly. Behavioral analytics are becoming an integral component of security decision-making, helping leaders identify and address poor decision-making within their organizations (Chen & Chen, 2023; Hassan, 2025). New tools utilize a combination of ML and NLP to review social media coverage and other predictive text resources, mapping these sources against market movements or identifying them as potential harbingers of risk. The objective is to employ behavioral analytics as predictive tools.

9.3.4.2 Personalized investment strategies

Influenced by biases and emotions, investment behavior frequently stems from prejudices, perceptions, and emotional responses. Consumers' animus or enthusiasm significantly influences their purchasing decisions and preferences. Natural sentiments can lead to excessive risk-taking or safety-seeking behavior. Additionally, social influences such as imitation or rejection play a crucial role in shaping consumer behavior (Kahneman et al., 1982; Shiller, 2003).

Investment decisions have consequences, and their benefits or detriments are contingent on the conscious evaluation of anticipated consequences, among other factors. Human irrationality in investment behavior can be analyzed using star rating, KNN, SVM, Decision Tree, and XGBoost. Incorporating a machine-learning method alongside traditional econometric techniques offers insights into the behavioral biases that affect investment decisions in the stock market. The algorithmic model can forecast whether the majority of investors are driven by rationality or behavioral biases (Assaf et al., 2021; Zhang et al., 2023).

9.3.4.3 Sentiment analysis tools

Behavioral biases appear in various forms across multiple domains. Analysis of social media can reveal emotional or behavioral tendencies. Within organizations or business sectors, such biases become apparent through analyst reports and financial news, which provide valuable insights for identifying recurring behavioral patterns. Additionally, biases linked to geopolitical events or specific nations and regions are observable in financial reports and Twitter data, underscoring the influence of these information sources. The richness of textual content, including sentiment and perspective, plays a crucial role in addressing risks stemming from social dynamics, recent developments, and global markets (Singh et al., 2023; Zoey et al., 2024). Behavioral analytics models interpret these well-structured textual sources and can alert investors, advisors, and financial experts regarding upcoming risks in investment strategies, financial markets, and the global economy as a whole. By promptly identifying emotional or behavioral biases embedded in social behavior, investment patterns, and the sentiments of investors, systematic risks within a business group, domain, or company, as reflected in the reports of investment analysts, market experts, and investors, can be effectively mitigated.

A variety of online financial services provide market intelligence to assist investors in evaluating opportunities. For instance, *Investing.com* provides GREED & FEAR gauges for markets like the S&P 500 and Forex, along with sentiment analysis tools for commodities and other assets. MarketBeat offers Market Sentiments and Sector Sentiments analyses. Skilling supports Stock Sentiment by displaying whether the latest news for particular stocks is "positive", "negative", "mixed", or "neutral". The Latest News Widget and Market News are also accessible on their platform. Stocktwits presents Market Sentiment tools for indices, cryptocurrencies, and specific stocks such as AAPL, TSLA, GOOGL, and AMZN (Chen & Chen, 2023; Hassan, 2025).

9.3.5 Systematic risks and AI mitigation strategies

Systematic risks affect the entire stock market or economy, regardless of the industry in which a company operates. When economic recessions or depressions occur, these risks affect almost every company, and investors are rarely willing to invest in such companies. The best way to avoid such risks remains well known: investors simply need to diversify their portfolio by reducing their exposure through holding assets in different sectors (Galaz et al., 2021; O'Halloran & Nowaczyk, 2019). However, most investors tend to choose asset portfolios limited only to high-growth stocks or dividend-payout stocks; in the process, they forgo diversification, leaving their portfolio vulnerable to systematic risks.

AI helps investors forecast economic and political scenarios; accordingly, they will know when to reduce their involvement in investment projects. Furthermore, by analyzing historical economic data and establishing relationships between all sectors during recessions and depressions, AI can help investors and portfolio managers make informed decisions to mitigate systematic risks (Sohail et al., 2023; Tanim & Ahmad, 2025). Beyond forecasting,

AI-based algorithmic trading enables market volatility trading in the future, contributing to the control of systematic risk in the financial investment market.

9.3.5.1 *Market volatility prediction*

The importance of portfolio diversification in reducing risk arises from the Optimization of the Standard Deviation of Portfolio returns. Investors make investment decisions considering risk (standard deviation) and expected return, according to the Capital Asset Pricing Model Guide. Systematic risk is also referred to as market risk, and market volatility is closely related to systematic risk. These factors have a direct impact on the investment decision. The degree of volatility determines whether an investment is undertaken or avoided. Systematic risk in investment can be reduced with the help of AI. Predicting market volatility helps investors make informed investment decisions. Expected future market volatility also influences investment decisions. AI methods, such as SVR, NARX, GBM, and LSTM, have been evaluated to determine the most effective technique for analyzing the relationship between expected and actual volatility in the stock market (Goutte, 2018; Zhang et al., 2023). The NARX model yielded the best results, followed by GBM and SVR.

9.3.6 Unsystematic risks and AI mitigation strategies

Unsystematic risks are specific to a company or industry. They can be reduced through diversification. However, AI can further aid in mitigating these risks by providing deep, granular analysis that is beyond human capability. AI algorithms can continuously monitor a company's financial health, supply chain stability, regulatory compliance status, and management effectiveness. NLP tools can scan thousands of news articles, earnings call transcripts, and regulatory filings in real-time to identify early warning signs of company-specific troubles, such as potential fraud, management scandals, or operational disruptions. This allows investors to make informed decisions about holding or divesting specific assets long before traditional analysis might detect an issue (Assaf et al., 2021; Zhang et al., 2023).

9.3.6.1 *Company-specific risk assessment*

AI-driven models can perform a comprehensive risk assessment for individual companies by analyzing their financial statements, cash flow patterns, debt levels, and market positioning. ML models can be trained to identify subtle patterns that precede financial distress or outperformance. For example, an AI model might detect that a company's accounts receivable are growing disproportionately to its revenue, a potential red flag for aggressive revenue recognition or future write-offs. By flagging such issues, AI enables a more proactive approach to managing unsystematic risk within a portfolio (Chen & Chen, 2023; Tanim & Ahmad, 2025).

9.3.6.2 Event-driven risk management

Specific events, such as a product recall, a key executive departure, or a major lawsuit, can significantly impact a company's value. AI-powered event-driven risk management systems use NLP to monitor news feeds and social media for such events in real-time. These systems can assess the potential impact of an event based on historical data and similar past occurrences, allowing for immediate analysis and response. This capability is crucial for managing unsystematic risk, as it provides the speed and scale necessary to react to fast-moving developments that could affect individual holdings (Singh et al., 2023; Zoey et al., 2024).

9.4 CONCLUSION

Integrating structured decision-making frameworks with advanced computational technologies offers a transformative approach to managing the complex risks inherent in financial investments. By harnessing capabilities such as pattern recognition, predictive modeling, and real-time data processing, investors and financial institutions can more effectively address behavioral, systematic, and unsystematic risks. The decision-making framework provides a structured method for translating these data-driven insights into actionable strategies, ensuring that investment choices remain aligned with overall risk tolerance and long-term financial objectives (Hassan, 2025; Yeomans & Wilson, 2021). The synergy between human expertise and AI augmentation is paramount. While AI excels at processing vast amounts of data and identifying complex, non-linear relationships, human judgment remains essential for contextual understanding, ethical considerations, and strategic oversight. The future of resilient financial systems lies in this collaborative model, where DI guides the application of AI to not only predict and react to risks but also to build more adaptive and robust investment strategies capable of weathering market uncertainties (Choi et al., 2025; Sarioguz, 2024).

REFERENCES

Assaf, L., Gillen, R. J., & O'Connell, J. F. (2021). An integrated financial risk assessment model using XGBoost. *Expert Systems With Applications*, *186*, 115832. https://doi.org/10.1016/j.eswa.2021.115832

Chen, A., & Chen, T. (2023). Multi-loss prediction for student loan credit risk. *Financial Innovation*, *9*(1), 28.

Choi, S., Kang, H., Kim, N., & Kim, J. (2025). How does artificial intelligence improve human decision-making? Evidence from the AI-powered go program. *Strategic Management Journal*. https://doi.org/10.1002/smj.3694

Faheem, M. A. (2021). AI-driven risk assessment models: Revolutionizing credit scoring and default prediction. *Iconic Research and Engineering Journals*, *5*(3), 177–186.

Galaz, V., Centeno, M. A., Callahan, P. W., Causevic, A., Patterson, T., Brass, I., Baum, S., Farber, D., Fischer, J., Garcia, D., McPhearson, T., Jimenez, D., King, B., Larcey, P., & Levy, K. (2021). Artificial intelligence, systemic risks, and sustainability. *Technology in Society*, *67*, 101741. https://doi.org/10.1016/j.techsoc.2021.101741

Goutte, C. (2018). Risk assessments: A range of models and strategies. *Journal of Financial Transformation*, *48*, 1–15.

Hassan, T. (2025). Augmented analytics in financial forecasting enhancing risk management and investment strategies through AI-driven insights. Available at SSRN 5179431.

Kahneman, D., Tversky, A. M., & Slovic, P. (1982). *Judgment Under Uncertainty: Heuristics and Biases*. Cambridge University Press.

O'Halloran, S., & Nowaczyk, N. (2019). An artificial intelligence approach to regulating systemic risk. *Frontiers in Artificial Intelligence*, *2*, 7. https://doi.org/10.3389/frai.2019.00007

Shiller, R. J. (2003). From efficient markets theory to behavioral finance. *Journal of Economic Perspectives*, *17*(1), 83–104. https://doi.org/10.1257/089533003321164967

Singh, S., Sharma, P. K., & Moon, R. (2023). Cybersecurity challenges and confidence in the financial industry. *Computers & Security*, *132*, 103388. https://doi.org/10.1016/j.cose.2023.103388

Sohail, M. K., Al-Zahrani, F. A., & Alharbi, S. S. (2023). A framework for cyber risk mitigation strategy selection in banking. *Journal of King Saud University - Computer and Information Sciences*, *35*(2), 295–304. https://doi.org/10.1016/j.jksuci.2022.12.009

Tanim, S. H., & Ahmad, M. S. (2025). AI driven strategic decision-making in IT project management: Enhancing risk assessment, cost control, and efficiency. *World Journal of Advanced Research and Reviews*, *25*(2), 247–268.

Unger, A., van Nederveen, F. C., & van der Spek, S. M. (2019). AI and portfolio risk: A comparative analysis. *Journal of Portfolio Management*, *45*(7), 123–135.

Yeomans, L. R., & Wilson, P. D. G. (2021). Decision intelligence: A human–machine partnership. *Business Horizons*, *64*(6), 761–770. https://doi.org/10.1016/j.bushor.2021.07.002

Zhang, Y., Li, H., & Wang, Q. (2023). A transfer learning and random forest DNN model for bank operational risk assessment. *Engineering Applications of Artificial Intelligence*, *123*(Part B), 106412. https://doi.org/10.1016/j.engappai.2023.106412

Zoey, A., Aria, D., Oscar, A., Marek, M., Julia, Z., Cora, L., & Ok, E. (2024). Blockchain and AI in financial risk management: A machine learning approach to credit risk mitigation. *Journal of Financial Technology*, *15*(4), 201–214.

Chapter 10

Algorithmic democracy

Ethical dilemmas of AI in public tax administration

Pascal Stiefenhofer and Cafer Deniz

10.1 INTRODUCTION

Artificial intelligence (AI) has become a constitutive element of contemporary public administration, transforming how discretionary authority is exercised, justified, and contested. No longer a neutral administrative instrument, algorithmic systems function as a normative infrastructure that redistributes power, reshapes discretion, and reconfigures the moral foundations of democratic governance (Wirtz et al., 2019; Yeung, 2018). These transformations are particularly visible in tax administration, where the state's coercive authority intersects directly with core democratic principles such as legality, proportionality, equality before the law, and public accountability (Braithwaite, 2009; Kirchler, 2007). As fiscal authorities increasingly rely on predictive analytics, automated risk scoring, and algorithmic fraud detection, administrative decision-making shifts from deliberative judgment to computational inference (Bovens and Zouridis, 2002; Bullock, 2019). While such systems promise gains in efficiency and analytical precision, they simultaneously disrupt the communicative and justificatory practices through which democratic authority is rendered intelligible and legitimate (Margetts and Dorobantu, 2019; Yeung, 2018).

This transformation marks more than a technical evolution in administrative practice. It signals a deeper reconfiguration of the democratic relationship between citizens and the state. In Habermasian terms, algorithmic systems risk displacing public reason with technical rationality, replacing dialogical justification with statistical prediction (Habermas, 1996). Decisions that were once embedded in reason-giving administrative processes increasingly appear as outputs of opaque computational architectures, difficult for affected citizens to understand, challenge, or attribute to accountable agents (Ananny and Crawford, 2018; Pasquale, 2015). What emerges is not merely automated administration, but a transformation in the normative conditions under which public authority is exercised and recognised within democratic societies.

Within public administration theory, this development intensifies a long-standing tension between efficiency and legitimacy, historically central to Max Weber's conception of rational–legal authority (Weber, 1978 [1922]). Classical bureaucracy derived its legitimacy from rule-bound reasoning, identifiable

DOI: 10.1201/9781003656463-10

officials, and the accountability of office. Under conditions of algorithmic governance, these foundations are unsettled. AI increasingly mediates core fiscal judgments—determining who is audited, on what grounds, and according to which inferred criteria of suspicion—yet it operates through probabilistic models and proprietary systems that lack discernible moral agency (Pasquale, 2015; Zouridis, van Eck and Bovens, 2019). As a result, administrative power risks becoming post-deliberative: decisions are executed without the communicative reasoning that traditionally linked authority to public justification and democratic consent (Bovens and Zouridis, 2002; Bullock, 2019). This shift challenges the normative core of democratic governance itself, particularly the conditions of intelligibility, contestability, and mutual recognition through which citizens and officials act as co-authors of legitimate rule (Habermas, 1996; Pettit, 2012).

10.1.1 Research gap

Despite the rapid diffusion of AI across public administration, existing scholarship has largely focused on technical performance, regulatory compliance, and ethical design, while paying comparatively limited attention to the democratic implications of algorithmic authority (Ananny and Crawford, 2018; Danaher, 2022; Margetts and Dorobantu, 2019; Stiefenhofer and Deniz, 2025). Much of the literature on digital governance adopts managerial or technocratic perspectives that prioritise efficiency, innovation, and risk management (Busch and Henriksen, 2018; Wirtz et al., 2019). These approaches often treat legitimacy as a derivative outcome of performance or procedural compliance, thereby overlooking the deliberative and justificatory dimensions that sustain democratic rule (Habermas, 1996; Pettit, 2012).

This omission is particularly consequential in the fiscal domain. Taxation represents a paradigmatic expression of state authority, combining coercive power with moral claims about fairness, reciprocity, and civic obligation (Braithwaite, 2009; Kirchler, 2007). Algorithmic tools in tax administration do not merely enhance detection or enforcement; they actively redefine the moral boundaries of fiscal citizenship and the conditions under which coercive authority can be democratically justified (Bullock, 2019; Yeung, 2018). Despite the widespread deployment of AI-driven tax systems across Europe, there remains no coherent theoretical framework that systematically links algorithmic discretion to democratic legitimacy, nor a sustained philosophical account of the ethical dilemmas that arise when public authority is exercised through computational means.

10.1.2 Research aim and question

This chapter addresses this gap by examining the democratic legitimacy of algorithmic decision-making in public tax administration. It asks:

> Under what democratic conditions can discretionary authority in tax administration be delegated to artificial intelligence, and what ethical dilemmas does this delegation generate for legitimacy, accountability, and equality before the law?

To answer this question, the chapter advances a novel analytical framework of *algorithmic democracy*. The framework identifies four interdependent conditions under which delegated algorithmic authority can be considered democratically legitimate. Intelligibility requires that administrative decisions remain comprehensible as reason-giving acts within a shared framework of public justification (Fuller, 1969; Habermas, 1996; Raz, 1986). Contestability demands effective and accessible institutional mechanisms through which citizens can challenge and seek redress for algorithmic decisions (Estlund, 2008; Pettit, 2012). Non-domination protects individuals from opaque, arbitrary, or unaccountable forms of computational control (Pettit, 2012; Yeung, 2018). Equality before the law requires that automated administrative processes operate impartially and without discrimination, addressing the documented risks of bias and structural injustice in algorithmic systems (Binns, 2018; Rawls, 1971; Sen, 2009). Together, these conditions constitute the normative grammar of algorithmic democracy and provide evaluative standards for assessing the legitimacy of algorithmic governance within democratic states.

10.1.3 The European context

The European Union provides a particularly revealing context for analysing these issues. Through legal and regulatory instruments such as the General Data Protection Regulation and the proposed Artificial Intelligence Act, the EU has articulated a shared normative vocabulary centred on transparency, accountability, and human oversight (European Commission, 2024). Yet national tax administrations interpret and operationalise these principles in markedly different ways. While some jurisdictions emphasise legal reflexivity, procedural safeguards, and human review, others prioritise efficiency, deterrence, and predictive control (Margetts and Dorobantu, 2019; Zouridis et al., 2019). This variation creates a fertile institutional landscape for examining how democratic principles are embedded, constrained, or diluted within algorithmic systems of fiscal governance.

10.1.4 Analytical approach and contribution

The chapter adopts a theoretical–philosophical and interpretive methodology. Rather than testing hypotheses empirically, it examines the moral and institutional conditions under which the delegation of administrative authority to AI can remain democratically legitimate (Habermas, 1996; Pettit, 2012). European governance frameworks are analysed as normative configurations—expressions of distinct ethical orientations towards discretion, accountability, and authority—rather than as datasets for statistical comparison (Bevir and Rhodes, 2006). Through normative framework development, interpretive analysis, and philosophical comparison, the chapter identifies recurring ethical tensions in algorithmic tax administration, particularly where predictive efficiency conflicts with procedural justice and democratic accountability.

The analysis identifies four moral configurations shaping European approaches to algorithmic taxation—pragmatic enforcement, rights-anchored governance, constitutional caution, and data-intensive profiling—each reflecting a distinct resolution of the tension between efficiency and legitimacy. These configurations expose three structural dilemmas at the core of algorithmic rule: opacity versus intelligibility, automation versus accountability, and efficiency versus equality before the law (Eubanks, 2018; Pasquale, 2015; Yeung, 2018). By theorising these dilemmas, the chapter advances a normative theory of algorithmic democracy and makes three original contributions: it develops a philosophical framework for assessing democratic legitimacy under algorithmic governance; it interprets European AI governance as a landscape of competing ethical architectures; and it identifies conceptual pathways for reconciling computational efficiency with the democratic requirements of public justification, contestation, and equality.

10.2 FRAMEWORK: ETHICS, DISCRETION, AND THE CONDITIONS OF LEGITIMATE AUTHORITY IN AI-GOVERNED TAX ADMINISTRATION

The integration of AI into public administration—most visibly in taxation—requires more than an assessment of technical performance or administrative efficiency. It demands a systematic inquiry into the normative conditions under which administrative authority can remain legitimate in a democratic state. Historically, tax administration has combined bureaucratic rationality with moral justification: its coercive power to collect revenue has depended on the state's capacity to provide reasons that citizens can recognise as lawful, fair, and non-arbitrary. The contemporary shift from embodied discretion to computational decision-making therefore represents not a mere technological refinement, but a fundamental reconfiguration of judgment, accountability, and legitimacy within democratic governance.

10.2.1 Discretion, authority, and the problem of delegation

Legitimate administrative authority presupposes identifiable agents who can exercise judgment, offer justification, and assume responsibility for their actions. Authority is not reducible to the mere capacity to decide; it is constituted through reason-giving within a shared normative order. Delegating decision-making power to AI transforms this structure. Where human officials deliberate, algorithmic systems infer—producing outcomes through probabilistic computation rather than intentional reasoning. Such systems may optimise prediction and consistency, but they cannot themselves satisfy the justificatory conditions that ground legitimacy.

The consequence is a displacement of discretion from deliberative judgment to procedural inference, accompanied by a diffusion of responsibility across technical, organisational, and institutional domains. As Zouridis et al. (2019) observe, discretion migrates from street-level bureaucrats to system-level architectures in which normative reasoning is embedded in code. Decision-making that was once dialogical and accountable becomes statistical and opaque. The central philosophical problem is therefore not whether algorithms *can* decide, but whether authority exercised through such systems can remain democratically legitimate when the capacity for judgment and justification is externalised to non-intentional artefacts.

10.2.2 From bureaucratic rationality to algorithmic governance

Classical administrative theory, most prominently articulated by Weber's account of rational–legal authority, reconciled efficiency (Deniz and Stiefenhofer, 2026) with legitimacy through rule-bound decision-making and the accountability of office. Bureaucracy derived its moral force from the predictability of rules and the visibility of responsibility. Algorithmic governance unsettles this equilibrium. Under conditions of automation, agency is distributed among designers, data infrastructures, administrative organisations, and software systems, rendering the locus of responsibility increasingly opaque.

The ethical implications of this shift are profound. As Danaher (2022) argues, automation generates a "responsibility gap" in which causal efficacy is distributed between human and non-human actors, weakening the moral connection between action and accountability. Algorithms lack moral agency, intentionality, and the capacity to respond to reasons. When administrative outcomes cannot be meaningfully attributed to an accountable subject, authority becomes detached from its normative foundations. What remains is an apparatus that performs the functions of authority without the justificatory practices that give it legitimacy, resulting in rule by code rather than rule by reasons.

This transformation reframes the democratic problem of administration. Where bureaucratic legitimacy rested on the rule of reasons, algorithmic governance threatens to substitute the rule of correlations. Public administration ethics (Stiefenhofer, 2025) must therefore specify the normative constraints under which delegating discretionary authority to artificial intelligence can remain compatible with democratic legitimacy.

10.2.3 The four democratic conditions of legitimate algorithmic authority

To evaluate legitimacy under algorithmic governance, this chapter advances four interdependent normative conditions. Each condition is individually necessary and jointly sufficient for the democratic legitimacy of delegated algorithmic authority. Together, they constitute the normative grammar of *algorithmic democracy.*

10.2.3.1 Condition 1: Intelligibility

Intelligibility denotes the capacity of administrative decisions to appear as reason-giving acts within a shared framework of public justification. Drawing on Fuller's internal morality of law and Habermas's discourse theory of legitimacy, authority is legitimate only when its directives can be understood as providing reasons for compliance (Fuller, 1969; Habermas, 1996; Raz, 1986). Algorithmic opacity undermines this condition. Where decision-making processes are inscrutable or irreconstructable, obligation loses its moral foundation and authority becomes epistemically arbitrary. Legitimacy failure occurs where affected individuals cannot understand *why* a decision applies to them.

10.2.3.2 Condition 2: Contestability

Contestability requires that those subject to administrative decisions possess both the formal right and the practical capacity to challenge them. Rooted in republican and procedural theories of non-domination, authority is legitimate only when it remains open to justification, revision, and correction through institutional channels (Estlund, 2008; Pettit, 2012). Algorithmic systems that foreclose review, obscure responsibility, or render appeal ineffective transform authority into domination—power exercised without recourse. Legitimacy failure occurs where decisions cannot be meaningfully contested or overturned.

10.2.3.3 Condition 3: Autonomy (including privacy)

Autonomy presupposes a protected informational sphere within which individuals can exercise moral agency. Extending Kantian respect for persons into the informational domain, autonomy depends on limits to surveillance, profiling, and data extraction (Floridi, 2013; Nissenbaum, 2004). When algorithmic governance relies on pervasive data aggregation and behavioural inference, it erodes the conditions of self-governing citizenship. Authority exercised through intrusive profiling compromises autonomy even when outcomes appear procedurally correct. Legitimacy failure occurs where governance undermines individuals' capacity for self-determination.

10.2.3.4 Condition 4: Fairness and equality before the law

Fairness requires that administrative systems allocate burdens and benefits impartially and without morally irrelevant discrimination. Drawing on Rawlsian and post-Rawlsian accounts of justice, equality before the law demands that like cases be treated alike and that structural bias be actively prevented (Rawls, 1971; Sen, 2009; Young, 2011). Algorithmic neutrality is often illusory; data-driven systems may reproduce historical inequalities unless fairness is institutionally enforced (Binns, 2018). Legitimacy failure occurs where algorithmic outcomes are systematically biased or disproportionate.

10.2.4 Formal legitimacy condition

The framework may be expressed formally:

Delegation of discretionary authority to AI is democratically legitimate if and only if:

(Intelligibility ∧ Contestability ∧ Autonomy ∧ Fairness)

Each condition is necessary: the violation of any single condition undermines legitimacy. Their conjunction is sufficient: when all four are satisfied, delegated algorithmic authority can be considered democratically justified. This formulation transforms abstract democratic values—reason-giving, participation, autonomy, and equality—into explicit evaluative criteria for algorithmic governance.

10.2.5 Authority as a performative and institutional practice

Administrative authority operates through performative acts that create obligations within institutional frameworks. As Austin (1962) demonstrated, authoritative utterances do not merely describe duties but enact them. Searle (1969, 1995) further conceptualised authority as a status function sustained by collectively recognised rules—"*X counts as Y in context C*." The legitimacy of administrative acts therefore depends on both procedural correctness and shared recognition.

Delegating discretionary authority to algorithmic systems destabilises this performative structure. Algorithms can compute outcomes but cannot perform illocutionary acts; they lack the intentional and normative orientation required to generate institutional commitments. Any legitimacy attaching to automated decisions must therefore be derivative—grounded in prior human authorisation and continuous institutional accountability (Searle, 2010).

Theories of collective intentionality reinforce this limitation. Institutional facts depend on mutual recognition among intentional agents who understand and endorse the commitments involved (Gilbert, 1990; Tuomela, 2002). Algorithms execute causal operations but cannot participate in such recognition. Algorithmic governance thus risks reproducing the *form* of authority while hollowing out its performative substance—decision without deliberation, enforcement without understanding.

10.2.6 Synthesis: From delegation to algorithmic democracy

The argument of this section can be stated conditionally. If legitimate authority requires both (a) satisfaction of the four democratic conditions and (b) attribution to accountable, performative agents, then delegation to

AI can remain legitimate only under derivative authorisation sustained by continuous human oversight. Where these conditions are absent, algorithmic execution ceases to constitute authority in the normative sense and becomes a mode of administrative coercion—action without justification, power without reason-giving.

This framework establishes the moral boundary between democratic automation and technocratic domination. It provides the evaluative foundation for the comparative analysis and grounds the identification of ethical dilemmas examined in the following sections.

10.3 ANALYTICAL APPROACH

This chapter adopts a philosophical and interpretive analytical approach to examine how democratic legitimacy can be sustained when administrative discretion is delegated to AI in public tax administration. Rather than testing hypotheses through quantitative measurement or causal inference, the analysis proceeds through conceptual reasoning, normative reconstruction, and structured interpretive comparison. Its purpose is not to measure the prevalence or performance of algorithmic systems, but to clarify the moral and institutional conditions under which algorithmic governance can remain compatible with democratic authority, and to diagnose the ethical dilemmas that arise when those conditions are weakened or violated.

10.3.1 Structure of the analysis

The analytical design integrates three interdependent stages that connect normative theory with the institutional realities of European tax governance.

10.3.1.1 Stage 1: Normative elaboration

The first stage develops the analytical framework of *algorithmic democracy* established in Section 10.2. It specifies four democratic conditions—intelligibility, contestability, autonomy, and fairness—as necessary and jointly sufficient conditions of legitimate administrative authority. These conditions function as evaluative criteria rather than abstract ideals: they define the standards against which algorithmic decision-making in tax administration is assessed throughout the chapter.

10.3.1.2 Stage 2: Interpretive comparison

The second stage applies the framework through a comparative interpretive analysis of European governance arrangements, including the GDPR, the proposed Artificial Intelligence Act, and national strategies for digital administration and taxation. These materials are analysed not as empirical datasets but as *normative texts* that articulate how democratic values are institutionalised, prioritised, or constrained in the governance of algorithmic systems. The comparison identifies recurring ethical orientations—precautionary, efficiency-driven, and rights-based—that structure how different jurisdictions justify the delegation of authority to AI.

10.3.1.3 Stage 3: Normative synthesis

The final stage synthesises these interpretive findings to articulate the core ethical dilemmas of AI-governed tax administration. These dilemmas—opacity versus intelligibility, automation versus accountability, and efficiency versus equality before the law—are analysed as structural tensions rather than contingent policy failures. The synthesis clarifies what must hold, both conceptually and institutionally, for algorithmic authority to remain democratically legitimate.

Together, these stages sustain a continuous dialogue between normative philosophy and administrative practice. European cases are treated not as data points for empirical generalisation, but as illustrative expressions of a broader moral problem: the tension between technological efficiency and democratic legitimacy in the exercise of public authority.

10.3.2 Comparative and interpretive method

The analysis draws on *interpretive institutionalism* (Bevir and Rhodes, 2006), which understands institutions as historically situated expressions of meaning and value rather than neutral instruments of policy implementation. From this perspective, frameworks for AI governance are read as normative artefacts that encode assumptions about discretion, accountability, citizenship, and authority. Methodologically, the analysis combines close textual reading, conceptual mapping, and analogical comparison to illuminate how democratic ideals are articulated, adapted, or displaced within algorithmic systems of tax administration.

10.3.3 Case selection and analytical scope

Fifteen European jurisdictions—Austria, the Czech Republic, Denmark, Finland, France, Germany, Italy, Latvia, the Netherlands, Norway, Poland, Spain, Sweden, Slovenia, and the United Kingdom—serve as reference cases. These jurisdictions were selected not for statistical representativeness but for *conceptual diversity*. Each reflects a distinct configuration of legal tradition, bureaucratic ethos, and digital modernisation, allowing the analysis to capture variation in how democratic values are interpreted and operationalised in algorithmic governance.

The purpose of case selection is therefore analytical rather than empirical: to reveal plural moral architectures of algorithmic authority rather than to establish causal generalisations.

10.3.4 Sources and interpretive corpus

The interpretive corpus combines primary legal and policy documents with secondary analytical materials relevant to AI governance in European tax administration.

Primary sources include European and national instruments such as the GDPR, the proposed Artificial Intelligence Act, national AI strategies, tax administration legislation, data-protection and oversight reports, and ethical or algorithmic accountability guidelines issued by public authorities. Secondary sources include analyses by European institutions (e.g. the European Commission and the OECD), academic research in public administration and digital ethics, and civil-society assessments produced by transparency and data-rights organisations.

All materials are examined hermeneutically as discursive artefacts through which public authorities articulate legitimacy claims, define safeguards, and justify the delegation of discretionary power to algorithmic systems.

10.3.5 Normative reasoning and evaluative logic

The analysis proceeds through a structured sequence of normative reasoning rather than procedural data analysis.

1. **Conceptual Clarification**
   Each of the four conditions of algorithmic democracy is refined through engagement with established traditions in political philosophy and public administration ethics. Intelligibility is grounded in theories of communicative rationality; contestability in republican theories of non-domination; autonomy in Kantian ethics and information privacy theory; and fairness in Rawlsian and post-Rawlsian accounts of justice. This step establishes the normative vocabulary through which legitimacy is evaluated.
2. **Interpretive Application**
   The clarified concepts are applied to governance texts to identify the moral assumptions embedded in regulatory language. The analysis examines, for example, whether transparency is framed as procedural disclosure or substantive reason-giving, and whether human oversight operates as genuine accountability or merely symbolic reassurance.
3. **Dialectical Evaluation**
   The final step evaluates where algorithmic governance satisfies or violates the four democratic conditions and how institutions seek to justify these outcomes. The objective is philosophical diagnosis rather than empirical measurement: to map where democratic reasoning is sustained and where it is displaced by instrumental rationality.

Through this iterative process, philosophical reflection and institutional interpretation remain mutually informative. The framework guides the analysis of governance practices, while observed variations across European contexts refine and deepen the theoretical understanding of legitimacy in the algorithmic age.

10.3.6 Methodological reflexivity and limitations

The study adopts a critical–hermeneutic methodological stance that acknowledges both its normative commitments and epistemic limits.

Methodological reflexivity is maintained by making explicit that concepts such as legitimacy, accountability, and equality are philosophically reconstructed rather than empirically measured. The argument proceeds through logical entailment—examining necessary and sufficient conditions of legitimacy—rather than causal inference.

Epistemic reflexivity recognises that the researcher's position mirrors that of democratic citizens confronting opaque algorithmic systems: reasoning under conditions of partial visibility. These limits are treated not as methodological deficiencies but as constitutive features of algorithmic governance itself.

The analysis is bounded by three limitations. First, it abstracts from empirical measurement in favour of normative clarification. Second, it interprets documentary sources rather than observing administrative practice directly. Third, it advances a democratic and deontological evaluative framework that contrasts with utilitarian or technocratic approaches. These boundaries clarify the scope of the contribution: not empirical generalisation, but normative elucidation of the ethical grammar of algorithmic governance.

10.4 INTERPRETIVE ANALYSIS OF EUROPEAN APPROACHES TO ALGORITHMIC TAX ADMINISTRATION

The European landscape of AI-driven tax administration provides a revealing context for examining how democratic values are translated into algorithmic governance. Across Europe, fiscal authorities deploy similar technological instruments—predictive analytics, automated risk scoring, and algorithmic audit selection—yet embed these tools within markedly different legal, institutional, and moral frameworks. These differences demonstrate that algorithmic governance is not normatively uniform: identical technologies may support divergent conceptions of legitimacy depending on how discretionary authority is justified, constrained, and rendered accountable.

Rather than constructing an empirical taxonomy or ranking national systems by performance, this section adopts an interpretive and evaluative approach. National frameworks are analysed as normative configurations—distinct ways of reconciling administrative efficiency with democratic legitimacy. Each configuration is assessed systematically using the four democratic conditions developed in Section 10.2: intelligibility, contestability, autonomy, and fairness. These conditions function as evaluative criteria, enabling structured comparison of how algorithmic authority is institutionalised across European tax administrations (Stiefenhofer et al., 2026).

Through this comparative analysis, four principal configurations of algorithmic governance in taxation can be identified:

1. **Pragmatic Enforcement:** efficiency as moral justification
2. **Rights-Anchored Governance:** ethics embedded in institutional design
3. **Constitutional Caution:** legality and due process prior to automation
4. **Data-Intensive Profiling:** authority exercised through correlation

These configurations are ideal types, not empirical clusters. They are analytical constructs that make visible the moral diversity of algorithmic governance in Europe and clarify how democratic legitimacy is variously sustained, weakened, or undermined.

10.4.1 Pragmatic enforcement: Efficiency as moral justification

The pragmatic enforcement configuration characterises systems in which efficiency, accuracy, and deterrence function as the primary justificatory grounds for algorithmic governance. In these systems, legitimacy is framed in outcome-oriented terms: an administrative system is considered legitimate insofar as it improves compliance, reduces costs, or enhances enforcement capacity.

Jurisdictions such as the Czech Republic, France, Italy, Latvia, Norway, and Poland exemplify this orientation. Their tax administrations employ predictive analytics and risk-scoring models to prioritise audits and detect irregularities, often presenting automation as a neutral enhancement of administrative rationality. Although official documents frequently invoke transparency, fairness, and accountability, these principles typically operate as secondary constraints on a managerial logic that equates legitimacy with performance.

Evaluated against the four democratic conditions, pragmatic enforcement exhibits systematic deficits:

- **Intelligibility:** Algorithmic decisions are presented as technical outputs rather than reasoned administrative acts, limiting citizens' ability to understand why particular decisions apply to them.
- **Contestability:** Formal appeal mechanisms exist, but they rarely expose the inferential logic of algorithmic systems, undermining effective challenge and redress.
- **Autonomy:** Individuals are primarily treated as data subjects rather than as deliberative agents capable of engaging with justificatory processes.
- **Fairness:** While formally affirmed, fairness is often subordinated to predictive optimisation and risk management.

The cumulative effect is a shift from reason-giving to outcome justification. Authority is validated by results rather than by communicative accountability. From the perspective of algorithmic democracy, pragmatic enforcement embodies a managerial conception of legitimacy that is administratively effective yet normatively thin.

10.4.2 Rights-anchored governance: Embedding ethics in institutional design

The rights-anchored governance configuration encompasses jurisdictions that embed algorithmic systems within robust frameworks of human rights, data protection, and procedural justice. Austria, Denmark, Germany, Sweden, Slovenia, and the United Kingdom exemplify this orientation.

In these systems, the deployment of AI in tax administration is accompanied by ethical guidelines, legal safeguards, and institutional oversight mechanisms. Instruments such as the Danish Tax Control Act (2017) and Austria's AI Mission 2030 (2021) establish transparency, equality, and accountability as prerequisites for automation. Germany and the United Kingdom further institutionalise ethical reflection through algorithmic audits, ethics councils, and coordination with data-protection authorities.

Assessed against the four democratic conditions, rights-anchored governance performs comparatively well:

- **Intelligibility:** Explainability requirements and human-in-the-loop decision structures preserve reason-giving practices.
- **Contestability:** Audit trails, appeal rights, and independent oversight bodies support effective challenge.
- **Autonomy:** Data-protection regimes constrain intrusive profiling and preserve informational self-determination.
- **Fairness:** Equality guarantees and anti-discrimination provisions actively address algorithmic bias.

This configuration is not without vulnerability. The institutionalisation of ethics risks reducing moral accountability to procedural compliance, in which ethical oversight becomes routinised and symbolic rather than substantively critical. From the perspective of algorithmic democracy, rights-anchored governance therefore constitutes a qualified success. It fulfils many of the conditions of democratic legitimacy but remains susceptible to bureaucratic formalism.

10.4.3 Constitutional caution: Legality before automation

The constitutional caution configuration is most clearly exemplified by Finland, where constitutional jurisprudence and administrative legal culture impose stringent constraints on automated decision-making. Finnish authorities have adopted a deliberately cautious approach in which algorithmic tools may be employed only when their reasoning can be explained, their errors corrected, and their compatibility with constitutional guarantees established.

Oversight by the Parliamentary Ombudsman has explicitly questioned whether opaque automation can coexist with due process and equality before the law. Automation is therefore treated as a conditional instrument rather than a default solution.

Evaluated against the four democratic conditions, constitutional caution satisfies all criteria at a high level. Intelligibility and contestability are prioritised through legal scrutiny; autonomy is protected through proportionality and data-minimisation requirements; and fairness is enforced through constitutional equality guarantees. Finland thus exemplifies a form of democratic reflexivity in which technological innovation remains subordinate to the rule of law.

10.4.4 Data-Intensive profiling: Authority by correlation

The data-intensive profiling configuration is most evident in the Netherlands and Spain, where tax administrations rely extensively on cross-database profiling and algorithmic risk assessment. These systems aggregate large volumes of data to identify irregularities, but they have produced significant legitimacy failures.

In the Netherlands, the child-benefits scandal revealed systemic discrimination generated by biased risk models, leading to widespread institutional and political reckoning. In Spain, multiple profiling systems—Zújar, Teseo, Dédalo, Prometeo, and Pandata—have raised persistent concerns about transparency, oversight, and procedural safeguards.

Evaluated normatively, this configuration exhibits severe legitimacy deficits:

- **Intelligibility:** Decision-making logic is opaque and difficult to reconstruct.
- **Contestability:** Affected individuals face substantial barriers to effective challenge.
- **Autonomy:** Extensive data aggregation erodes informational self-determination.
- **Fairness:** Profiling reproduces structural inequalities and discriminatory outcomes.

Here, authority shifts from government under law to governance by correlation, testing the limits of democratic legitimacy and illustrating how algorithmic power can undermine foundational democratic norms.

10.4.5 Comparative synthesis: Divergent moral architectures

Across these four configurations, European states share a rhetorical commitment to transparency, accountability, and equality, yet diverge sharply in how these values are institutionalised. Table 10.1 summarises the comparative evaluation of democratic legitimacy in algorithmic tax governance.

Rather than converging towards a single model, European algorithmic governance exhibits democratic divergence. Efficiency may function as a surrogate for legitimacy (pragmatic enforcement), ethics may be proceduralised (rights-anchored governance), innovation may be constitutionally restrained (constitutional caution), or authority may be exercised through opaque correlation (data-intensive profiling).

From a normative standpoint, algorithmic legitimacy emerges not as a fixed achievement but as a spectrum of democratic reasoning. The closer an administrative system comes to satisfying the four democratic conditions—intelligibility, contestability, autonomy, and fairness—the more its reliance on AI can be considered morally justified. Where these conditions are neglected, automation substitutes for authority rather than serving it.

Table 10.1 summarises the comparative evaluation of European approaches to algorithmic tax administration using the four democratic conditions developed in Section 10.2. The table is not intended as an empirical ranking but as a normative assessment that visualises how different governance configurations satisfy—or fail to satisfy—the conditions of intelligibility, contestability,

Table 10.1 Comparative evaluation of democratic legitimacy in algorithmic tax governance

Configuration	*Intelligibility*	*Contestability*	*Autonomy*	*Fairness*	*Approximate democratic legitimacy*	*Normative character*
Pragmatic Enforcement	Low	Low	Low	Moderate	Weak	Performance-based, outcome-driven legitimacy
Rights-Anchored Governance	High	Moderate–High	Moderate	High	Relatively Strong	Proceduralised ethics with substantive safeguards
Constitutional Caution	High	High	High	High	Strong	Legal reflexivity and due process before automation
Data-Intensive Profiling	Very Low	Low	Very Low	Low	Fragile/ Illegitimate	Technocratic opacity and systemic bias

autonomy, and fairness. It represents the formal analytical output of the framework of algorithmic democracy.

The table makes visible that algorithmic legitimacy is not binary but graduated. Systems that satisfy all four conditions approximate democratic authority, while those that violate multiple conditions fall below the threshold of legitimacy. This confirms the central claim of the chapter: algorithmic governance becomes democratically legitimate only when efficiency is institutionally subordinated to public justification, accountability, and equality before the law.

This comparative analysis maps the moral architectures of European algorithmic governance and prepares the ground for the ethical evaluation that follows. Section 10.5 examines the deeper normative tensions—opacity versus intelligibility, automation versus accountability, and efficiency versus equality—that define the moral politics of algorithmic democracy in contemporary public administration.

10.5 ETHICAL DILEMMAS AND NORMATIVE TENSIONS IN ALGORITHMIC TAX GOVERNANCE

The interpretive analysis in Section 10.4 demonstrated that European tax administrations do not converge on a single moral architecture of algorithmic governance. Instead, they differentiate into four normative configurations—pragmatic enforcement, rights-anchored governance, constitutional caution, and data-intensive profiling—each representing a distinct strategy for reconciling administrative efficiency with democratic legitimacy. These configurations are not merely institutional variants; they expose structural ethical tensions that arise when discretionary authority is delegated to AI.

As democratic principles are translated into algorithmic infrastructures, their normative substance is transformed. Deliberative justification is displaced by procedural inference, and accountability is redistributed across layers of code, organisational design, and data systems. From this transformation emerge three constitutive dilemmas that define the moral landscape of algorithmic tax administration:

1. **Opacity versus intelligibility:** the tension between computational complexity and the democratic requirement of reason-giving;
2. **Automation versus accountability:** the conflict between delegated efficiency and moral responsibility;
3. **Efficiency versus fairness:** the struggle to reconcile predictive optimisation with equality before the law.

These dilemmas are not contingent policy failures but structural features of algorithmic governance, marking fault lines in the normative foundations of democratic authority.

10.5.1 Opacity and the failure of intelligibility

Transparency has become a central normative demand of digital governance, yet in practice it often collapses into disclosure without comprehension. Across Europe, governments emphasise transparency in regulatory frameworks and policy documents, while delivering decision-making systems whose internal logic remains inaccessible to those subject to them. Predictive systems deployed in jurisdictions such as Austria, France, and Germany—frequently based on proprietary software and complex statistical inference—illustrate this paradox: procedural openness does not guarantee intelligible reasoning.

As Floridi and Cowls (2019) argue, intelligibility requires more than access to information. It requires that affected individuals can reconstruct the reasons guiding administrative decisions. In algorithmic governance, however, inference substitutes for reasoning. Outputs are correlations rather than justifications. When citizens cannot understand why they have been selected for audit or classified as high risk, the deliberative relationship between ruler and ruled collapses.

The normative logic can be stated conditionally:

If administrative authority is legitimate only when its reasoning is publicly intelligible, and if algorithmic decision-making remains opaque to those affected, then algorithmic authority fails the condition of legitimacy.

Opacity, therefore, is not a technical limitation but a moral failure of public reason. It transforms citizens into governable data subjects, ruled through patterns they cannot interrogate or contest. In place of communicative justification, algorithmic governance offers statistical explanation—an epistemic shift that erodes the normative basis of democratic legitimacy.

10.5.2 Automation and the diffusion of accountability

A second dilemma arises from the displacement of moral responsibility in automated governance. In classical public administration, accountability was anchored in identifiable officials capable of reasoning, explanation, and answerability. In algorithmic systems, causal efficacy is dispersed among designers, data engineers, institutional actors, and software artefacts, producing what Danaher (2022) describes as a *responsibility gap*.

In pragmatic-enforcement regimes such as those operating in Poland or Germany, audit priorities are set by machine-learning pipelines that no single actor fully understands or controls. In the Netherlands, this diffusion culminated in the child-benefits scandal, where opaque algorithmic systems produced wrongful accusations without clear avenues for redress. When no agent can meaningfully answer for an outcome, authority loses its moral anchor in accountability.

This dilemma can be expressed formally:

Accountability $\Leftrightarrow$ (Identifiable agent $\wedge$ Capacity to justify $\wedge$ Capacity to rectify).

Where any of these conditions fails—when agents are unidentifiable, unable to explain decisions, or incapable of correcting errors—accountability collapses into procedural responsibility devoid of moral substance. Automation thus converts the *ethics of office* into the *logistics of management*. Decisions are executed rather than justified, and responsibility is reduced to compliance with process rather than answerability to citizens.

10.5.3 Efficiency and the erosion of fairness

The third dilemma concerns the tension between administrative efficiency and substantive fairness. Artificial intelligence promises optimisation—faster audits, targeted enforcement, and predictive allocation of resources—but, as Eubanks (2018) demonstrates, such optimisation often automates inequality by embedding historical bias and structural disadvantage into data and models.

Rights-anchored and constitutionally cautious systems—such as those in Denmark, Sweden, and Finland—seek to mitigate this risk through human-in-the-loop procedures and constitutional oversight. By contrast, data-intensive and enforcement-driven regimes, including Spain and Poland, frequently privilege throughput and predictive accuracy at the expense of equality before the law. The resulting governance structure approximates what Rawls (1971) would describe as *procedural rationality without substantive justice*: decisions are consistent yet normatively asymmetrical.

The moral logic is straightforward:

If fairness is a necessary condition of justice, and if algorithmic efficiency systematically disadvantages the least advantaged, then the resulting governance arrangement is unjust—regardless of its administrative gains.

When pursued without ethical constraint, efficiency undermines the distributive neutrality that sustains democratic legitimacy. It replaces the impartiality of rule with the partiality of optimisation, redefining justice as throughput rather than equity.

10.5.4 Synthesis: Legitimacy under algorithmic authority

Taken together, these dilemmas confirm the theoretical argument developed in Section 10.2. Democratic legitimacy in algorithmic governance is sustained only when the conditions of intelligibility, contestability, autonomy, and fairness are jointly fulfilled. When any of these conditions is weakened, the moral coherence of administrative authority deteriorates. Efficiency may increase, but legitimacy becomes derivative—maintained through legal form rather than democratic justification.

This diagnosis aligns with Habermas's (1996) account of legitimacy as redeemability through public reason. Algorithmic systems that act without intelligible reasoning or effective contestation instantiate what Searle (2010) describes as *simulated performatives*: actions that reproduce the form of authority while lacking its normative force. They mimic rule while hollowing out its justificatory substance.

The European experience thus reveals a central paradox of algorithmic democracy: the state gains epistemic power while losing justificatory depth. As administrative decisions become more computationally precise, they risk becoming politically unintelligible. Procedural efficiency can coexist with, and even accelerate, the erosion of the moral grammar that makes public authority legitimate.

10.6 CONCLUSION: RECLAIMING LEGITIMACY IN THE ALGORITHMIC STATE

This chapter has examined the ethical and philosophical conditions under which artificial intelligence may exercise delegated authority within democratic public administration, focusing on European tax governance. Through interpretive comparison and normative analysis, it has been shown that algorithmic decision-making in Europe does not follow a single trajectory but unfolds across four distinct moral configurations—pragmatic enforcement, rights-anchored governance, constitutional caution, and data-intensive profiling—each reflecting a different resolution of the tension between efficiency and democratic legitimacy.

Across these configurations, a shared rhetorical commitment to human-centred AI masks deep divergence in institutional practice. Some administrations embed automation within frameworks of oversight, justification, and procedural justice; others prioritise predictive control at the expense of intelligibility, accountability, and equality. These contrasts demonstrate that legitimacy cannot be inferred from legal compliance or ethical codification alone. It depends on whether administrative systems continue to satisfy the normative conditions identified in this analysis:

Legitimate algorithmic authority $\Leftrightarrow$ (Intelligibility $\wedge$ Contestability $\wedge$ Autonomy $\wedge$ Fairness).

When these conditions are fulfilled, automation can extend administrative capacity without undermining democratic justification. When they are violated, authority becomes merely instrumental—efficient but normatively hollow.

Philosophically, the analysis affirms that democratic legitimacy arises not from technical performance but from communicative justification. Algorithms that decide without intelligible reasoning or contestable procedures reproduce the *form* of authority without its moral content. They instantiate a post-deliberative bureaucracy—precise in function, yet impoverished in meaning.

The broader implication is that the ethics of public administration must be re-founded for the algorithmic age. Regulatory instruments such as the

GDPR and the forthcoming EU AI Act are necessary but insufficient. What is required is a renewed normative vocabulary that re-centres:

- **Intelligibility** as public reason,
- **Contestability** as democratic participation,
- **Autonomy** as informational self-determination, and
- **Fairness** as equality before the law.

These are not auxiliary safeguards but constitutive conditions of legitimate authority.

The task ahead for democratic institutions is therefore twofold. Firstly, *institutional design* must embed human oversight, ethical reasoning, and effective contestation within the architectures of automated governance. Secondly, *normative renewal* must reaffirm that algorithmic systems derive their authority only through continuous accountability to the public they govern.

The central challenge for democracy in the age of artificial intelligence is not to resist automation, but to civilise it—to ensure that every algorithmic act of governance remains intelligible, contestable, and just. Authority will endure as legitimate only so long as it can be understood, questioned, and held to account within the shared space of democratic reason.

REFERENCES

Ananny, M. and Crawford, K. (2018) 'Seeing without knowing: Limitations of the transparency ideal and its application to algorithmic accountability', *New Media & Society*, 20(3), pp. 973–989.

Austin, J.L. (1962) *How to Do Things With Words*. Oxford: Clarendon Press.

Austria AI Mission 2030. (2021) *Artificial Intelligence Strategy of the Austrian Federal Government*. Available at: https://digital-skills-jobs.europa.eu/sites/default/files/2023-10/Artificial%20Intelligence%20Mission%20Austria%202030_AIM_AT_2030.pdf (Accessed: 20 December 2025).

Bevir, M. and Rhodes, R.A.W. (2006) 'Interpretive approaches to British government and politics', *British Politics*, 1(1), pp. 84–112. https://doi.org/10.1057/palgrave.bp.4200001

Binns, R. (2018) 'Fairness in machine learning: Lessons from political philosophy', *Proceedings of the 2018 Conference on Fairness, Accountability, and Transparency (FAT)*, pp. 149–159. Available at: https://papers.ssrn.com/sol3/papers.cfm?abstract_id=3086546 (Accessed: 20 August 2025).

Bovens, M. and Zouridis, S. (2002) 'From street-level to system-level bureaucracies: How information and communication technology is transforming administrative discretion and constitutional control', *Public Administration Review*, 62(2), pp. 174–184. https://doi.org/10.1111/0033-3352.00168

Braithwaite, V. (2009) *Defiance in Taxation and Governance: Resisting and Dismissing Authority in a Democracy*. Cheltenham: Edward Elgar Publishing.

Bullock, J.B. (2019) 'Artificial intelligence, discretion, and bureaucracy', *The American Review of Public Administration*, 49(7), pp. 751–761. https://doi.org/10.1177/0275074019856123

Busch, P.A. and Henriksen, H.Z. (2018) 'Digital discretion: A systematic literature review of ICT and street-level discretion', *Information Polity*, 23(1), pp. 3–28. https://doi.org/10.3233/IP-170050
Danaher, J. (2022) 'Tragic choices and the virtue of techno-responsibility gaps', *Philosophy & Technology*, 35(2), p. 26. https://doi.org/10.1007/s13347-022-00519-1
Danish Tax Control Act. (2017) *Danish Tax Control Act (Skattekontrolloven)*, Lov nr. 1535 af 19. December 2017. Available at: https://www.retsinformation.dk/eli/lta/2017/1535 (Accessed: 20 December 2025).
Deniz, C. and Stiefenhofer, P. (2026) 'The algorithmic conscience: reconciling AI efficiency with human dignity', Journal of Chinese Economic and Business Studies, 1–33. https://doi.org/10.1080/14765284.2026.2640533
Estlund, D. (2008) *Democratic Authority: A Philosophical Framework*. Princeton, NJ: Princeton University Press.
Eubanks, V. (2018) *Automating Inequality: How High-Tech Tools Profile, Police, and Punish the Poor*. New York, NY: St. Martin's Press.
European Commission. (2024) *The EU AI Act*. Available at: https://eur-lex.europa.eu/legal-content/EN/TXT/?uri=CELEX:32024R1689 (Accessed: 20 December 2025).
Floridi, L. (2013) *The Ethics of Information*. Oxford: Oxford University Press.
Floridi, L. and Cowls, J. (2019) 'A unified framework of five principles for AI in society', *Harvard Data Science Review*, 1(1), pp. 2–15. https://doi.org/10.1162/99608f92.8cd550d1
Fuller, L.L. (1969) *The Morality of Law*. New Haven, CT: Yale University Press.
Gilbert, M. (1990) 'Walking together: A paradigmatic social phenomenon', *Midwest Studies in Philosophy*, 15(1), pp. 1–14.
Habermas, J. (1996) *Between Facts and Norms: Contributions to a Discourse Theory of Law and Democracy*. Cambridge, MA: MIT Press.
Kirchler, E. (2007) *The Economic Psychology of Tax Behaviour*. Cambridge: Cambridge University Press.
Margetts, H. and Dorobantu, C. (2019) 'Rethink government with AI', *Nature*, 568(7751), pp. 163–165. https://doi.org/10.1038/d41586-019-01099-5
Nissenbaum, H. (2004) 'Privacy as contextual integrity', *Washington Law Review*, 79(1), pp. 119–158. Available at: https://digitalcommons.law.uw.edu/wlr/vol79/iss1/10 (Accessed: 21 December 2025).
Pasquale, F. (2015) *The Black Box Society: The Secret Algorithms That Control Money and Information*. Cambridge, MA: Harvard University Press.
Pettit, P. (2012) *On the People's Terms: A Republican Theory and Model of Democracy*. Cambridge: Cambridge University Press.
Rawls, J. (1971) *A Theory of Justice*. Cambridge, MA: Harvard University Press.
Raz, J. (1986) *The Morality of Freedom*. Oxford: Clarendon Press.
Searle, J.R. (1969) *Speech Acts: An Essay in the Philosophy of Language*. Cambridge: Cambridge University Press.
Searle, J.R. (1995) *The Construction of Social Reality*. New York, NY: Free Press.
Searle, J.R. (2010) *Making the Social World: The Structure of Human Civilization*. Oxford: Oxford University Press.
Sen, A. (2009) *The Idea of Justice*. Cambridge, MA: Harvard University Press.
Stiefenhofer, P. (2025) 'The role of ethical consumption in promoting democratic sustainability: Revisiting neoclassical economics through Kantian ethics', *The Journal of Philosophical Economics*, XVIII, pp. 74–123. https://doi.org/10.46298/jpe.15427
Stiefenhofer, P. and Deniz, C. (2025) 'The Role of AI in the Rise of the Ethical Consumer', in Düzenli, F. and Ertürk, E. (eds.) *International Social Policies Congress: Proceedings I*, 17–18 May 2025, Sarajevo. Istanbul: Filiz Kitabevi. (ISBN: 978-625-5697-83-7).

Stiefenhofer, P., Gergerlioğlu, U. and Deniz, C. (2026) 'Delegating authority to algorithms: Legitimacy and public values in European tax administrations', *Philosophy and Realistic Reflection*, 3(1). DOI: https://doi.org/10.55121/prr.v3i1.757

Tuomela, R. (2002) *The Philosophy of Social Practices: A Collective Acceptance View*. Cambridge: Cambridge University Press.

Weber, M. (1978) *Economy and Society: An Outline of Interpretive Sociology* (Vol. 2). Berkeley, CA: University of California Press.

Wirtz, B.W., Weyerer, J.C. and Geyer, C. (2019) 'Artificial intelligence and the public sector—Applications and challenges', *International Journal of Public Administration*, 42(7), pp. 596–615. https://doi.org/10.1080/01900692.2018.1498103

Yeung, K. (2018) 'Algorithmic regulation: A critical interrogation', *Regulation & Governance*, 12(4), pp. 505–523. https://doi.org/10.1111/rego.12158

Young, I.M. (2011) *Responsibility for Justice*. Oxford: Oxford University Press.

Zouridis, S., van Eck, M. and Bovens, M. (2019) 'Automated Discretion', in Hupe, P. and Evans, T. (eds.) *Palgrave Handbook on Discretion: The Quest for Controlled Freedom*. Basingstoke: Palgrave Macmillan. DOI: https://doi.org/10.2139/ssrn.3453068

Chapter 11

Revolutionizing financial technologies through artificial intelligence modeling

Nidhi Arora, Poonam Arora, and Swati Mehta

11.1 CHAPTER OVERVIEW

Artificial Intelligence (AI) in financial technology (fintech) has emerged as a significant transformative force. The fintech sector is currently witnessing a significant shift with integration of AI as a fundamentally transforming enabler to deliver financial services. This chapter examines the paradigm shift introduced by AI in the fintech sector, from the viewpoint of both the theoretical and practical applications, as well as the challenges it poses in effectively harnessing its benefits.

Continuous progress in AI technologies has made it an integral part of the essential operations of fintech, covering areas such as customer service, risk assessment, fraud prevention, and investment strategies. This chapter presents a comprehensive analysis of these state-of-the-art applications, underscoring their relevance and potential. Significant trends discussed in this study include other advanced technologies like cloud computing, blockchain and big data, with the growing focus on data security and privacy, customer engagement, and personalized service in the view of global expansion of AI-driven financial solutions. Furthermore, the chapter investigates the paradigm shift brought by AI in fintech, as well as the possible ways to deal with the current issues. This thorough examination of AI's impact on fintech aims to provide a holistic perspective on the current landscape while offering insights into the future trajectories of this interrelated and mutually beneficial relationship. A sample use case is presented to demonstrate practical AI-based application in financial lending. Such use cases addressed by AI algorithms can serve as crucial resources for industry stakeholders, policymakers, and researchers interested in leveraging the transformative potential of AI in the fintech field.

11.2 INTRODUCTION: BACKGROUND AND DRIVING FORCES

Numerous groundbreaking and novel innovations in technology are changing the world. Ease of network connections and accessibility of the internet is

DOI: 10.1201/9781003656463-11

the reason that different groups of individuals are able to use internet-based services through their smartphones. The admittance of technology-enabled high-speed advancements have propeled these services. Industry 4.0 is synonymous to the paradigm shift and transformations in society thereby impacting the economy. This technology enabled changes are reshaping the world facilitating and enhancing the interactions between the intrinsic and extrinsic world within the digital process (Kumari & Devi, 2022). Additionally, the shift from traditional systems to modern systems is attributed to the changed economic scenario leading to new consumption patterns. This shift is leading to a convergence of technological, economic, and sociocultural factors that have led to the change in traditional methods of financial services and money exchange (Ertz & Boily, 2019; Limna et al., 2022). To add further, the most innovative technology i.e. fintech, which is commonly referred to as fintech, includes the introduction of technology in the system of designing, delivering, and disbursing finance-related products and services. This has impacted the way businesses used to work across various sectors. The finance industry; one of the most vibrant industries, is known to have one of the crucial pillars of the Indian economy, reasoned for the increasing businesses and expanding innovations, all due to application of smart technology such as AI. AI is ushering in a wave of opportunities in the financial sector by getting embedded into their operations, whether through in-house initiatives, outsourcing, or ecosystem collaborations.

New digital technologies are questioning the fundamentals of still sticking to traditional policies and systems paving ways to modern systems making old systems obsolete (Leong et al., 2017). In comparison to old traditional systems, the designing, launch, awareness, promotion, disbursement, delivery and post-feedback systems have been transformed by fintech leading to the changed perception of financial services (Mention, 2021). The acceptance of fintech innovation is a summation of digitization, openness of stakeholders, social media awareness, credit platforms, smart technology and AI, and big data analytics. While existing businesses are addressing the need to integrate technology in businesses, fintech startups are on the way to pose threat to financial institutions still working on traditional systems as fintech startups offer personalized services, customized products, data-driven solutions, cloud-based storage and a tech-savvy culture, aligning systems with upcoming technology securing a competitive edge for themselves over others in market. This has increased the seriousness to regard fintech as a strategic aspect by market leader financial institutions; changing, formulating and building collaborations with fintech startups (Lee & Shin, 2018).

The fintech sector is showing promising leverage and growth in the years to come with forecasted benefits to all the stakeholders, owners and businesses (Karim et al., 2022; Nathan et al., 2022). Making fintech an interesting area of study (Limna & Kraiwanit, 2022). Customers usually face several challenges and issues relating to financial and commercial dealings and transactions. fintechs promise to have solutions for all the challenges making it safe and secure for customers. Along with customer support and acceptance, fintechs are also getting a push because of changes in market conditions, government policies, and amendments in regulatory frames. (Mirchandani et al., 2020). This chapter aims to delve into the latest innovations in fintech, driven by sophisticated AI and related techniques that model complex interactions, relationships, and their dynamics.

11.3 EVOLUTION AND DEVELOPMENT OF FINTECH

Fintech, which stands for fintech, is increasingly turning into a global trend, inspired by the latest innovations and also gaining the attention of regulators. In general, fintech serves as an umbrella term for innovative, technology-driven financial services and the corresponding business models. Simply put, fintech encompasses any innovation aimed at enhancing the process, delivery, and utilization of financial services.

Ernst and Young characterized fintech as an innovation in financial services, with technology serving as the primary enabler where financial solutions are enabled by technology (Arner et al., 2015; Mirchandani et al., 2020). Lee and Kim (2015) noted that fintech represents the technical processes that arise from the development and implementation of new financial software, which has the potential to impact the entire traditional financial system. For facilitating better use of financial services and automating processes, the novel technology created is termed as fintech (Al-Okaily et al., 2021). fintech encompasses secure communication with others in a market, facilitating the rapid dissemination of information and news, whether public or private, through a communication network (Mirchandani et al., 2020). Fintech is a distinct category of fintech, defined as the technology utilized to offer financial markets a financial product or service, distinguished by its advanced technology compared to existing solutions in that market.

Companies that predominantly utilize fintech are categorized as fintech firms. Based on these definitions, the next part of the chapter outlines a framework for the developments in the fintech industry (Knewtson & Rosenbaum, 2020). One of the most expeditious and crucial innovations in financial sector which is equivalently perceived and accepted by industry and customers is financial technology i.e. fintech. The precipitation of this technology is screaming because of an inflated economy, higher dependence on technology, and supportive government regulations (Lee & Shin, 2018). Research in 2022 by Giglio and Limna & Kraiwanit has concluded that the ascent of fintech in market is due to various business models such as insurance processes, capital market, crowdfunding, fee and payments, management of wealth, and lending business payments (Giglio, 2022; Limna & Kraiwanit, 2022).

In recent years, the rise of digital technologies in the financial sector has led to the emergence of fintech, resulting in a swift and dynamic transformation that both business operators and regulatory bodies in the banking sector are finding challenging to keep up with. This is particularly due to issues impacting financial intermediaries and customers, alongside potential risks to the stability of the financial system (Elia et al., 2023). The growing fintech segment is an indispensable category of the financial market as the cardinal technology in this digital era has impacted the financial processes significantly, making it one of the crucial segments of the market. Businesses, be it the owner or the stakeholders such as clients, customers, marketers, or employees, can reap benefits by enhancing their productivity, achieving higher performance, and gaining superior success by aligning their moves and strategies with the demand and expectation of their clients with the application of fintech (Limna & Kraiwanit, 2022).

From 1860 to 1990, the financial sector has seen continuous changes from its initiation to the crisis in 2008. Initially, fintech was linked to three main services: lending, capital raising, and payment solutions. The recent developments point to the emergence of a second wave that introduces fintech to areas like international money transfers, wealth management, and insurance. The overall impact of fintech on small businesses and the economy appears to be substantial (Mirchandani et al., 2020).

The introduction of fintech in the industry has created a lot of unsettling and obstreperous changes. These innovations are the result of continuous application of fintech in the day-to-day operations (Schueffel, 2016) of even those firms that provide financial services by applying technology in providing financial services. As technology has enabled integrating and unifying services to businesses and clients by converging the finance-related transactions, fintech companies have proved to play an important role in streamlining services. These services comprise of solutions related to mobile banking, client-based payment systems and usage of investment platforms (Lee & Shin, 2018; Limna & Kraiwanit, 2022; Soloviev, 2018). AI's exceptional promise of cost reduction coupled with enhanced differentiation makes it broadly appealing. However, with the exception of some applications like fraud detection, the realization of these benefits is often dependent on the organization's scale.

11.4 RECENT TRENDS IN FINTECH

Fintech relies on technical components that constitute the foundational infrastructure supported by modern technologies. The integration of AI, Blockchain, and 5G technology characterizes fintech. AI and cloud computing, in conjunction with blockchain technology, facilitate automation by delivering improved accuracy, security, and transparency across services. The simultaneous rise of all these technologies has generated a transformative momentum for fintech, showcasing its developed potential applications.

The future of global fintech initiative examines both global and regional market trends as well as the emerging needs of Industry 5.0. Following decades of rapid expansion, fintech companies have transitioned into a new phase of value generation, emphasizing sustainable and profitable growth. Fintech revolutionizes financial delivery mechanisms, and a new wave of independence and ease of use is being brought about in traditional financial market constructions (Datta, 2023). Evidently, in the last ten years, acceptance of technology and ease of use have dominantly accelerated the advancements in the fintech sector in financial services which have been found to be expeditiously speedy. McKinsey's research in 2023 shows that in comparison to traditional banking, the fintech industry is forecasted to intensify its revenue almost three times higher between 2022 and 2028.

In comparison to revenue growth for traditional banking, which is reported to be 6% annually, fintech has shown a potential annual revenue growth of 15 percent in a gap of six years from 2022 to 2028 (Anam et al., 2023). The revenue growth is expected due to consumers' fintech Adoption across leading markets.

According to the Fintech Adoption Index for 2022, around 87% of Indians have adopted fintech, which is the highest adoption rate in comparison to other countries and hence is globally the highest global adoption rate. The above graph shows the Consumer fintech adoption across ten leading markets as a percentage of the digitally active population in each market. India is sharing the first spot with around 87% of the people adopting fintech. India's fintech market is projected to reach $155.67 billion in 2025 and $990.45 billion by 2032, growing at a CAGR of 30.26% (Naker, 2022).

A report from Statista indicates the global adoption rate of consumer fintech. The primary categories where fintech is predominantly utilized are money transfers, payments, and insurance (Sujoy, 2024).

Fintech is also revolutionizing money transfers and payments by providing innovative digital solutions that are quicker, more convenient, and more cost-effective than traditional methods. Fintech firms leverage digital platforms and mobile applications to optimize processes, lower fees, and broaden access to financial services, particularly for those who are unbanked or underbanked. The advancement of technology has facilitated a better understanding of the fundamental aspects of insurance processes (Arora & Mehta, 2010), which have collided with persistent customer issues, resulting in a series of profound, enduring, systemic challenges for the insurance sector. Fintech innovations can streamline the insurance experience and improve customer satisfaction. It aids in optimizing insurance premiums (Arora & Arora, 2014), expediting underwriting processes (Arora, 2012), and predicting bankruptcy, (Arora 2017; Arora & Vij, 2010).

11.5 FACTORS DRIVING FINTECH ADOPTION

There are numerous factors that have propagated the acceptance and development of fintech in the market. One of the most spanking factors leading to growth of fintech in the country is the rise in the use of digital payments. The acceptance among smartphone users is nimble in the nation as a rise in digital platforms have been observed which has facilitated the ease in payment transactions through technology-based systems. The second factor leading to the growth of lending technology platforms which have leveraged credit systems, optimized risk evaluations, enhanced loan processing and disbursement, and facilitated financial products through properly aligned algorithms and technology codes. Though the reach of technology is extensive, there is still a mass population which is not using digital technology-based platforms for payments, and hence poses a significant opportunity for the financial institutions to increase their business by tapping them and introducing digitech systems to them. Fintech companies can provide easy systems and user-friendly financial services and bank on these unbanked people of India. To expand their reach, fintech companies are expected to have partner ventures and collaboration with e-commerce platforms. Among all the other factors driving the development of fintech, one of the potentially dominant factors is the introduction of AI and innovations in blockchain technology. These technologies are setting the stage on fire with their novel, more secure, easy, and smart systems in fintech services. Technology is cherishing a more intelligent and faster system by introducing AI-driven chatbots to verification systems to identify digital introduction through blockchain technology. The AI/ machine learning (ML)-driven technology in fintech is in naïve stage and has the potential of providing numerous benefits, including provision of identity checks, enhancing customization, and bringing personalization along with the potential of mitigating fraud and increasing operational efficiency (SNS Insider, 2025).

11.6 EMERGING TECHNOLOGIES IN FINTECH

The integration of AI in the fintech industry encompasses the utilization of cognitive computing, natural language processing, blockchain technology, IoT, cloud computing, predictive analytics, and learning through machines to enhance the capabilities of financial institutions. Through the implementation of AI-driven technologies, fintech companies are giving a new meaning to personalized and customized services, making financial services more optimized. AI is swiftly establishing itself as the foundation of the next generation of fintech enterprises. AI and ML are predominantly applied in the following domains of financial digital transformation:

As shown in Figure 11.1, AI and ML are predominantly applied in security and investment services along with providing superior customer service and maintaining productivity. AI is being applied across various fintech functions, leading to substantial improvements in areas like data processing, customer service, fraud detection, and risk mitigation. The AI in the fintech market is projected to reach a valuation of USD 18.31 billion in 2025, with projections indicating growth up to $52.19 billion in 2029 at a compound annual growth rate (CAGR) of 30.9% (AI in FinTech Global Market Report, 2025), with

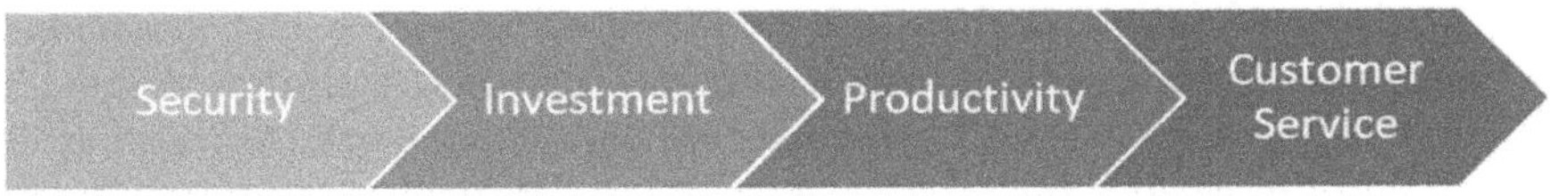

Figure 11.1 Foundational services of AI in fintech.

expectations to grow to USD 53.30 billion by 2030, reflecting a CAGR of 23.82% (Mordor Intelligence, 2025). The AI in the fintech market is becoming increasingly fragmented due to the presence of numerous global players operating worldwide. Various acquisitions and collaborations among major companies are expected to take place soon, with a focus on innovation. Some key players in the market include IBM Corporation, Intel Corporation, Narrative Science, and Microsoft Corporation (Globenewswire, 2024).

The growth of AI in the fintech market is driven by the increasing demand for intelligent financial solutions that enhance customer experience, lower risks, and improve decision-making in real time. Driven by the growing adoption of AI for fraud detection and risk management, the AI in fintech market is anticipated to touch USD 61.6 billion by 2032 (Globenewswire, 2024).

In conclusion, AI is not just an accessory within the fintech sector; it serves as a vital cornerstone that signifies the trajectory of modern innovations within the sector. With continued integration of AI in fintech companies, its role in promoting the progress of industry in improving operational efficiency and offering enhanced security is undeniable.

In the rapidly changing realm of fintech, big data serves as a catalyst for the development of financial products and services, making a considerable impact. As stated by PwC, big data encompasses the vast quantities of structured and unstructured data generated by humans and machines—amounting to petabytes daily (Chen, 2024). This data not only drives the R & D initiatives improving risk management and enhancing the overall operational efficiency, but also fosters financial inclusion. Notably, big data's ability to provide valuable insights into customer behavior is recognized as a significant factor in developing inclusive financial services (Mhlanga, 2024).

The use of big data in the fintech industry can influence various aspects of the sector, such as decision-making, innovation around new products, development of new services, and of course the advancement of new technologies. By scrutinizing large data volumes in real-time, fintech companies can uncover patterns leading to improved decision-making, such as predicting the customers which are most likely to default on the loans or detecting the financial fraudulent activities. This allows companies to make more accurate forecasts (Mhlanga, 2024). There has been a considerable rise in the utilization of big data within the fintech sector, and it is expected that this trend will continue to play a crucial role in the industry (Allen et al., 2022; Johnson et al., 2021; Mhlanga, 2020; Mhlanga & Dunga, 2020).

Cloud computing is becoming a primary focus in the financial services sector. Leaders in banking and capital markets are increasingly acknowledging that cloud represents more than just a technology; it serves as a destination for banks and other financial institutions to store data and applications, as well as to access sophisticated software applications through the internet. By leveraging AI in various business avenues, financial institutions may enhance operational efficiency, thereby optimizing organizational effectiveness in dealing with clients (Tang, 2019).

11.7 APPLICATIONS OF RECENT TECHNOLOGIES IN FINTECH

Over the past few years, AI has reshaped the fintech industry and various financial aspects surrounding it in a variety of ways, from generating faster financial reports, analyzing them, predicting more efficiently, forecasting for the financial markets, more accurate credit assessment, to automated customer support using virtual agents and chatbots. All these insights by leveraging AI capabilities have led to making smart strategic decisions, continuous monitoring for fraud protection, and enhanced customer experience. AI has revolutionized the financial industry by providing new opportunities for innovation, managing processes smoother, efficient, and faster. Accessibility is improved by using robo-advisors to help customers by providing personalized financial advice catered to their preferences and needs to achieve their financial goals. Figure 11.2 shows some of the prominent applications areas of AI in the fintech world.

Big Data, on the other hand, forms the foundation of the modern fintech industry. It facilitates collecting data from a variety of sources, processing various types of data and analyzing voluminous data speedily helping

Figure 11.2 Applications of AI in fintech.

financial institutions to take advantage in terms of active customer engagement, improved financial services, and foster innovation. Big data can be used in customer segmentation, providing them with personalized services like investment portfolio management and quick support. This can be achieved by historical data analysis comprising history of spending patterns and transactions, their online behavior, and demographics, thereby classifying the customers in specific groups and catering to their needs and goals. Figure 11.3 shows that Big Data plays a significant role in predicting various financial risks by analyzing market conditions, operational data, and a number of economic factors to help develop strategies for financial risk mitigation. By supplying enormous amounts of data to algorithms in the form of alternating market trends, diverse economic indicators, and behavioral data extracted from social media, big data can help discover probabilistic opportunities in trading. Big Data incorporates a number of different data sources to assess the creditworthiness of customers comprehensively and automate loan approvals.

Cloud computing is the backbone of the current fintech industry, driving innovation and growth. Its capability to help modernize financial platforms like banking and insurance is proving to be massively transformative. It has provided the infrastructure to the fintech industry in the form of remote servers and other resources to develop and deploy services and provide robust security of financial data without the need for expensive hardware and on-premises IT infrastructure. Cloud computing supports the integration of blockchain technology and cryptocurrency services by providing distributed and powerful architecture. By embracing cloud platforms, the process of adhering to stringent financial regulations becomes simplified due to reliance on built-in tools for compliance monitoring and reporting by the cloud provider. Cloud-based CRM systems deliver enhanced customer experience by managing customer interactions, electronic KYC, and other services in a centralized location. Listed below in Figure 11.4 are some of the application areas of cloud computing in fintech.

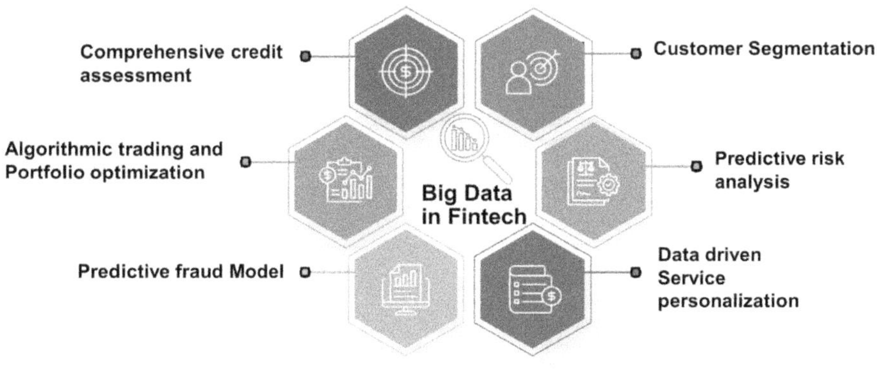

Figure 11.3 Applications of big data in Fintech.

Figure 11.4 Applications of cloud computing in fintech

Another emerging technology, blockchain, is a decentralized system to record and store data across computers in a transparent, secure, and chronological way. It is a fundamental technology underlying cryptocurrencies and contributes to numerous benefits and uses in the fintech world. It provides the opportunity to address challenges in the financial world because of its key characteristics of decentralization, transparency, and immutability. Given its decentralized nature the risk of fraud and cyber-attacks decreases, resulting in higher security. It also helps maintain smart contracts and the process of digital identity verification.

By integrating blockchain in fintech (Figure 11.5), it also facilitates cross-border payments and remittances securely and quickly. Decentralized finance (DeFi) provides better access to financial services without the intermediaries.

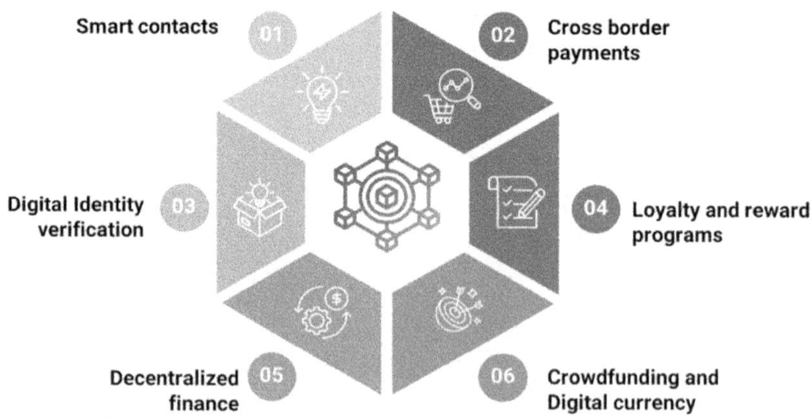

Figure 11.5 Applications of blockchain in fintech.

11.8 BENEFITS OF ARTIFICIAL INTELLIGENCE IN FINTECH

AI in fintech can lead to an overall improved customer experience through 24-hour support, streamlined processes for credit and loan approval, customized investment recommendations, budgetary insights, and continuous application of monitoring fraudulent behavior or activities to proactively prevent fraud. Figure 11.6 depicts the AI automation for the generation of reports and detecting anomalies in compliance data, thereby ensuring efficient adherence to the financial regulations.

These use AI algorithms to leverage historical reports and data to predict economic conditions, market trends, and customer behavior in the fintech industry and ultimately deliver cost savings and revenue maximization by giving them competitive advantage in the industry.

Looking from the various benefits accrued by using big data capabilities in the fintech landscape, it can be seen from Figure 11.7 that collecting massive volumes of structured and unstructured data and analyzing it at high speed makes it useful for overall transactional efficiency, optimized trading strategies, and enhanced customer experience for fintech. It also contributes to significantly reduced transaction costs and revenue maximization by effective resource allocation. Big data provides the information from vast datasets, helping financial companies to make data-driven strategically aligned decisions. Real-time fraud monitoring with the help of data processing capabilities result in better customer engagement and builds trust.

The third technology under discussion, Cloud computing, unlocks significant uses and benefits across the fintech landscape. It empowers companies to evolve faster, innovate, and operate more efficiently to deliver a robust and secure platform for a wide audience.

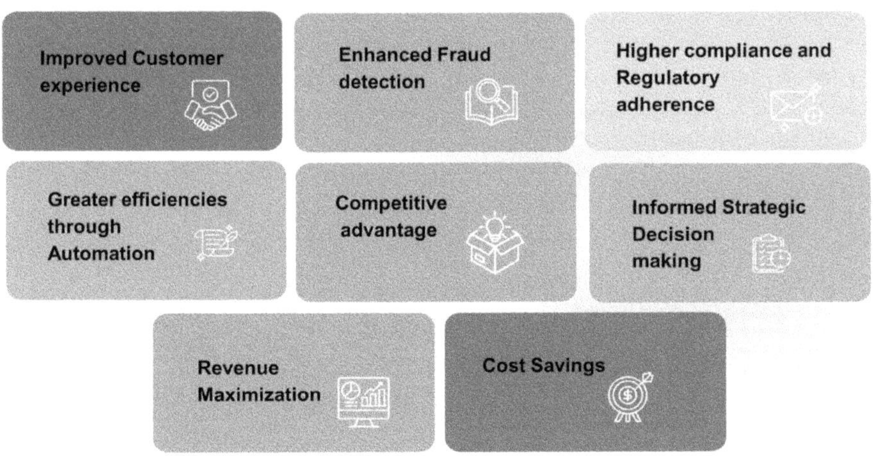

Figure 11.6 Benefits of AI in fintech.

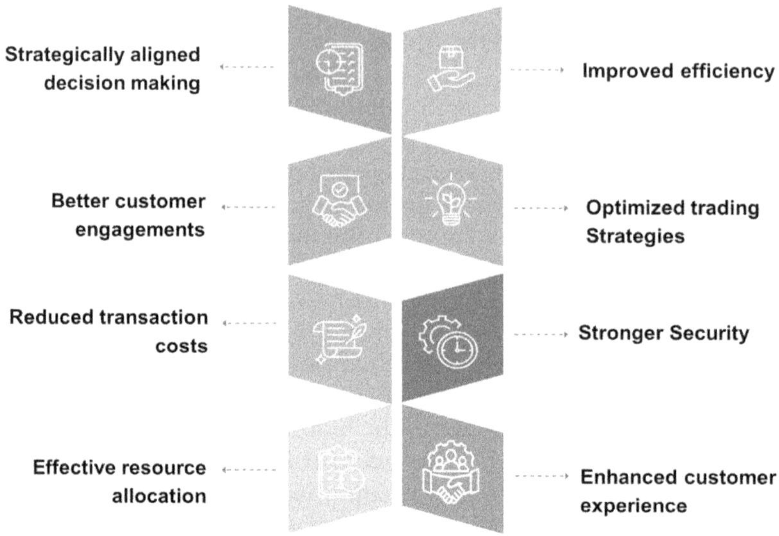

Figure 11.7 Benefits of big data in fintech.

Figure 11.8 shows that cloud computing allows fintech to deploy scalable products and services catering to fluctuating demands, resulting in low operational cost and subsequent savings. Regional regulatory compliance for global customers is simplified by integrating cloud technologies, leading to improved accessibility and faster deployment.

Fintech benefits the most from blockchain in the banking industry due to its characteristics of being secure, transparent, and immutable. It provides easier buying and selling of assets, faster remittances with a high level of traceability, resulting in cost and time savings and enhanced trust of the customers.

Embracing this modern technology leads to increased access to new markets and opportunities by eliminating third-party intermediaries (Figure 11.9). Owing to its decentralized structure, there is a significantly higher security level, which is paramount due to the sensitive nature of personal and financial data of the customers.

Figure 11.8 Benefits of cloud computing in fintech.

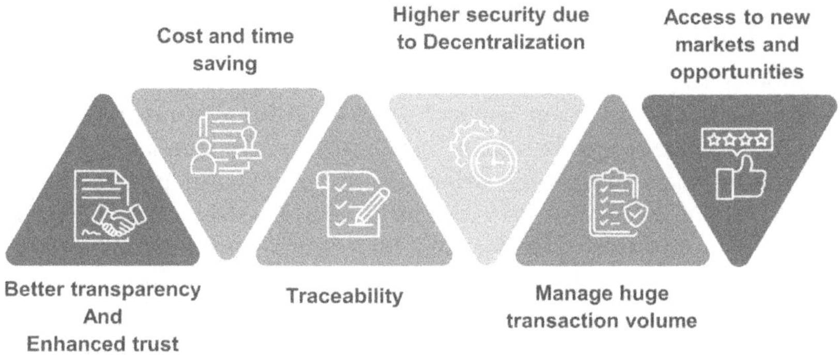

Figure 11.9 Benefits of blockchain in fintech.

11.9 ARTIFICIAL INTELLIGENCE IN FINTECH

A large number of industries across the world have successfully shifted to digital platforms embracing AI to reinforce their operational intelligence and at the same time, invest in the technology to predict and combat potential challenges. The financial sector has also gained substantial advantages from this ongoing transformation, marking a notable advancement attributed to the rise of financial technologies. The ever-growing area of AI is undergoing a significant transformation aimed at redefining the essential practices and operational strategies used within the financial industry aiming to establish contemporary pathways for innovation. Simultaneously, there exists a notable level of reluctance and skepticism regarding the authenticity and reliability of these groundbreaking innovations, which could potentially obstruct their widespread acceptance and integration into routine practices.

Fintech signifies the application of modern technology in financial service products, which seeks to improve the automation of financial service delivery. Fintech functions as a specialized tool that enhances financial management for both businesses and consumers through software and algorithmic systems. Through its effective service management, fintech cultivates global financial literacy and enables universal financial access. This framework is heavily relied upon by capital markets as it offers powerful tools to enhance transparency in AI-driven innovations in fintech: applications, challenges, and future trends. Let's consider a use case in fintech in the next section.

11.10 USE CASE IN FINTECH

11.10.1 AI in combating financial frauds in lending

Financial institutions heavily depend on lending as a primary source of revenue. However, a number of considerable risks can be involved for these institutions when granting loans, which eventually can lead to financial losses. To reduce such capital losses, an appropriate process of evaluation of the credibility of individuals including their analysis, is required before the loans are sanctioned. In the absence of these careful measures, the likelihood of turning these loans into bad loans in the future may increase.

Throughout the history of lending, the loan approval process has been focused on the challenge of differentiating creditworthy borrowers from a large pool of applicants. The demand for effective loan default prediction has become more critical in today's financial systems. Failures in predicting loan defaults have led to significant consequences, including the lending crisis. The task of identifying loan defaulters is quite complex, considering the intricacies of the current finance landscape and the ever-growing demand for loans.

In this view, the challenge lies in distinguishing deserving applicants who will reliably repay loans. The loan approval process is fundamentally concerned with the challenge of differentiating creditworthy borrowers from a huge number of applicants. Thus, the importance of an effective loan default prediction has become increasingly important in modern banking systems. Failures in predicting loan defaults can have significant repercussions, including banking crises. Traditional selection processes often struggle to identify the most appropriate candidates from loan applicants.

With the recent technological developments in AI, availability of relevant data, and higher computing power, many banks have started reviving their traditional business models. Credit risk prediction is crucial for decision-making on the part of financial institutions to make the process more convenient and transparent. In the past decade, AI-based algorithms have attracted considerable attention for their ability to automate and refine loan approval processes.

11.10.2 Dataset description

The dataset considered for the use case consists of a large collection of data consisting of anonymized loan applicants from financial institutions. The dataset comprises 255347 instances with features belonging to categorical, integer, and real values. Some of the feature names and their corresponding values in the dataset have been kept anonymous to maintain the data privacy. The dataset has features like Gender, Age, Education, Marital Status, Employment Type, Months Employed, Income, Loan Amount, Loan Purpose, Has Mortgage, Has Dependents, Has Co-signer, Number of Credit Lines, Interest Rate, Loan Term, and one class, Defaulter. The dataset is well balanced, which makes it appropriate for training classifiers through supervised learning algorithms to make the classifiers perform effectively.

The initial and crucial step entails preprocessing the raw dataset to convert it into a clean, comprehensive, and high-quality format that is suitable for ML analysis. This stage encompasses cleaning, normalizing, encoding, and creating new features. Issues such as missing, inconsistent, and erroneous entries in the dataset are resolved. For the data processing tasks, standard Python libraries such as NumPy, pandas, and scikit-learn are utilized. Ultimately, we divide the dataset into 70% training and 30% testing subsets. We introduced two additional derived features, viz., credit score and DTI ratio, to enhance the predictive capability of the models. Credit score is calculated to represent a score to reflect the applicant's creditworthiness based on their credit history, while DTI ratio is computed to help assess the ability of the applicant to handle additional loans which can act as an indication of applicant's strength of repayment. Factors like number of dependents, employment type, and employment duration are important for this assessment. Figure 11.10 represents the number of applicants in various categories of employment like part-time, unemployed, self-employed, and full-time employment.

The data distribution among different age groups is shown in Figure 11.11. It is evident that there is disparity between the paid loans and unpaid loans by applicants. The dataset contains highest defaulters from the youngest age group of 21–30, followed by the age group 31–40.

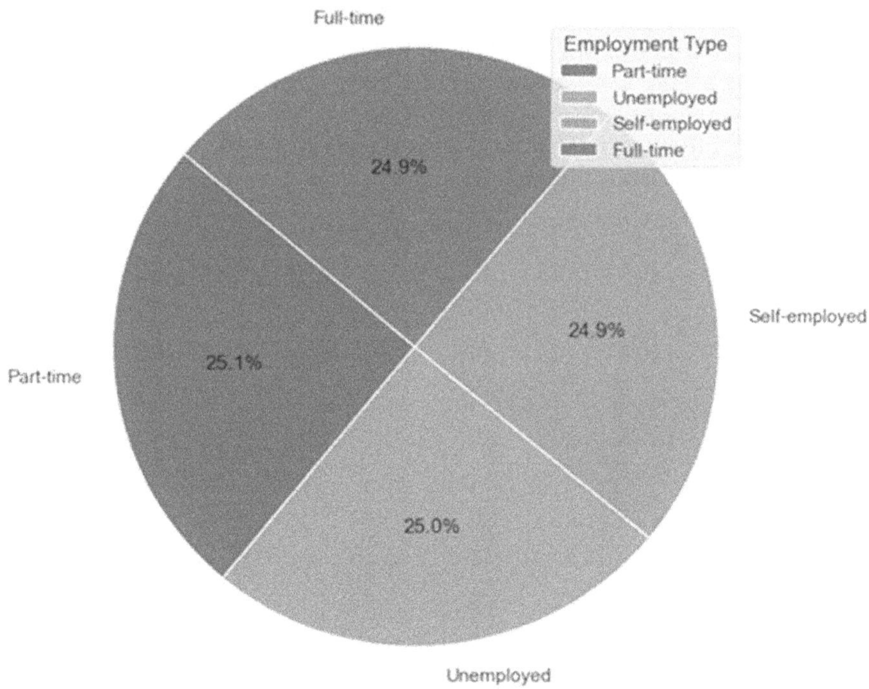

Figure 11.10 Distribution of employment type of applicants.

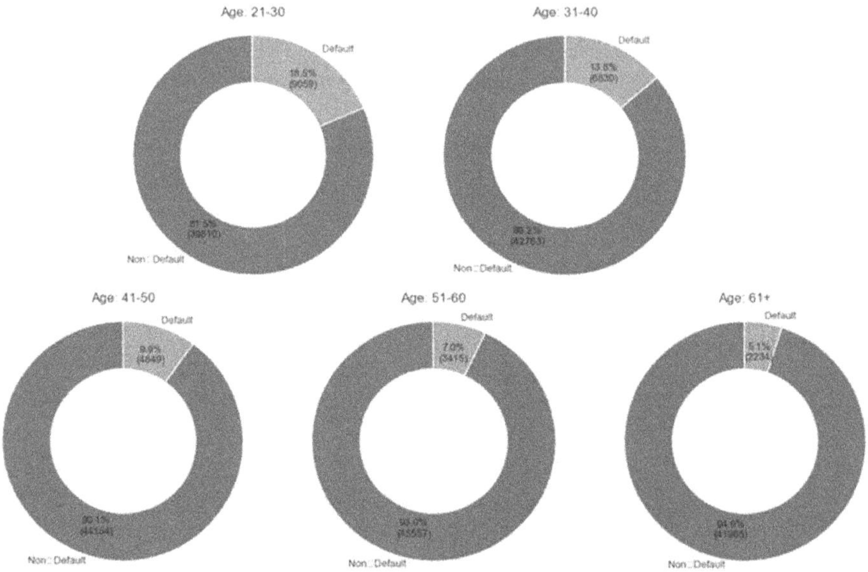

Figure 11.11 Defaulter distribution based on age group.

The income group and age group of the applicant together also confirm the most defaulters from the initial age and income groups leading to least with maturity and stability of applicants seen in Figure 11.12.

By adopting a quantitative strategy, the data is meticulously screened and filtered to ensure consistency, unbiasedness, and relevance. Statistical methods are applied to analyze the data, with the goal of understanding the relationship between various factors.

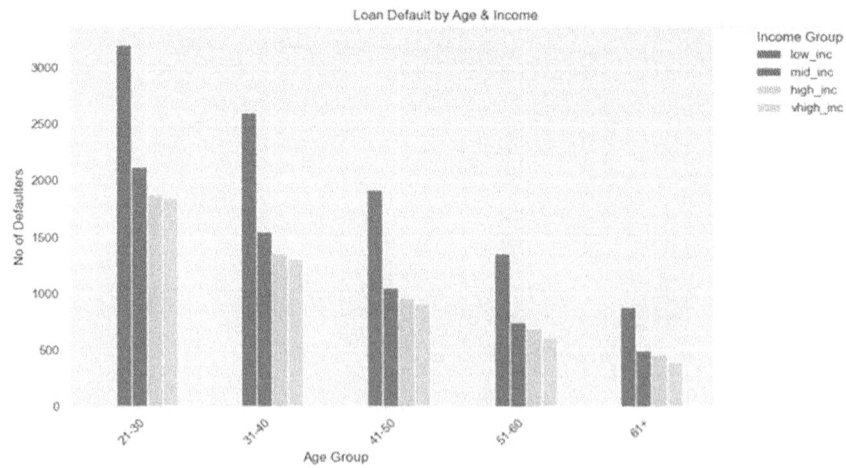

Figure 11.12 Defaulters based on age group and income.

11.10.3 AI modeling for fintech

The process of loan eligibility identification is gaining increasing importance as a pivotal technology in revolutionizing the lending industry by integration of predictive analytics with machine learning. These technologies facilitate smooth loan processing, minimize waiting durations and enhance customer satisfaction through the faster evaluation of applications.

In this regard, an AI-based solution is presented that utilizes technology in the financial services domain, as these concepts are systematically modeled and investigated in the context of financial lending. Following the careful development of a theoretical framework, a thorough implementation is carried out with the aim of assessing the level of trust and confidence that can be cultivated in users within the technological landscape. This comprehensive analysis attempts not only to shed light on the strengths of AI-based solutions in fintech, but also to provide valuable insights into the effectiveness of these emerging technologies and their utilization to augment customer engagement and satisfaction across the financial sector.

Hence, in this section, we explore a fintech application aimed at approving lending requests based on predictions made through machine learning. The prediction of whether a financial institution will approve an applicant's request for loan depends on predicting whether a borrower will default or not if the loan is approved. For this task, we have experimented with four classifiers: AdaBoost, XGBoost, Light Gradient Boosting, and CatBoost, to make predictions on the dataset. There are specific reasons for selecting Boosting methods over other classifiers. Firstly, these classifiers have shown their effectiveness in industry-level systems due to their computational efficiency. Secondly, they are known for their generalization abilities and exceptional predictive performance, and finally, they excel at working with structured data.

11.11 RESULTS AND DISCUSSION

This section presents a comprehensive analysis of the performance of above ML models. The analysis covers capturing key factors influencing identification of a defaulter and determining model accuracy. We also offer insights into the comparative analysis of the said classifiers on performance metrics like accuracy, precision, recall, F1 score, and graphically including area under curve (AUC) and ROC curve. As shown in Figure 11.13, all classifiers exhibit similar accuracy scores on the same dataset, with CatBoost slightly outperforming the others.

Figure 11.14 depicts the classification accuracy of the model by a value of 0.74 for AUC, which tells that the model is good at classifying applicants into defaulter and non-defaulter categories.

After training the model, we generated predictions for 76605 data points in the validation dataset as shown in Figure 11.15. As the actual labels are known, the quality of the model predictions can be evaluated. The top left

Model	Accuracy	Precision	Recall	F1
AdaBoostClassifier	0.809608	0.246140	0.310027	0.274414
XGBClassifier	0.881248	0.452074	0.106565	0.172473
LGBMClassifier	0.883089	0.482838	0.094874	0.158587
CatBoostClassifier	0.884694	0.520820	0.088579	0.151407

Figure 11.13 Comparative summary of classifiers.

corner of the matrix represents True Positives which reveals the number of correctly identified positive cases. Here, the number of true positives is 67063. Looking at the bottom right corner of the matrix which shows the number of correctly identified negative cases, known as True Negatives, the values are found to be 752. The other two corners hold the incorrectly identified cases. The bottom left corner of the matrix shows Type 1 error understood to be false alarms generated by the model. There are 8144 wrongly predicted positive cases where the actual label is negative, but the model predicts it to be positive. On the other hand, the top right corner represents Type 2 error put as missed cases. There are 752 applicants which are legitimate but misunderstood to be defaulters.

There is potential to optimize the presented machine learning model with a dataset consisting of more relevant parameters, optimizing the selection of

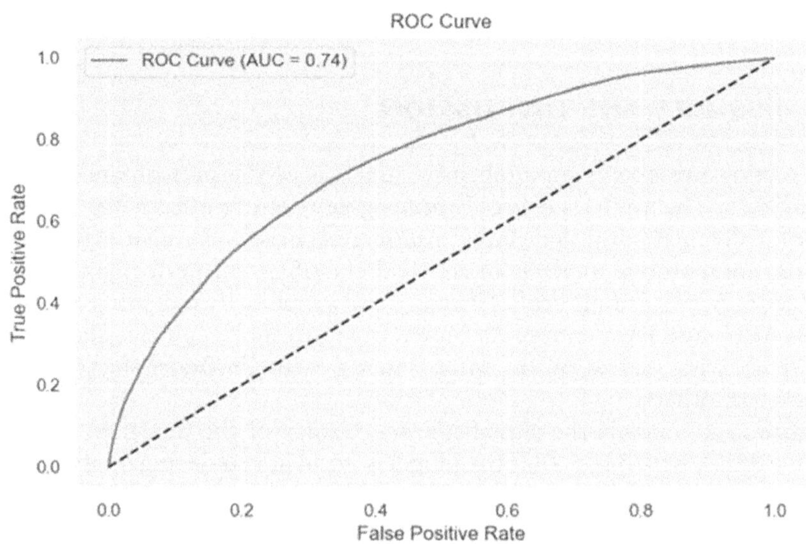

Figure 11.14 Area under ROC curve

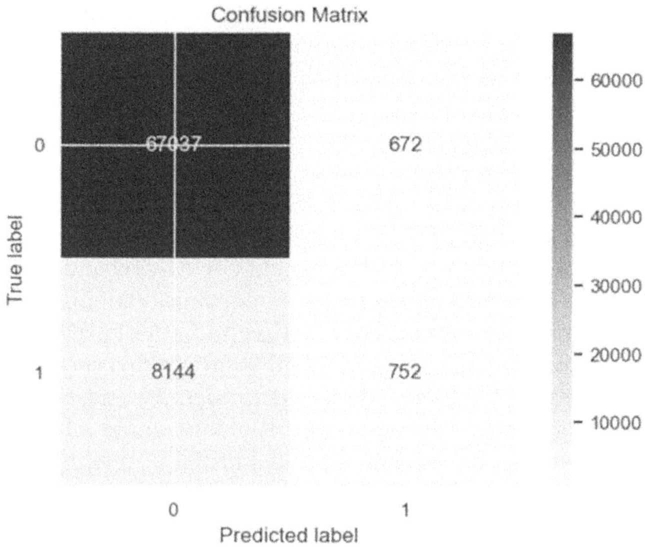

Figure 11.15 Confusion matrix for prediction.

features, and adjusting hyperparameters, the model can attain more accurate predictions and strong generalization across various datasets. Moreover, the inclusion of a bigger and better training data and the implementation of advanced methods like regularization or ensemble learning could further embellish its reliability. With these enhancements, the model can be better positioned to align the requirements of real-world applications, ensuring the fulfillment of intended goals with increased efficiency. Ongoing development and iterative improvements will certainly boost its capacity to produce exceptional outcomes.

State-of-the-art algorithms provide unbiased and accurate credit assessments, thereby reducing the risk of possible human biases. Automated technologies empower lending institutions to consider a wider pool of applicants, further promoting financial inclusion. Moreover, this technology is crucial for modern lending organizations seeking to optimize routine operations to meet the needs of a wide range of clients offering them personalized services, time and cost savings, and efficient processes.

11.12 CONCLUSION

The field of AI is transforming many sectors and finance is not an exception to this. There is substantial evidence present in the literature about AI-driven methods which indicates that AI is set to become the driving technology for the financial industry in the foreseeable future. AI algorithms have the potential to upgrade financial services and boost client value by leveraging the promise of large-scale automation, resulting in significant cost reductions. However, in spite of the expected positive implications for businesses, a variety of challenges exist within fintech that not only affect the customers of fintech services but also the financial institutions themselves. We have sought to merge the principles of traditional finance with modern advanced technologies like AI to transform it into fintech. A rigorous study is done to create a cohesive narrative regarding AI's current condition and recent trends in fintech along with other prominent technologies. Moreover, the emphasis on machine learning aims to combine the benefits of AI-driven decision-making, such as cost and time benefits on top of conventional financial decision-making, thereby increasing its efficacy leading to better customer satisfaction and enhanced customer engagement. To substantiate this claim, we have presented an AI-based methodology designed to identify and tackle challenges in decision-making within fintech, specifically concerning a lending use case. The process of developing a predictive model utilizing cutting-edge ML algorithms has been illustrated. Various classifiers based on machine learning models are showcased to forecast loan default probabilities. The most relevant features from various models are chosen and then applied in the modeling process to evaluate the classifiers. In conclusion, this chapter investigates the dynamic landscape of AI in fintech, scrutinizing the latest developments and its influential applications.

From a managerial perspective, such AI models can assist financial institutions, including banks and fintech companies, in conducting compliant credit scoring while evaluating loan applicants' applications. The combination of credit score calculations and data analysis can assist lenders and financial institutions in recognizing patterns and trends, evaluating borrower creditworthiness, and reducing credit risk. This methodology emphasizes the importance of effective credit risk management while ensuring the financial stability of both lenders and borrowers.

REFERENCES

AI in FinTech Global Market Report 2025. Retrieved on 13th June 2025 from https://www.thebusinessresearchcompany.com/report/ai-in-fintech-global-market-report

Allen, F., Gu, X., & Jagtiani, J. (2022). Fintech, cryptocurrencies, and CBDC: Financial structural transformation in China. Journal of International Money Finance 124,102625. 10.1016/j.jimonfin.2022.102625

Al-Okaily, M., Al Natour, A. R., Shishan, F., Al-Dmour, A., Alghazzawi, R., & Alsharairi, M. (2021). Sustainable FinTech innovation orientation: A moderated model. Sustainability, 13(24), 13591.

Anan, L., Castellanos Isaza, D., Figueiredo, F., Flötotto, M., Jerenz, A., Krivkovich, A., Nadeau, M.-C., Olanrewaju, T., Orlando, Z., & Vassallo, A. (2023, October 24). *Fintechs: A new paradigm of growth.* McKinsey & Company. Retrieved on 12th June 2025 from https://www.mckinsey.com/industries/financial-services/our-insights/fintechs-a-new-paradigm-of-growth

Arner, D. W., Barberis, J. N., & Buckley, R. P. (2015), The Evolution of Fintech: A New Post-Crisis Paradigm? Hong Kong: University of Hong Kong. p 1–46.

Arora, N., & Arora, P. (2014). Insurance premium optimization: Perspective of insurance seeker and insurance provider. Journal of Management and Science, 4(1), 43–53. https://doi.org/10.26524/jms.2014.6
Arora, N. (2012). Neuro-fuzzy approach for insurance underwriting. International Journal of Advanced Research in Computer Science. 3.
Arora, N. (2017). Soft Computing Methodologies for Bankruptcy Prediction. LAP Lambert Academic Publishing.
Arora, N., & Vij, S. K. (2010). A novel independent component analysis approach for bankruptcy prediction using neuro-fuzzy networks. International Journal of Commerce and Management Research, 1(4).
Arora, P., & Mehta, P. (2010, January–June). Rudiments of insurance. The Journal, 35, 69–76.
Chen (2024). Content Strategist. What is Big data? Retrieved on 15th June 2025 from https://www.oracle.com/in/big-data/what-is-big-data/
Datta, D. (2023). The future of financial inclusion through FinTech: A conceptual study in post pandemic India. Sachetas, 2(1), 11–17.
Dublin (2025). Firms Eye Untapped Indian Digital Payments Market with Secure, Low-Cost Digital Financial Solutions. Global news wire. Retrieved on 13th June 2025 from https://www.globenewswire.com/news-release/2025/05/09/3077984/28124/en/India-s-Fintech-Market-to-Reach-990-Billion-by-2032-at-30-2-CAGR-Fintech-Firms-Eye-Untapped-Indian-Digital-Payments-Market-with-Secure-Low-Cost-Digital-Financial-Solutions.html
Elia, G., Stefanelli, V., & Ferilli, G. B. (2023). Investigating the role of fintech in the Banking industry: What do we know. European Journal of Innovation Management, 26(5), 1365–1393.1393.
Ertz, M., & Boily, É. (2019). The rise of the digital economy: Thoughts on blockchain technology and cryptocurrencies for the collaborative economy. International Journal of Innovation Studies, 3(4), 84–93.
Giglio, F. (2022). Fintech: A literature review. International Business Research, 15(1), 80–85. Canadian Center of Science and Education.
Johnson, M., Jain, R., Brennan-Tonetta, P., Swartz, E., Silver, D., & Paolini, J., et al. (2021). Impact of big data and artificial intelligence on industry: Developing a workforce roadmap for a data driven economy. Global Journal of Flexible Systems Management. 22, 197–217. 10.1007/s40171-021-00272-y
Karim, S., Naz, F., Naeem, M. A., & Vigne, S. A. (2022). Is FinTech providing effective solutions to small and medium enterprises (SMEs) in ASEAN countries? Economic Analysis and Policy, 75, 335–344.
Knewtson, H. S., & Rosenbaum, Z. A. (2020). Toward understanding FinTech and its industry. Managerial Finance, 46(8), 1043–1060.
Kumari, A., & Devi, N. C. (2022). The impact of FinTech and blockchain technologies on Banking and financial services. Technology Innovation Management Review, 12(1/2)
Lee, I., & Shin, Y. J. (2018). Fintech: Ecosystem, business models, investment decisions, and challenges. Business Horizons, 61(1), 35–46.
Lee, T. H., & Kim, H. W. (2015), An Exploratory Study on Fintech Industry in Korea: Crowdfunding Case. Bangkok: Proceedings in International Conference on Innovative Engineering Technologies.
Leong, C., Tan, B., Xiao, X., Tan, F. T. C., & Sun, Y. (2017). Nurturing a FinTech ecosystem: The case of a youth microloan startup in China. International Journal of Information Management, 37(2), 92–97.
Limna, P., & Kraiwanit, T. (2022). The rise of fintech: A review article. *STOU Academic Journal of Research and Innovation in Humanities and Social Sciences*, 2(2), 35–46.

Limna, P., Kraiwanit, T., & Siripipatthanakul, S. (2022). The growing trend of digital economy: A review article. International Journal of Computing Sciences Research, 6, 1–11.
Mention, A. L. (2021). The age of FinTech: Implications for research, policy and practice. The Journal of FinTech, 1(01), 2050002.
Mhlanga, D. (2020). Industry 4.0 in finance: The impact of artificial intelligence (ai) on digital financial inclusion. International Journal of Financial Studies, 8, 45. 10.3390/ijfs8030045
Mhlanga, D. (2024). The role of big data in financial technology toward financial inclusion. Retrieved on 15th June 2025 from https://pmc.ncbi.nlm.nih.gov/articles/PMC11106479/. PMCID: PMC11106479 PMID: 38774056
Mhlanga, D., & Dunga, S. H. (2020). Measuring financial inclusion and its determinants among the smallholder farmers in Zimbabwe: An empirical study. Eurasian Journal of Business and Management, 8, 266–281. 10.15604/ejbm.2020.08.03.008
Mirchandani, A., Gupta, N., & Ndiweni, E. (2020). Understanding the fintech wave: A search for A theoretical explanation. International Journal of Economics and Financial Issues, 10(5), 331.
Mordor Intelligence (2025). AI in Fintech Market Size & Share Analysis - Growth Trends & Forecasts (2025–2030). Retrieved on 12th June 2025 from https://www.mordorintelligence.com/industry-reports/ai-in-fintech-market
Naker, N. (2022). 7 trends shaping the future of Fintech. EY. Partner, Technology Consulting, EY India. Retrieved on 12th June 2025 from https://www.ey.com/en_in/insights/consulting/seven-key-trends-shaping-the-future-of-fintech-industry
Nathan, R. J., Setiawan, B., & Quynh, M. N. (2022). Fintech and financial health in Vietnam during the COVID-19 pandemic: In-depth descriptive analysis. Journal of Risk and Financial Management, 15(3), 125.
Schueffel, P. (2016). Taming the beast: A scientific definition of fintech. Journal of Innovation Management, 4(4), 32–54.
SNS Insider. (2025). Artificial Intelligence in Fintech Market to Reach USD 61.6 Billion by 2032, Driven by Increasing Adoption of AI for Fraud Detection and Risk Management. Globenews Wire Retrieved on 13th June 2025 from https://www.globenewswire.com/news-release/2024/12/07/2993334/0/en/Artificial-Intelligence-in-Fintech-Market-to-Reach-USD-61-6-Billion-by-2032-Driven-by-Increasing-Adoption-of-AI-for-Fraud-Detection-and-Risk-Management-Research-by-SNS-Insider.html
Soloviev, V. (2018). Fintech Ecosystem in Russia. 2018 Eleventh International Conference "Management of Large-Scale System Development" MLSD, pp. 1–5. IEEE
Sujoy, V. (2024). Adoption rate of financial technology worldwide in 2024, by software application. Statista. Retrieved on 12th June 2025 from statista.com/statistics/1331176/fintech-adoption-rate
Tang, M. (2019). Delloitte Report. Cloud banking: More than just a CIO conversation. Retrieved on 15th June 2025 from https://www.deloitte.com/za/en/Industries/financial-services/perspectives/bank-2030-financial-services-cloud.html

Chapter 12

Smart governance for smart money

AI-enabled monitoring of Indonesian Digital Rupiah (CBDC)

Muhammad Syauqi Bin-Armia

12.1 INTRODUCTION

The rapid digitalisation of money and payments has transformed how central banks, financial institutions, and consumers conceptualise the role of sovereign currency in the modern economy. Over the past decade, interest in central bank digital currencies (CBDCs) has intensified across advanced and emerging economies, driven by shifts in payment preferences, declining cash usage, rising digital platforms, and concerns regarding monetary sovereignty (BIS, 2022; Brunner et al., 2019; Goodhart, 2010). CBDCs have emerged as a strategic response to technological disruption, with multiple jurisdictions experimenting with retail and wholesale models that embed programmability, enhanced settlement finality, and data-rich transaction structures (G7, 2021; Soderberg et al., 2022).

Growing empirical work highlights the diverse motivations and potential risks associated with CBDC adoption. Cross-country analyses document that CBDCs influence payment competition, bank intermediation, capital flows, and financial stability in varied ways depending on institutional quality and market structure (Ayadi et al., 2023; Aysan, & Syarif, 2025; Bas et al., 2024; Lee et al., 2023; Li et al., 2022; Luu et al., 2023; Rehman et al., 2023; Son et al., 2023; Tian et al., 2023; Xin, & Jiang, 2023). Research also shows that CBDC-related news affects asset prices, crypto spillovers, and systemic risk sentiment (Akin et al., 2023; Helmi et al., 2023; Mzoughi et al., 2022; Tercero-Lucas, 2023; Wang et al., 2022, 2023). Meanwhile, design principles – including caps, tiered remuneration, privacy architectures, and cybersecurity protocols – shape the balance between monetary policy effectiveness, user acceptance, and banking-sector resilience (Agur et al., 2022; Davoodalhosseini, 2022; Schilling et al., 2024; Zhou, 2024).

At the global level, CBDC implementation trajectories vary widely. Countries such as China, the Bahamas, Jamaica, and select African nations have reached advanced pilot or deployment stages, providing early evidence on economic, behavioural, and governance impacts (Allen et al., 2022; Shen & Hou, 2021; Wu et al., 2024; Xiao et al., 2024). China's e-CNY experiments offer insight into programmability, payment-platform competition,

DOI: 10.1201/9781003656463-12

tax compliance, cross-border integration, and macroeconomic implications. Other jurisdictions – including the European Union, the United Kingdom, Middle East, South Asia, and Latin America – continue to explore design options, institutional trade-offs, and political economy factors shaping adoption (Alora et al., 2024; Chua et al., 2025; Corbet et al., 2024; Desai, 2025; Hemingway, 2025; Minesso et al., 2022). Simultaneously, several projects have stalled or been discontinued due to governance concerns, limited user demand, cybersecurity risks, or institutional constraints (Bhaskar et al., 2022; Conlon et al., 2024; Mishra & Prasad, 2024). These global experiences produce valuable lessons about sequencing, regulatory harmonisation, and the importance of building public trust through transparency and robust oversight (Nyffenegger, 2024).

As CBDCs evolve, artificial intelligence (AI) has emerged as a foundational layer enabling real-time monitoring, auditability, and supervisory analytics. Advances in explainable AI, machine-learning validation, risk scoring, anomaly detection, and policy modelling have expanded the toolkit available to central banks (Cil & Yildiz, 2025; Estrada et al., 2023; Kumari et al., 2022). AI promises to enhance the capacity of central banks to detect illicit activity, systemic vulnerabilities, compliance breaches, behavioural anomalies, and model instability in a CBDC environment. Yet integrating AI within sovereign monetary infrastructures raises new concerns regarding model risk, transparency, explainability, and governance (Maryaningsih et al., 2022; Zams et al., 2020).

Indonesia's CBDC initiative – Project Garuda – situates itself within this global landscape of experimentation and innovation. Bank Indonesia has completed proof-of-concept testing for the wholesale Digital Rupiah focusing on the Digital Cash Ledger and the interbank settlement architecture, while outlining a roadmap towards the Securities Ledger and full retail CBDC implementation (Maryaningsih et al., 2022; Zams et al., 2020). The Garuda framework emphasises interoperability, privacy protection, programmability, and cross-border use cases consistent with BIS and G20 principles. However, as the ecosystem grows in complexity, AI-assisted auditing and supervisory frameworks become essential for ensuring reliability, transparency, and policy alignment.

Despite a rapidly expanding literature, three critical gaps remain. First, existing studies provide limited evidence on how AI can be embedded within CBDC infrastructures to support real-time auditability, macroprudential monitoring, and automated compliance verification. Second, few analyses integrate cross-country CBDC lessons with Indonesia's regulatory, institutional, and technological realities. Third, the literature has not yet articulated a structured AI-governance model tailored for a hybrid wholesale – retail CBDC transitioning economy.

This study addresses these gaps by synthesising global CBDC developments, evaluating Indonesia's Digital Rupiah architecture, and proposing an AI-enabled supervisory and auditing framework tailored to Bank Indonesia's next developmental stage Digital Cash and Securities Ledger integration. By connecting international empirical evidence with Indonesia's institutional context, the article advances a model of "smart governance for smart money," where AI functions not merely as a technological tool but as an institutional capability that enhances financial stability, regulatory oversight, and policy precision in the era of sovereign digital currency.

12.2 LITERATURE REVIEW

This section synthesises the global, technological, and country-specific strands of the CBDC literature with a focus on the evolving role of AI in supervision, auditing, and financial services governance. The VOSviewer bibliometric map (Figure 12.1) visually illustrates the conceptual clusters linking AI, financial services, explainability, credit-risk modelling, and policy modelling demonstrating that CBDC research increasingly intersects with AI governance and systems-thinking approaches.

12.2.1 Global CBDC findings: Adoption, stability, and policy design

The global CBDC literature reflects significant heterogeneity in motivations, design choices, financial stability consequences, and behavioural responses. Early theoretical work establishes foundational frameworks for CBDC design, bank intermediation effects, and monetary-policy transmission (Agur et al., 2022; Barrdear & Kumhof, 2022; Davoodalhosseini, 2022; Kumhof & Noone, 2021; Mishra & Prasad, 2024). These models highlight how CBDC interest-rate structures, remuneration tiers, caps, and privacy options shape the degree of bank disintermediation and liquidity substitution.

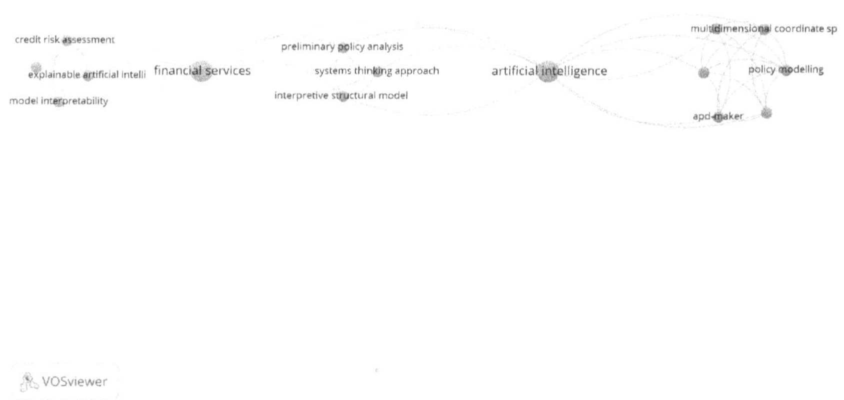

Figure 12.1 VOSviewer bibliometric map of AI–CBDC literature.

Empirical studies show that CBDC announcements and policy signals often generate measurable effects in financial markets. Research documents spillovers into equity volatility (Wang et al., 2024), fintech stocks (Li et al., 2022), banking-sector stability (Heitmann et al., 2025; Luu et al., 2023), cryptocurrency markets (Akin et al., 2023; Ayadi et al., 2023; Mzoughi et al., 2022), and digital-asset attention cycles (Wang et al., 2023). The behavioural dimensions of CBDC acceptance – such as technology perceptions, trust, and switching intention – are shown to be critical determinants of adoption (Liu et al., 2025; Sha et al., 2024; Söilen & Benhayoun, 2022; Umar et al., 2024). Country-level evidence further enriches this landscape. China's e-CNY pilot offers the most extensive real-world empirical evidence to date, with research documenting its effects on corporate debt financing (Xiao et al., 2024), cash-management behaviour (Zhang & Chan, 2025b), tax compliance (Umar, 2025), overseas investment (Zhu & Zhou, 2025), and macroeconomic adjustments (Xiang et al., 2024). Other regional perspectives highlight rollout challenges in emerging markets (Alora et al., 2024), tourism and retail payment adoption (Chua et al., 2025), and comparative digital-rupee experiences (Balasubramanian & Thirumaran, 2025).

A separate emerging stream investigates why some jurisdictions stalled or abandoned their CBDC projects, identifying issues such as low public trust, unclear value propositions, institutional fragility, and cybersecurity vulnerabilities (Bhaskar et al., 2022; Conlon et al., 2024). These findings provide important lessons for countries still designing their CBDC architectures.

12.2.2 AI in financial supervision, audit, and policy modelling

AI applications in financial-sector governance have expanded substantially in recent years. The bibliometric clusters in Figure 12.1 highlight key thematic areas: *explainable artificial intelligence (XAI)*, *financial services*, *credit-risk assessment*, *model interpretability*, and *policy modelling*. These high-coherence clusters suggest that CBDC infrastructures, with their rich data flows and programmable features, are likely to become fertile environments for AI-enabled oversight.

In financial services, AI has been widely adopted for risk scoring, fraud detection, behavioural profiling, and credit-risk modelling (Cil & Yildiz, 2025; Wang et al., 2024). Explainable AI methods specifically enhance model transparency and accountability, addressing concerns about algorithmic opacity and decision-making bias (Estrada et al., 2023; Fan et al., 2021). Studies on machine-learning-driven lending and financial risk assessment show that AI improves predictive accuracy but introduces model risk challenges requiring robust supervisory oversight (Kumari et al., 2022).

AI has also been proposed as an essential component of public-sector macro-financial surveillance. AI-enabled policy modelling, systems-thinking approaches, and structural modelling techniques aim to enhance scenario analysis, forecasting accuracy, and stress-testing frameworks for digital financial ecosystems (Blinder, 2010; Estrada et al., 2023). These tools are increasingly relevant as CBDCs generate high-volume, high-granularity transactional data well-suited for real-time monitoring.

Despite its promise, the integration of AI into financial governance raises several risks. The literature underscores concerns regarding explainability, auditability, regulatory compliance, privacy, embedded bias, and systemic interconnectedness (Berger & Humphrey, 1997; Cil & Yildiz, 2025). These risks imply that AI auditing frameworks – covering data validation, model testing, risk scoring, compliance review, and continuous monitoring – are necessary to ensure responsible adoption.

12.2.3 Indonesia's Digital Rupiah (Project Garuda): Motivations, architecture, and gaps

Indonesia's CBDC development has advanced significantly through Bank Indonesia's *Project Garuda*, which outlines a phased approach beginning with the wholesale Digital Cash Ledger and progressing towards a Securities Ledger and retail CBDC. Indonesian studies identify key adoption drivers such as financial inclusion, efficiency gains, cross-border payment integration, and monetary-policy modernisation (Maryaningsih et al., 2022; Zams et al., 2020).

Delphi and analytic network process analyses emphasise stakeholder preferences for privacy safeguards, interoperability, programmable features, and strong governance mechanisms (Zams et al., 2020). Other Indonesian research stresses the importance of institutional trust, technological readiness, and consumer behaviour in shaping adoption outcomes factors that mirror global findings (Maryaningsih et al., 2022).

Despite these advances, gaps remain. Indonesia has not yet incorporated a systematic framework for AI-enabled financial oversight into its CBDC architecture. While the Garuda roadmap acknowledges programmability and data governance, it does not yet specify how AI will support real-time monitoring, compliance verification, anomaly detection, macro-financial surveillance, or auditability of CBDC transactions. International experience suggests that such frameworks will become essential as Indonesia transitions towards the Digital Cash and Securities Ledger stages.

Thus, a key contribution of this paper is to propose an integrated supervisory and auditing model tailored to Indonesia's regulatory context, leveraging AI to strengthen governance, resilience, and policy effectiveness in the Digital Rupiah ecosystem.

12.3 METHODOLOGY

This study adopts a mixed qualitative – analytical methodology designed to evaluate the development of CBDCs globally, derive lessons across jurisdictions, and develop an AI-enabled supervisory and auditing framework applicable to Indonesia's Digital Rupiah (Project Garuda). The methodological approach integrates four complementary components: (1) cross-country comparative analysis, (2) structured document and grey-literature review, (3) case-study methodology for Indonesia, and (4) bibliometric mapping using VOSviewer to contextualise AI–CBDC research linkages.

12.3.1 Cross-country comparative analysis

The first methodological pillar involves a structured comparative analysis of global CBDC trajectories. Countries are classified into three groups based on publicly available datasets and CBDC development portals, including the BIS, IMF, and CBDC Tracker databases:

a. Jurisdictions that have *implemented* CBDCs (e.g., China, the Bahamas, Jamaica). (Umar, 2025; Xiao et al., 2024; Zhang & Chan, 2025a)
b. Jurisdictions that are *actively studying or piloting* CBDCs (e.g., EU, UK, Singapore, Saudi Arabia). (Alora et al., 2024; Hemingway, 2025; Kamin, & Zampolli, 2025)
c. Jurisdictions that have *halted, cancelled, or deprioritised* CBDC initiatives (e.g., some Nordic and African economies) due to weak demand, governance constraints, or operational challenges. (Bhaskar et al., 2022; Conlon et al., 2024)

Comparisons are developed through thematic dimensions derived from the literature, including:

- Design choices (retail vs. wholesale, remuneration, privacy, caps).
- Institutional readiness and governance.
- Financial-stability implications.
- Technological design and cybersecurity considerations.
- Behavioural and adoption factors.
- Macroeconomic and policy outcomes.

This synthesis enables extraction of cross-country lessons relevant to Indonesia's institutional and policy context.

12.3.2 Document and grey-literature review

Given the fast-evolving nature of CBDCs, much of the authoritative guidance arises from central banks, BIS working groups, G7/G20 policy papers, and IMF technical notes. Accordingly, this study incorporates a structured review of grey literature, including:

- BIS foundational reports on CBDC design, payments, and policy principles (Auer & Böhme, 2020; BIS, 2022; Eriksson et al., 2008);
- G7 public policy frameworks for retail CBDCs (G7, 2021);

- IMF technical papers and "behind the scenes" operational analyses (Soderberg et al., 2022);
- Regional studies such as Latin America's CBDC readiness (Kamin & Zampolli, 2025).

These documents complement peer-reviewed research by describing operational realities, risk management frameworks, pilot outcomes, cybersecurity incidents, and institutional-level challenges that academic studies rarely capture. The grey-literature review therefore informs the practical policy recommendations developed for Bank Indonesia.

12.3.3 Case-study methodology for Project Garuda

To analyse Indonesia's CBDC development, this study applies an embedded case-study design consistent with qualitative international-business and policy research (Tsang & Colpan, 2025). This approach is appropriate when the objective is to balance contextual specificity with theoretical generalisation.

The case study draws on:

1. Official reports from Bank Indonesia on Project Garuda, including wholesale proof-of-concept documentation and roadmap publications;
2. Academic studies on Indonesian CBDC design, adoption drivers, and governance considerations (Maryaningsih et al., 2022; Zams et al., 2020);
3. Comparative ASEAN and Asia-Pacific studies that illuminate regional CBDC dynamics (Aysan & Syarif, 2025).

The analytical framework focuses on key dimensions:

- Institutional governance and regulatory capacity.
- Wholesale market structure and settlement design.
- Data architecture and programmability needs.
- Potential risks and bottlenecks in scaling towards the Securities Ledger.

The case-study results later inform the AI governance model proposed for the Indonesian context.

12.3.4 Bibliometric mapping and knowledge-structure identification

To contextualise the conceptual evolution of AI and CBDC research, this study incorporates a bibliometric analysis using VOSviewer. A curated dataset of peer-reviewed publications and institutional reports was analysed to identify thematic clusters. The resulting map (Figure 12.1) reveals three dominant clusters:

a. **Financial-services AI and explainability** (credit-risk assessment, model interpretability);
b. **Policy-modelling and systems-thinking approaches** (AI for public decision-making);
c. **Core AI methodologies** linking the two domains.

The bibliometric evidence validates the conceptual integration pursued in this study: AI is simultaneously shaping micro-level financial analytics and macro-level policy modelling, a duality essential for designing AI-enabled CBDC oversight mechanisms.

12.3.5 Development of the AI supervisory and auditing framework

The final methodological step synthesises insights from the prior stages to construct a conceptual model for AI-enabled CBDC supervision tailored to Indonesia. This model integrates:

- **AI Supervision Layer:** macro-financial monitoring, anomaly detection, early-warning indicators, liquidity and flow analytics, and behavioural surveillance.
- **AI Audit Layer:** data validation, model testing, explainability assessment, compliance verification, and continuous monitoring.

The design follows best practices from AI auditing and explainable machine-learning literature (Cil, & Yildiz, 2025; Kumari et al., 2022) and incorporates lessons from jurisdictions with advanced CBDC analytics.

The proposed framework is intended not as a prescriptive technological roadmap, but as a conceptual tool to support Bank Indonesia's transition to the next developmental milestone: the Digital Cash and Securities Ledger integration phase.

12.4 DISCUSSION: INTEGRATING THE CONCEPTUAL FRAMEWORK WITH GLOBAL CBDC PATHWAYS

This section synthesises the conceptual foundations of CBDC governance with global comparative developments and applies these insights to the context of Indonesia's Digital Rupiah (Project Garuda). The goal is to articulate how an AI-enabled governance architecture can enhance supervisory robustness, auditability, and policy responsiveness as Indonesia advances towards an interoperable, programmable sovereign digital currency.

12.4.1 Lessons from global CBDC implementation pathways

The global distribution of CBDC activity reveals a heterogeneous landscape characterised by divergent technological priorities, institutional capacities, and policy motivations. While CBDCs are often framed as a natural evolution of digital payment ecosystems, cross-country evidence shows that their development is far from linear. Instead, jurisdictions are navigating a complex interplay of technological feasibility, regulatory preparedness, financial stability concerns, geopolitical considerations, and public acceptance (Auer & Böhme, 2020; BIS, 2022b). This diversity underscores that CBDCs do not represent a single model but rather a spectrum of design choices shaped by each country's economic structure and policy objectives.

A significant proportion of jurisdictions remain in the *research phase*, where central banks are conducting conceptual analyses, industry consultations, and cross-border experiments to understand programmability, privacy configurations, settlement efficiency, and macro-financial transmission implications. These early-stage efforts reflect a cautious and analytical approach: central banks aim to avoid premature commitments while ensuring that any future digital currency aligns with monetary sovereignty, payment resilience, and financial integrity.

A second group of countries has moved towards *proof-of-concept* experimentation. These projects – often carried out in partnership with technology providers, fintech, and academic institutions – test the performance of distributed ledger architectures, token-based settlement schemes, interoperability modules, and regulatory sandboxes. PoC environments serve as controlled settings to evaluate technical reliability, examine tokenised asset settlement, and explore how wholesale or retail CBDCs interact with existing financial infrastructures.

Only a smaller subset has advanced to *pilot implementations.* These jurisdictions typically combine strong state capacity, advanced digital identity infrastructure, and high mobile payment penetration. They demonstrate the operational feasibility of digital legal tender, though often under tightly constrained conditions (e.g., transaction caps, limited users, controlled geographic areas). At the same time, pilots reveal the complexity of scaling CBDCs nationally-requiring coordination across commercial banks, payment service providers, telecom operators, and regulatory institutions (Alora et al., 2024; Hemingway, 2025; Kamin & Zampolli, 2025).

Finally, a notable number of countries have *cancelled, suspended, or deprioritised* their CBDC plans. Reasons vary: some experienced weak user demand due to existing efficient payment systems; others encountered high operational burdens, institutional fragmentation, cybersecurity concerns, or unclear value propositions. These cases demonstrate that CBDCs are not universally necessary and that, without strong domestic justification, the risks may outweigh the benefits (Bhaskar et al., 2022; Conlon et al., 2024).

A critical insight from this global comparison is that CBDCs operate within socio-technical systems where institutional trust, governance frameworks, and public acceptance are as crucial as technological sophistication. The global experience suggests that success hinges on clarity of policy objectives, iterative pilot testing, and the ability to integrate automated supervision and compliance tools into real-time digital infrastructures. These lessons directly inform Indonesia's roadmap for the Digital Rupiah and highlight the importance of building robust supervisory and auditing capabilities from the outset.

To complement the qualitative discussion, Table 12.1 organises CBDC initiatives by geographical region. The classification is based on the most recent

Table 12.1 CBDC Development Worldwide by region

Region	*Countries and CBDC Projects*
South America	Argentina (Digital Peso – Research); Brazil (DREX Phases 1–3 – PoC); Chile (CBDC – Research); Peru (CBDC – Research); Ecuador (Dinero Electrónico – Cancelled); Uruguay (e-Peso – Pilot).
North America	United States (Digital Dollar – Cancelled; Project Hamilton – PoC); Canada (Jasper; Jasper –Ubin – PoC).
Europe	Euro Area (Digital Euro – Research); France (Project Prosperus – Pilot; Jura – Research); Switzerland (e-Franc – Research); Germany (Trigger Solution – Pilot); Spain (Wholesale CBDC – Research); Italy (TIPS Hash-Link – Pilot); Sweden (e-Krona – PoC); Norway (CBDC – PoC); Poland (Digital Zloty – Research); Czech Republic (CBDC – Research); Hungary (CBDC – Pilot); Luxembourg (Project Venus – Pilot); Finland (Avant – Cancelled); Iceland (Rafkróna – Research); Austria (DELPHI – Research).
Middle East & North Africa (MENA)	United Arab Emirates (Digital Dirham – Pilot; Aber – Pilot); Saudi Arabia (Wholesale CBDC – Research; Retail CBDC – Research; mBridge – Pilot); Qatar (Wholesale CBDC – PoC; CBDC – Research); Bahrain (Digital Dinar – Research); Morocco (CBDC – Research); Egypt (CBDC – Research); Algeria (Digital Dinar – Research); Tunisia (e-Dinar – Research).
Central Asia	Kazakhstan (Digital Tenge – Pilot); Kyrgyzstan (Digital Som – PoC); Uzbekistan (CBDC – Research); Tajikistan (CBDC – Research).
South Asia	India (Digital Rupee – Pilot); Pakistan (CBDC – Research); Sri Lanka (CBDC – Research); Bangladesh (CBDC – Research); Nepal (CBDC – Research); Bhutan (Digital Ngultrum – Research); Maldives (CBDC – Research).
Southeast & Pacific Asia	Indonesia (Digital Rupiah/Project Garuda – PoC); Singapore (Ubin+ – Pilot; Orchid – Cancelled; Project Mariana – Research); Malaysia (E-Ringgit – Research); Thailand (CBDC – PoC; Inthanon – PoC); Philippines (Agila – PoC; CBDC – Cancelled); Vietnam (CBDC – Research); Laos (CBDC – Research); Cambodia (Bakong – Domestic blockchain payment system); Timor-Leste (eCentavos – Research).
East Asia	China (e-CNY – Pilot); Hong Kong (e-HKD – Pilot; Ensemble – Research; Inthanon-LionRock Joint project with Thailand – PoC); South Korea (Wholesale CBDC – Research; Digital Won – Pilot); Japan (Digital Yen – PoC; Stella – Research); Taiwan (CBDC – Research); Mongolia (CBDC – Research); Macau (e-MOP – PoC).
Oceania	Fiji (CBDC – Cancelled); Papua New Guinea (CBDC – PoC); Vanuatu (CBDC – Research); Solomon Islands (CBDC – Research; Bokolo Cash – PoC); Tonga (CBDC – Research).
Australia-New Zealand	Australia (eAUD – Research; Project Atom – PoC; Project Acacia – Research); New Zealand (CBDC – Re- search/PoC).

Source: CBDCTracker.org

dataset from cbdctracker.org, which compiles and updates CBDC development statuses globally. Countries are grouped into: South America, North America, Europe, MENA, Central Asia, South Asia, Southeast Asia and Pacific Asia, Oceania, and Australia – New Zealand.

12.4.2 China's CBDC development: Institutional, technological, and policy insights

China represents the most advanced and comprehensive CBDC initiative globally, offering valuable lessons for jurisdictions designing large-scale digital currency ecosystems. The development of the digital renminbi (e-CNY) has unfolded through extensive pilot programs, multilayered coordination between public and private actors, and progressive refinement of payment infrastructure. The Chinese model provides an empirical benchmark for understanding how CBDCs can be operationalised at scale, particularly within complex and digitally mature economies.

China's CBDC strategy is rooted in its long-standing efforts to modernise its financial structure, expand digital payments, and strengthen monetary sovereignty. Early regulatory initiatives on fintech and platform finance created the institutional foundations for CBDC adoption (Zhang & Zhang, 2025). The central bank's leadership – combined with broad cooperation from commercial banks, fintech platforms, and technology providers – has allowed the e-CNY to embed itself within an already dynamic digital payment ecosystem, complementing rather than displacing private-sector innovations (Allen et al., 2019).

Empirical studies consistently show that China's CBDC pilots have generated tangible financial and economic effects. For example, CBDC trials have reduced corporate debt financing costs by enhancing transaction transparency and lowering information asymmetries (Xiao et al., 2024). Other analyses reveal changes in firms' liquidity decisions, with the availability of e-CNY influencing corporate cash holdings and working capital strategies (Zhang & Chan, 2025a). Digital currency pilots have also encouraged outward investment behaviour, particularly among firms participating in cross-border e-CNY initiatives (Zhu & Zhou, 2025).

These developments reflect China's comprehensive CBDC design, which integrates supply, demand, and infrastructure considerations (Zheng et al., 2025). On the supply side, the People's Bank of China (PBoC) has deployed a two-tiered architecture combining centralised issuance with commercial bank distribution. On the demand side, incentives for adoption have been aligned with existing digital services, enabling seamless integration with widely used platforms such as WeChat Pay and Alipay. On the infrastructure side, China employs a hybrid ledger model, and programmable payment features to support offline payments, traceability, interoperability, and high-volume retail transactions (Wang et al., 2023).

The Chinese CBDC model also illustrates the strategic use of CBDCs in platform competition and financial governance. Studies demonstrate how e-CNY interacts with dominant private payment providers in a Stackelberg-style competitive framework, balancing innovation with public oversight (Wu et al., 2024). Additionally, analyses of regulatory and political economy factors show how fintech regulation shapes the broader ecosystem in which CBDCs operate (Zhang & Chan, 2025b). These dynamics highlight how CBDCs can be leveraged not only as payment instruments but also as tools for strengthening regulatory visibility and public-sector control over digital financial infrastructures.

China's approach further demonstrates the importance of macro-monetary design in CBDC policy. Research shows that uncertainty surrounding CBDC development has implications for international financial markets, reflecting the geopolitical and macro-financial sensitivity of digital currency initiatives (Lü et al., 2025). Similarly, macroeconomic modelling indicates that CBDC tools – such as programmable interest or negative interest policies – can influence open-economy dynamics, policy transmission, and financial stability (Hua et al., 2025).

Taken together, China's CBDC development offers several key lessons:

- Large-scale CBDC deployment requires coordinated institutional design integrating legal, technological, and operational dimensions.
- CBDCs can meaningfully affect firm-level behaviour, financial market expectations, and monetary policy channels.
- Integration with existing digital platforms promotes adoption but necessitates strong regulatory capacity to maintain market balance.
- Programmability and hybrid ledger architectures enhance CBDC flexibility across use cases, including cross-border applications.

These insights provide comparative value for Indonesia's Digital Rupiah initiative, especially in understanding the institutional, technological, and governance requirements associated with national-scale CBDC implementation.

12.4.3 Conceptual framework: AI-enabled CBDC governance

The conceptual framework developed in this study positions AI as a foundational enabler of CBDC governance, bridging technological infrastructure, supervisory capacity, and policy execution. The framework is built on the premise that CBDCs generate continuous, high-frequency data across wholesale, retail, and interbank layers, which require automated monitoring and structured auditability to maintain system integrity. Consistent with global CBDC and digital financial governance literature (Auer & Böhme, 2020; BIS, 2022b; Brunner et al., 2019), our model divides AI participation into two complementary pillars: *AI supervision* and *AI auditing*. These two layers align with the clusters identified in our VOSviewer mapping – "financial services," "explainable AI," and "policy modelling" – which highlight the interdisciplinary nature of AI-enabled CBDC oversight.

AI Supervision Layer: The AI Supervision Layer provides real-time, data-driven oversight across the CBDC life cycle. Drawing on systems-thinking approaches (Goodhart, 2010), interpretive structural models (Soderberg et al., 2022), and recent advances in AI-enabled monitoring for financial stability, this layer is responsible for detecting, classifying, and assessing operational and systemic risks within the CBDC ecosystem. In practice, AI supervision performs four core functions.

Firstly, AI enhances *continuous anomaly detection* by identifying irregular transaction flows, suspicious wallet behaviour, liquidity abnormalities, or deviations from expected settlement patterns. These capabilities have been emphasised in the BIS foundational papers (Auer & Böhme, 2020) and recent digital risk analyses (Aramonte et al., 2021), which outline the need for supervisory technology (Sup-Tech) that operates at the speed and scale of digital money.

Secondly, AI supports *behavioural and pattern analysis*, enabling central banks to monitor transaction clusters, payment network concentration, and usage segmentation. This aligns with the literature on CBDC demand prediction (Li, 2023) and payment ecosystem competition (Wang et al., 2024; Wu et al., 2024).

Thirdly, the supervision layer contributes to *risk scoring and prioritisation*. Machine learning-based scoring models synthesise heterogeneous data – transaction flows, network dependencies, and institution-level risk indicators – to generate continuous risk profiles, supporting macroprudential oversight and monetary transmission analysis (Agur et al., 2022; Keister & Monnet, 2022; Nyffenegger, 2024).

Finally, AI assists in *compliance and regulatory validation*. This includes automated checking of transaction rules, monitoring adherence to AML/CFT requirements, validating programmed policy instruments (e.g., holding limits or interest-bearing CBDCs), and ensuring operational consistency. As CBDCs increasingly incorporate programmability and policy levers, AI becomes essential for verifying rule execution and detecting unintended consequences.

AI Audit Procedures: While AI supervision addresses real-time operations, the AI Audit Cycle introduces a structured and transparent mechanism for ex-post verification and system integrity assurance. CBDCs, as programmable financial infrastructures, require auditing frameworks that go beyond traditional financial auditing and incorporate checks on algorithmic behaviour, data provenance, and system governance (Bernini et al., 2022). The AI Audit Cycle formalises this need through a six-stage workflow:

1. *Audit Planning* – Defining the audit scope, risk areas, and data domains based on CBDC operational objectives.
2. *Data Review* – Validating data sources, ensuring data quality and integrity, and detecting anomalies or missing values.
3. *Model and Algorithm Audit* – Reviewing AI models used in transaction monitoring, risk scoring, or policy automation; verifying fairness, interpretability, and performance consistency.

4. *Risk Assessment* – Evaluating exposures related to cyber risks, liquidity risks, interoperability dependencies, and policy implementation risks.
5. *Compliance Review* – Assessing adherence to regulatory principles, privacy requirements, and CBDC design constraints, as well as verifying programmed rules.
6. *Reporting and Feedback Loop* – Generating explanations, traceability outputs, and recommendations that feed back into system improvements and supervisory recalibration.

This cyclic structure reflects best practices in digital platform auditing (Zheng et al., 2025) and case study evidence from digitalisation in financial institutions (Bernini et al., 2022). The circular format emphasises *continuous improvement*, which is essential for CBDCs undergoing multi-phase piloting or iterative functional expansion. In highly interconnected ecosystems – such as Indonesia's Digital Rupiah architecture, which integrates distributed ledger components (Corda, Besu) with banking intermediaries – such iterative auditing ensures resilience and adaptability.

Together, the AI Supervision Layer and AI Audit Cycle form a unified governance architecture capable of monitoring CBDC operations at scale while ensuring accountability, explainability, and regulatory compliance. They operationalise the "smart governance" principle central to digital currency infrastructures, ensuring that CBDCs can evolve safely and transparently as their complexity increases.

12.4.4 Integrating global insights into the Indonesian context

The Digital Rupiah (Project Garuda) shares structural features with other CBDC initiatives yet exhibits unique challenges stemming from Indonesia's dual-track design involving a *Wholesale Digital Rupiah* and a future *Retail Digital Rupiah* (BIS, 2022b). Indonesia's CBDC model also features the *Khazanah Digital Rupiah* (KDR) architecture integrating distributed ledger technologies (DLT) such as Corda and Besu.

Insights from global CBDC pathways inform several key areas:

- **Interoperability and ecosystem maturity.** Lessons from China and EU pilots suggest that a multi-tier system requires seamless integration between central banks, commercial institutions, and payment service providers (Allen et al., 2022). AI-enabled supervision can manage these expanded interconnections by monitoring transactional flows across layers.
- **Public acceptance and institutional trust.** Studies on CBDC adoption highlight the importance of transparency, privacy, and trust (Ngo et al., 2023). AI auditing can reinforce these attributes by ensuring visible, evidence-based integrity of CBDC operations.

- **Operational and cyber resilience.** Failures observed in countries that halted CBDC plans frequently relate to operational risks and insufficient digital infrastructure (Bhaskar et al., 2022). AI-driven risk assessment can proactively identify vulnerabilities within Indonesia's Digital Rupiah network.
- **Governance and monetary policy design.** Research demonstrates that CBDC design significantly shapes monetary transmission, financial stability, and bank intermediation (Agur et al., 2022; Keister & Monnet, 2022; Nyffenegger, 2024). Embedding AI in supervisory pipelines ensures that impacts on liquidity, credit creation, and market dynamics can be monitored continuously.

12.5 INDONESIA'S DIGITAL RUPIAH (CBDC) ARCHITECTURE AND AI-ENABLED GOVERNANCE

Indonesia's CBDC initiative – *Project Garuda* – has progressed into one of the most structured and technically mature CBDC programmes in emerging economies. Bank Indonesia (BI) articulates a dual wholesale–retail Digital Rupiah vision supported by a multilayered architecture consisting of: (1) economic actors issuing and transacting Digital Rupiah, (2) the KDR ledger and digital infrastructure, (3) an embedded AI Supervision Layer for real-time oversight, and (4) governance and legal foundations aligning privacy, AML/CFT, and interoperability requirements. This section presents the reconstructed architecture using three detailed diagrams visualising the operational, supervisory, and audit dimensions.

12.5.1 Digital Rupiah ecosystem overview

The Digital Rupiah architecture developed under Project Garuda reflects one of the most structurally coherent CBDC frameworks among emerging economies. As illustrated in Figure 12.2, Bank Indonesia adopts a multi-layered, modular design that connects economic agents, programmable ledger infrastructure, supervisory analytics, and the broader governance and legal foundations required for national-scale deployment. At the top of the ecosystem are the *economic agents* – households, firms, commercial banks, and the central bank – whose interactions constitute the core payment flows and monetary transmission channels. These agents interface with the Digital Rupiah via intermediated distribution, ensuring continuity with the existing two-tiered financial system and mitigating risks of disintermediation and liquidity shocks. This design parallels international practices emphasising indirect CBDC distribution to preserve banking stability and credit creation (Agur et al., 2022; Barrdear & Kumhof, 2022; Kumhof & Noone, 2021).

At the centre of the architecture lies the *KDR (Central Bank Digital Rupiah) ledger*, which forms the technological backbone of issuance,

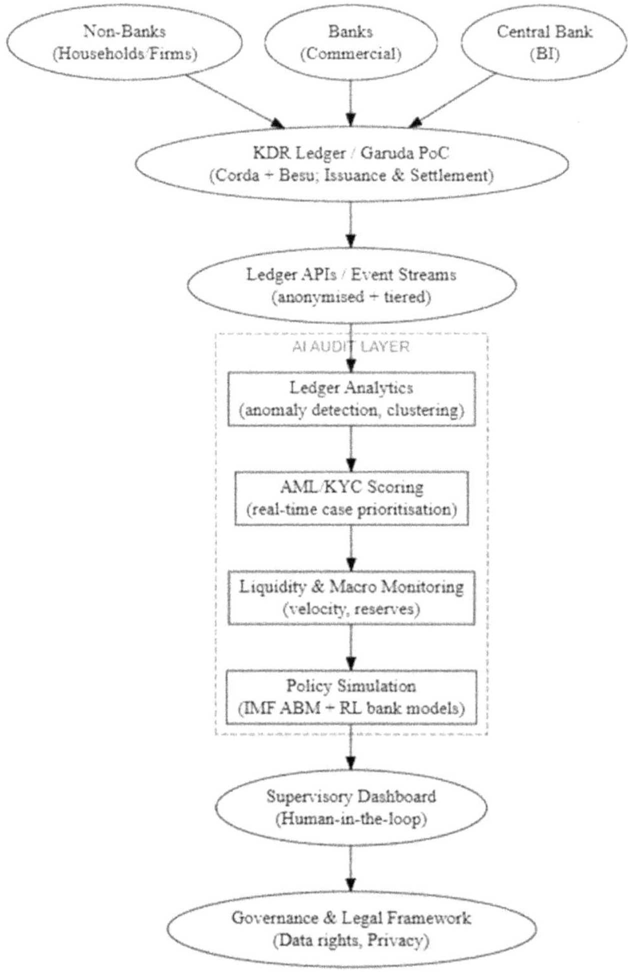

Figure 12.2 Digital Rupiah ecosystem overview (Project Garuda).

redemption, settlement, and programmability. Bank Indonesia deploys a hybrid dual-ledger system using *Corda* for wholesale transactions – leveraging permissioned workflows, identity-based ledgers, and deterministic settlement – and *Hyperledger Besu* for token-based retail programmability. This combination aligns with global trends favouring modularity and interoperability across wholesale and retail infrastructures (Auer & Böhme, 2020; BIS, 2022b). It also reflects lessons from other multi-ledger pilots such as mBridge, Project Helvetia, and the EU's wholesale CBDC experiments.

Digital Rupiah is distributed through a secure *API/PSP interface layer* that allows the KDR ledger to integrate with the national payment ecosystem, including QRIS, e-wallets, and banking applications. This ensures a smooth transition between existing digital payments and CBDC-based instruments, thereby reducing adoption frictions and enabling programmability in a controlled environment. Such interoperability is consistent with international recommendations emphasising flexible, layered infrastructure for CBDCs (Auer & Böhme, 2020; G7, 2021).

A defining feature of the Indonesian model is the intentional inclusion of an *AI Supervision Channel* embedded directly into the system architecture. Unlike many jurisdictions where AI is envisioned merely as an analytical add-on, Bank Indonesia explicitly allocates a dedicated supervisory layer with read-only or controlled-write access to the ledger. This AI Supervision Layer supports:

- *AI-driven anomaly and pattern detection* for suspicious or systemic-risk-related behaviour;
- *Real-time AML/KYC scoring* aligned with international AML standards;
- *Liquidity and macro-financial monitoring*, including velocity tracking and early-warning indicators;
- *Policy simulation and counterfactual stress testing* to assist monetary and macroprudential decision-making.

This design reflects broader trends in the literature advocating the use of AI for financial stability monitoring, real-time oversight, and model transparency in digital financial infrastructures(Aramonte et al. 2021; Goodhart, 2010; Soderberg et al., 2022). By integrating these tools at the architectural level rather than as ex-post enhancements, Bank Indonesia aligns its CBDC with emerging models of *smart supervision* within digital monetary systems.

12.5.2 AI supervisory overlay for digital rupiah

The second diagram (Figure 12.3) illustrates the supervisory architecture underpinning the Digital Rupiah and highlights a central innovation of Project Garuda: the integration of an *AI Supervisory Layer* between the KDR ledger and the human-in-the-loop supervisory dashboard.

While global CBDC research often discusses AI as a peripheral analytical tool, Indonesia's model embeds AI directly into the supervisory stack, positioning it as a core enabler of real-time oversight, financial integrity, and macroprudential responsiveness. This approach reflects emerging international debates on the role of AI in central banking supervision and the need for automated yet accountable oversight systems (Aramonte et al., 2021; BIS, 2022a; Goodhart, 2010; Soderberg et al., 2022).

The supervisory layer performs four major monitoring and analytical functions, each designed to reduce latency, enhance analytic precision, and

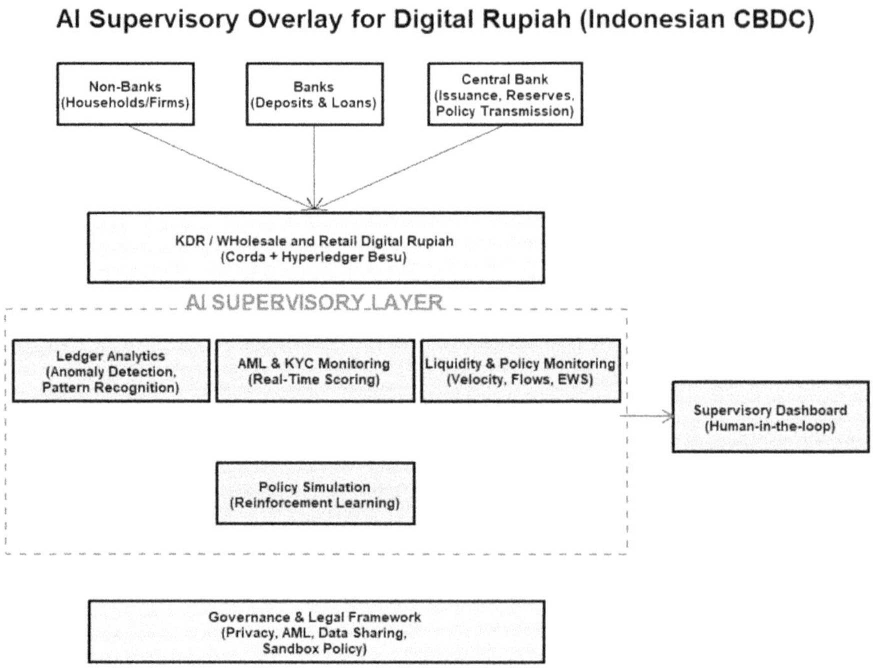

Figure 12.3 AI supervisory layer for Digital Rupiah (Project Garuda).

align supervisory capabilities with the high-frequency nature of CBDC transaction flows:

1. **Ledger Analytics:** This module continuously analyses transaction-level microdata to detect anomalies, behavioural irregularities, and outlier patterns. Machine-learning models support early detection of fraud, abnormal fund movements, and network-pattern irregularities. This component reflects the shift in global central banking towards granular, data-driven supervisory strategies as CBDC infrastructures dramatically increase the availability of real-time, high-resolution transaction data (Auer & Böhme, 2020).
2. **AML/KYC Monitoring:** A dedicated AI-based compliance layer conducts identity consistency verification, risk-scoring, clustering of suspicious activities, and cross-institution correlation analysis. By automating components of AML/KYC screening, the system enhances the precision and speed of financial integrity monitoring while preserving regulatory standards. The approach aligns with Financial Action Task Force (FATF) recommendations on leveraging Reg-Tech and Sup-Tech tools for anti-money laundering in digital finance ecosystems.
3. **Liquidity and Policy Monitoring:** AI models track liquidity conditions across institutions, payment velocity, the distribution of Digital Rupiah

balances, network congestion, and systemic interlinkages. The output can be used to identify early-warning indicators, liquidity mismatches, or deviations in money flow patterns relevant to monetary transmission. Global research emphasises that CBDCs – particularly those with programmability – require more dynamic and high-frequency monitoring frameworks to maintain macro-financial stability (BIS, 2022b).

4. **Policy Simulation and Stress Testing:** The supervisory layer incorporates simulation modules using counterfactual modelling, agent-based techniques, and shock propagation analysis. These tools allow Bank Indonesia to test alternative policy settings (e.g., CBDC interest-bearing features, holding limits, or tiered remuneration) under varying scenarios of adoption, liquidity stress, or operational disruption. Such capabilities align with calls in the governance literature to build forward-looking supervisory capacity in the face of rapidly evolving digital monetary infrastructures (G7, 2021).

All analytical outputs feed into a *human-in-the-loop supervisory dashboard*, ensuring that ultimate decision authority remains with Bank Indonesia. This hybrid model – combining automation with central bank discretion – responds directly to concerns about algorithmic opacity, explainability, and the preservation of public accountability in AI-assisted supervision. As noted in the literature, effective CBDC governance requires maintaining the primacy of human judgment while harnessing AI for enhanced efficiency and early detection of risks (Goodhart, 2010; Soderberg et al., 2022).

Finally, underpinning the entire AI Supervisory Layer is a robust *governance and legal framework* that ensures the safe, accountable, and policy-aligned use of AI within the Digital Rupiah ecosystem. This foundational layer establishes the rules that govern data access, model usage, system interoperability, and supervisory authority. It includes legally binding data-sharing arrangements, privacy and confidentiality protections, digital identity standards, and regulatory sandbox mechanisms that allow controlled testing of AI-enabled supervisory tools.

In the context of AI-driven oversight, the governance framework also addresses issues of explainability, auditability, liability allocation, and human-in-the-loop control dimensions that the emerging literature identifies as essential for preventing automation bias, reinforcing institutional legitimacy, and ensuring model accountability in critical financial infrastructures (BIS, 2020; Brunner et al., 2019; G7, 2021).

By embedding these safeguards at the architectural level rather than treating them as post-deployment add-ons, Indonesia strengthens its capacity to deploy AI systems that enhance supervisory intelligence without undermining trust, privacy, or legal certainty. The explicit codification of governance principles within Project Garuda reflects an institutional commitment to creating a resilient, transparent, and future-proof CBDC ecosystem capable of supporting both domestic monetary stability and cross-border interoperability.

12.5.3 AI audit procedure: Circular workflow for Digital Rupiah

Beyond ongoing supervision, Bank Indonesia requires mechanisms ensuring *auditability*, *model accountability*, and *regulatory compliance* across both the ledger and AI components. While the AI Supervisory Layer provides continuous oversight, the *AI Audit Cycle* offers an additional layer of ex-post and ex-ante assurance that the Digital Rupiah ecosystem remains transparent, explainable, and resilient. This cycle mirrors advanced practices in algorithmic auditing and digital financial governance (Bernini et al., 2022; Zheng et al., 2025), particularly in systems where automated or semi-automated mechanisms influence real-time financial decision-making.

Figure 12.4 illustrates a circular workflow consisting of six recurring phases. The circular structure emphasises that CBDC audits are not discrete, annual procedures but part of an ongoing assurance loop integrated directly into the technical architecture. Four of the six stages involve AI-enabled processes, which increase the frequency, depth, and precision of audits without removing the role of human oversight.

1. *Data Review (AI-Assisted):* AI-assisted data validation tools perform completeness checks, identify missing or anomalous records, and verify data lineage across the Corda–Besu ledger structure. These techniques

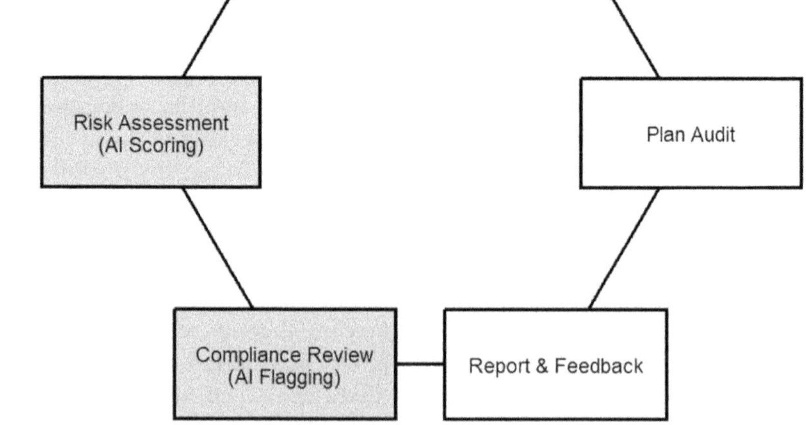

Figure 12.4 Circular workflow of AI audit for Digital Rupiah.

support high-frequency auditing by reducing manual verification burdens and ensuring that downstream models operate on consistent, high-quality data. This step is aligned with emerging requirements for data-centric governance in CBDC environments, where data quality directly affects real - time scoring, compliance analytics, and policy simulations (BIS, 2022b).

2. *Model Audit (AI Testing):* This phase focuses on the integrity and performance of AI models embedded in the Digital Rupiah supervisory architecture. Techniques such as drift detection, adversarial testing, counterfactual evaluation, and fairness diagnostics ensure that models behave consistently over time and do not introduce bias through learning dynamics or environmental changes. Consistent with AI governance principles highlighted by Bernini et al. (2022), this step provides documentation and explainability inputs necessary for regulatory compliance and internal validation.
3. *Risk Assessment (AI Scoring):* The risk assessment phase leverages machine learning systems to generate dynamic AML/CFT risk scores, systemic risk indicators, liquidity stress markers, and behavioural anomaly signals. Compared to rule-based methods, AI-based scoring significantly enhances sensitivity to emerging threats, transaction-layer irregularities, and novel patterns that may not be captured in preprogrammed rules. Literature on macro-financial AI emphasises the value of pattern-recognition systems in delivering early warning signals and stress-testing insights for central banks (Aramonte et al. 2021; Auer & Böhme, 2020).
4. *Compliance Review (AI Flagging):* This stage focuses on automated rule-checking, threshold detection, and regulatory compliance verification for both the ledger operations and AI models. AI flagging systems contrast observed behaviours with encoded policy rules, enabling quicker identification of violations such as transaction limit breaches, cross-border flows inconsistent with policy guidance, or model decisions that lack adequate documentation. This aligns with the compliance-oriented frameworks proposed in the algorithmic auditing literature (Zheng et al., 2025), which emphasises continuous monitoring to maintain trust and accountability.
5. *Reporting and Feedback:* The final stage synthesises AI-generated audit outputs into dashboards and technical reports interpretable by human auditors. These reports document model performance, system behaviours, deviations from expected patterns, and required corrective actions. Feedback loops ensure updates to policies, model parameters, and ledger governance protocols. This human-in-the-loop structure is essential in maintaining central bank authority and avoiding over-automation of critical oversight decisions. Taken together, these six stages create an iterative assurance mechanism that operates in parallel with ongoing supervision. The result is a hybrid auditing approach in

which AI augments traditional audit functions while ensuring explainability, traceability, and alignment with the regulatory mandates central to CBDC governance. These practices align with the broader shift towards continuous, data-driven audit systems advocated in digital finance oversight research (Bernini et al., 2022; Zheng et al., 2025).

12.6 POLICY IMPLICATIONS FOR AI-AUGMENTED CBDC GOVERNANCE

The integration of AI-enabled supervision and audit mechanisms within the Digital Rupiah architecture carries significant policy implications that extend far beyond technological design. As Bank Indonesia advances Project Garuda from proof-of-concept towards broader deployment, the central bank must address governance, regulatory, institutional, and cross-border considerations that collectively define the trajectory of a sustainable CBDC ecosystem. The adoption of AI-driven oversight highlights the need for clearer regulatory governance frameworks, particularly those outlining model accountability, supervisory escalation procedures, and audit trails that capture both machine-generated insights and human decision-making. This ensures that AI strengthens supervisory precision without undermining central bank discretion, in line with emerging global principles on explainability, transparency, and proportional use of automated monitoring (Goodhart, 2010; Soderberg et al., 2022).

Financial integrity represents another central policy concern. AI-enhanced AML and KYC systems offer unprecedented capacity for real-time monitoring, but their deployment must be accompanied by standards governing model validation, fairness testing, and anti-bias mechanisms. These safeguards become crucial as CBDC adoption accelerates and the transaction volume increases, requiring alignment with FATF recommendations and Indonesia's broader financial integrity framework. Simultaneously, the CBDC environment generates high-frequency transactional data that necessitates robust data governance policies, including access controls, retention rules, anonymisation procedures, and secure inter-agency data sharing. Ethical considerations regarding surveillance and proportional oversight must also be addressed to maintain public trust, consistent with trends in global CBDC development (BIS, 2022b; G7, 2021).

To operationalise these innovations, significant institutional capacity building is required. AI-based supervision and auditing cannot function effectively without specialised expertise in machine learning, model risk management, digital forensics, and cyber-resilience. This underscores the need for long-term investment in Sup-Tech capabilities, staff training, and collaboration with academia and industry to ensure that supervisors can meaningfully interpret AI-generated signals. In parallel, digital infrastructures must be enhanced to ensure operational resilience. Continuous monitoring, adversarial testing, redundancy mechanisms, secure data pipelines, and failure-mode management systems form the foundation of a resilient supervisory ecosystem capable of supporting the Digital Rupiah at scale.

Finally, the policy implications extend to cross-border interoperability and regional monetary cooperation. As Project Garuda evolves, AI-driven monitoring can play a key role in supporting cross-border settlement risk analysis, fraud detection, and regulatory harmonisation across initiatives such as mBridge, Project Dunbar, or ASEAN payment integration. To participate effectively in the emerging global CBDC landscape, Indonesia will need policies that address cross-border data exchange, shared supervisory standards, and interoperability frameworks. Collectively, these implications suggest clear priorities for the next stage of Project Garuda, including the development of a Digital Cash and Securities Ledger, expansion of AI audit governance rules, and deeper integration of programmable policy tools. Embedding these principles at the design stage will strengthen financial stability, regulatory coherence, and long-term public trust in Indonesia's next-generation CBDC infrastructure.

12.7 CONCLUSION AND RECOMMENDATIONS

The findings of this study demonstrate that Indonesia's Digital Rupiah initiative stands at the forefront of AI-augmented CBDC governance, integrating a dual-ledger architecture with supervisory and audit mechanisms that are technologically sophisticated and institutionally grounded. The empirical analysis shows that embedding AI into both real-time oversight and cyclical auditing offers a viable pathway for enhancing financial integrity, operational resilience, and policy responsiveness within a high-frequency digital payment ecosystem. The Indonesian approach, particularly through the KDR ledger and AI Supervisory Layer, illustrates how central banks can balance innovation with prudential safeguards, ensuring that technological capabilities are matched with clear governance structures and human-in-the-loop oversight.

As Bank Indonesia transitions towards subsequent phases of Project Garuda, several strategic directions naturally emerge. Strengthening regulatory clarity – especially regarding data governance, model accountability, and supervisory escalation – will be essential to ensure that AI-enabled monitoring operates with transparency and fairness across the ecosystem. Enhancing institutional capacity, particularly in machine learning supervision, model validation, and cyber-resilience, will determine whether the central bank can fully harness AI-driven insights while maintaining interpretability and control. Further development of resilient digital infrastructures, including redundancy systems, stress-testing frameworks, and secure API governance, will also be critical to support large-scale adoption of the Digital Rupiah.

Moreover, the Indonesian CBDC trajectory will increasingly intersect with regional and global payment integration initiatives. Cross-border interoperability shared supervisory standards, and the ability to analyse cross-jurisdictional data flows using AI will shape Indonesia's role in platforms such as mBridge, Project Dunbar, or ASEAN payment corridors. Building on the progress achieved in the current phase, future development should focus on expanding the Digital Cash and Securities Ledger, operationalising programmable policy tools, and strengthening AI audit governance to ensure that oversight remains robust as system complexity grows. Taken together, these insights affirm that Indonesia is well positioned not only to advance its national CBDC infrastructure but also to contribute meaningfully to the emerging global architecture of AI-enabled digital money.

REFERENCES

Agur, I., Ari, A., & Dell'Ariccia, G. (2022). Designing central bank digital currencies. *Journal of Monetary Economics*, *125*, 62–79.

Akin, I., Khan, M. Z., Hameed, A., Chebbi, K., & Satiroglu, H. (2023). The ripple effects of CBDC-related news on bitcoin returns: Insights from the DCC-GARCH model. *Research in International Business and Finance*, *66*, 102060.

Allen, D. W. E., Lane, A. M., & Poblet, M. (2019). The governance of blockchain dispute Resolution. *Harvard Negotiation Law Review*, *25*, 75.

Allen, F., Gu, X., & Jagtiani, J. (2022). Fintech, cryptocurrencies, and CBDC: Financial structural transformation in China. *Journal of International Money and Finance*, *124*, 102625.

Alora, A., Sahoo, P., & Sasidharan, A. (2024). Central Bank digital currency adoption challenges-the case of an emerging nation. *Finance Research Letters*, *59*, 104756.

Aramonte, S., Huang, W., & Schrimpf, A. (2021). *DeFi risks and the decentralisation illusion 1 The DeFi ecosystem: An overview.* Retrieved from https://www.bis.org/publ/qtrpdf/r_qt2112b.htm

Auer, R., & Böhme, R. (2020). *The technology of retail central bank digital.* Retrieved from https://www.bis.org/publ/qtrpdf/r_qt2003j.htm

Ayadi, A., Ghabri, Y., & Guesmi, K. (2023). Directional predictability from central bank digital currency to cryptocurrencies and stablecoins. *Research in International Business and Finance*, *65*, 101909.

Aysan, A. F., & Syarif, M. F. (2025). *Future of money and central bank digital currency.*

Balasubramanian, S. A., & Thirumaran, P. (2025). Understanding enablers and inhibitors of digital rupee: A dual-factor theory perspective. *Digital Policy, Regulation and Governance*, *27*(5), 507–522.

Barrdear, J., & Kumhof, M. (2022). The macroeconomics of central bank digital currencies. *Journal of Economic Dynamics and Control*, *142*, 104148.

Bas, T., Malki, I., & Sivaprasad, S. (2024). Connectedness between central bank digital currency index, financial stability and digital assets. *Journal of International Financial Markets, Institutions and Money*, *92*, 101981.

Berger, A. N., & Humphrey, D. B. (1997). Efficiency of financial institutions: International survey and directions for future research. *European Journal of Operational Research*, *98*(2). https://doi.org/10.1016/S0377-2217(96)00342-6

Bernini, F., Ferretti, P., & Angelini, A. (2022). The digitalization-reputation link: A multiple case-study on Italian Banking groups. *Meditari Accountancy Research*, *30*(4), 1210–1240.

Bhaskar, R., Hunjra, A. I., Bansal, S., & Pandey, D. K. (2022). Central Bank digital currencies: Agendas for future research. *Research in International Business and Finance*, *62*, 101737.
BIS. (2020). *Central banks and payments in the digital era: Money and payment systems: the foundation*. Retrieved from https://www.bis.org/publ/arpdf/ar2020e3.htm
BIS. (2022a). *Annual Economic Report 2022*. Retrieved from https://www.bis.org/publ/arpdf/ar2022e.pdf
BIS. (2022b). *The future monetary system*. Retrieved from https://www.bis.org/publ/arpdf/ar2022e3.htm
Blinder, A. S. (2010). How central should the central bank be? *Journal of Economic Literature*, *48*(1), 123–133.
Brunner, A., Decressin, J., Hardy, D., & Kudela, B. (2019). Germany's three-pillar Banking system: Cross-country perspective in Europe. *IMF Occasional Papers*, *233*, 1–44.
Chua, B.-L., Ayalew, Z. A., Kim, S., Han, H., & Ha, H. (2025). Consumer multifaceted trust of central bank digital currency (CBDC) payment in travel and tourism. *Technological Forecasting and Social Change*, *217*, 124166.
Cil, A. E., & Yildiz, K. (2025). A systematic literature review on applications of explainable artificial intelligence in the financial sector. *Internet of Things*, *33*, 101696. https://doi.org/10.1016/j.iot.2025.101696
Conlon, T., Corbet, S., Hou, Y. G., Hu, Y., Larkin, C., & Oxley, L. (2024). Understanding sentiment shifts in central bank digital currencies. *Journal of Behavioral and Experimental Finance*, *44*, 100988.
Corbet, S., Cumming, D., Glatzer, Z., & Johan, S. (2024). Understanding the rapid development of CBDC in emerging economies. *Finance Research Letters*, *70*, 106226.
Davoodalhosseini, S. M. (2022). Central Bank digital currency and monetary policy. *Journal of Economic Dynamics and Control*, *142*, 104150.
Desai, R. (2025). Analysing consumer switching behaviour and financial antecedents to determine the intention to use central bank digital currency: Evidence from the Indian economy. *Asia Pacific Journal of Marketing and Logistics*, *37*(7), 2048–2074.
Eriksson, K., Kerem, K., & Nilsson, D. (2008). The adoption of commercial innovations in the former Central and Eastern European markets: The case of internet banking in Estonia. *International Journal of Bank Marketing*, *26*(3), 154–169. https://doi.org/10.1108/02652320810864634
Estrada, M. A. R., Park, D., & Staniewski, M. (2023). Artificial intelligence (AI) can change the way of doing policy modelling. *Journal of Policy Modeling*, *45*(6), 1099–1112. https://doi.org/10.1016/j.jpolmod.2023.11.005
Fan, Y., Gan, L., Hong, C., Jessup, L. H., Jin, X., Pijanowski, B. C., & Lv, L. (2021). Spatial identification and determinants of trade-offs among multiple land use functions in Jiangsu province, China. *Science of the Total Environment*, *772*, 145022.
G7. (2021). *Public Policy Principles for Retail Central Bank Digital Currencies (CBDCs) Foreword Chancellor of the Exchequer*. Retrieved from https://www.gov.uk/government/publications/g7-public-policy-principles-for-retail-central-bank-digital-currencies-and-g7-finance-ministers-and-central-bank-governors-statement-on-central-bank
Goodhart, C. (2010). *The changing role of central banks*. Retrieved from https://www.bis.org/publ/work326.htm
Heitmann, D., Koch, J.-A., Islam, M. S., & Eva, S. A. (2025). The impact of central bank digital currencies on the financial stability of banks: Dynamic panel estimation. *Finance Research Letters*, *84*, 107791.

Helmi, M. H., Çatık, A. N., & Akdeniz, C. (2023). The impact of central bank digital currency news on the stock and cryptocurrency markets: Evidence from the TVP-VAR model. *Research in International Business and Finance*, *65*, 101968.

Hemingway, B. (2025). The role of central bank digital currency in an increasingly digital economy. *Journal of Economic Dynamics and Control*, *179*, 105161.

Hua, Q., Qiu, Z., Jiang, T., & Tang, K. (2025). Macroeconomic effects of CBDC negative interest policy in an open economy: A comparison of quantity and price rules. *International Review of Economics & Finance*, *100*, 104119. https://doi.org/10.1016/j.iref.2025.104119

Kamin, S., & Zampolli, F. (2025). Central Bank digital currencies (CBDCs) in Latin America and the Caribbean. *Latin American Journal of Central Banking*, *6*(1), 100140.

Keister, T., & Monnet, C. (2022). Central Bank digital currency: Stability and information. *Journal of Economic Dynamics and Control*, *142*, 104501.

Kumari, B., Kaur, J., & Swami, S. (2022). Adoption of artificial intelligence in financial services: A policy framework. *Journal of Science and Technology Policy Management*, *15*(2), 396–417. https://doi.org/10.1108/JSTPM-03-2022-0062

Kumhof, M., & Noone, C. (2021). Central Bank digital currencies—Design principles for financial stability. *Economic Analysis and Policy*, *71*, 553–572.

Lee, C.-C., Wang, C.-W., Hsieh, H.-Y., & Chen, W.-L. (2023). The impact of central bank digital currency variation on firm's implied volatility. *Research in International Business and Finance*, *64*, 101878.

Li, J. (2023). Predicting the demand for central bank digital currency: A structural analysis with survey data. *Journal of Monetary Economics*, *134*, 73–85.

Li, Z., Yang, C., & Huang, Z. (2022). How does the fintech sector react to signals from central bank digital currencies? *Finance Research Letters*, *50*, 103308.

Liu, X., Wu, J., & Zhang, C. (2025). Antecedents of consumers' acceptance of central bank digital currency: The role of technology perceptions, social influence and personal traits. *Technological Forecasting and Social Change*, *217*, 124192.

Lü, Z., Ozcelebi, O., & Yoon, S.-M. (2025). Impact of central bank digital currency uncertainty on international financial markets. *Research in International Business and Finance*, *73*, 102627. https://doi.org/10.1016/j.ribaf.2024.102627

Luu, H. N., Nguyen, C. P., & Nasir, M. A. (2023). Implications of central bank digital currency for financial stability: Evidence from the global banking sector. *Journal of International Financial Markets, Institutions and Money*, *89*, 101864.

Maryaningsih, N., Nazara, S., Kacaribu, F. N., & Juhro, S. M. (2022). Central Bank digital currency: What factors determine its adoption? *Bulletin of Monetary Economics and Banking*, *25*(1), 1–24.

Minesso, M. F., Mehl, A., & Stracca, L. (2022). Central Bank digital currency in an open economy. *Journal of Monetary Economics*, *127*, 54–68.

Mishra, B., & Prasad, E. (2024). A simple model of a central bank digital currency. *Journal of Financial Stability*, *73*, 101282.

Mzoughi, H., Benkraiem, R., & Guesmi, K. (2022). The bitcoin market reaction to the launch of central bank digital currencies. *Research in International Business and Finance*, *63*, 101800.

Ngo, V. M., Van Nguyen, P., Nguyen, H. H., Tram, H. X. T., & Hoang, L. C. (2023). Governance and monetary policy impacts on public acceptance of CBDC adoption. *Research in International Business and Finance*, *64*, 101865.

Nyffenegger, R. (2024). Central Bank digital currency and Bank intermediation: Medium of exchange vs. savings vehicle. *European Economic Review*, *170*, 104890.

Rehman, M. A., Irfan, M., Naeem, M. A., Lucey, B. M., & Karim, S. (2023). Macro-financial implications of central bank digital currencies. *Research in International Business and Finance*, *64*, 101892.

Schilling, L., Fernández-Villaverde, J., & Uhlig, H. (2024). Central Bank digital currency: When price and Bank stability collide. *Journal of Monetary Economics*, *145*, 103554.
Sha, C., Che, T., Xu, T., & Yang, Z. (2024). Antecedents of users' switching intention to Central bank digital currency: A push-pull-mooring model perspective. *Electronic Commerce Research and Applications*, *68*, 101467.
Shen, W., & Hou, L. (2021). China's central bank digital currency and its impacts on monetary policy and payment competition: Game changer or regulatory toolkit? *Computer Law & Security Review*, *41*, 105577.
Soderberg, G., Bechara, M., Bossu, W., Che, N., Davidovic, S., Kiff, J., & Yoshinaga, A. (2022). *Behind the Scenes of Central Bank Digital Currency: Emerging Trends, Insights, and Policy Lessons*.
Solberg Söilen, K., & Benhayoun, L. (2022). Household acceptance of central bank digital currency: The role of institutional trust. *International Journal of Bank Marketing*, *40*(1), 172–196.
Son, J., Ryu, D., & Webb, R. I. (2023). Central Bank digital currency: Payment choices and Commercial Bank profitability. *International Review of Financial Analysis*, *90*, 102874.
Tercero-Lucas, D. (2023). Central Bank digital currencies and financial stability in a modern monetary system. *Journal of Financial Stability*, *69*, 101188.
Tian, S., Zhao, B., & Olivares, R. O. (2023). Cybersecurity risks and central banks' sentiment on central bank digital currency: Evidence from global cyberattacks. *Finance Research Letters*, *53*, 103609.
Tsang, E. W. K., & Colpan, A. M. (2025). Reconciling the tension between contextualization and generalization in qualitative international business research. *International Business Review*, *34*(2), 102383.
Umar, M. (2025). Does CBDC launch increase tax collection? Empirical evidence from China. *Finance Research Letters*, *71*, 106486.
Umar, M., Shahzad, F., Iqbal, A., & Tong, F. (2024). Does institutional quality matter for central bank digital currency adoption? *Economic Analysis and Policy*, *83*, 378–389.
Wang, X., Tang, Y., & Quaranta, A. G. (2024). Machine learning-driven lending decisions in bank consumer finance. *International Journal of Information Systems and Supply Chain Management*, *17*(1). https://doi.org/10.4018/IJISSCM.348337
Wang, Y., Lucey, B. M., Vigne, S. A., & Yarovaya, L. (2022). The effects of central bank digital currencies news on financial markets. *Technological Forecasting and Social Change*, *180*, 121715.
Wang, Z., Samuel, R.-N., Chen, X., Xu, B., & Huang, W. (2023). Central Bank digital currencies: Consumer data-driven sustainable operation management policy. *Technological Forecasting and Social Change*, *196*, 122867.
Wu, J., Liu, X., & Zhang, C. (2024). Unveiling the influencing mechanism underlying users' adoption and recommend intentions of central bank digital currency: A behavioral reasoning theory perspective. *Journal of Retailing and Consumer Services*, *81*, 104050.
Wu, W., Chen, X., Zvarych, R., & Huang, W. (2024). The Stackelberg duel between Central bank digital currencies and private payment titans in China. *Technological Forecasting and Social Change*, *200*, 123169.
Xiang, L., Feng, C., Xiao, Z., & Liu, J. (2024). The impact of central bank digital currency on macroeconomic dynamics: A DSGE analysis. *Economic Modelling*, *141*, 106930.
Xiao, Z., Niu, Y., Xiang, L., & Cui, Y. (2024). Central Bank digital currency and corporate debt financing costs: Empirical evidence from China. *Finance Research Letters*, *69*, 106195.

Xin, B., & Jiang, K. (2023). Economic uncertainty, central bank digital currency, and negative interest rate policy. *Journal of Management Science and Engineering*, *8*(4), 430–452.

Zams, B. M., Indrastuti, R., Pangersa, A. G., Hasniawati, N. A., Zahra, F. A., & Fauziah, I. A. (2020). Designing central bank digital currency for Indonesia: The Delphi–analytic network process. *Bulletin of Monetary Economics and Banking*, *23*(3), 413–440.

Zhang, G., & Chan, K. C. (2025a). Central Bank digital currency and corporate cash holdings: Evidence from China's e-CNY pilot. *Journal of Corporate Finance*, *94*, 102847.

Zhang, G., & Chan, K. C. (2025b). Tracing tax transparency: The effect of central bank digital currency on corporate tax avoidance. *Journal of Accounting and Public Policy*, *54*, 107377.

Zhang, M., & Zhang, C. (2025). The political economy of the fintech regulation in China and its implications. *Computer Law & Security Review*, *56*, 106089.

Zheng, J., Zhang, J. Z., Kamal, M. M., Liang, X., & Alzeiby, E. A. (2025). Unpacking human-AI interaction: Exploring unintended consequences on employee well-being in entrepreneurial firms through an in-depth analysis. *Journal of Business Research*, *196*, 115406.

Zhou, C. (2024). Evaluating the effectiveness of monetary policy for retail central bank digital currency. *Latin American Journal of Central Banking*, *5*(3), 100111.

Zhu, Z., & Zhou, X. (2025). How does digital RMB encourage enterprises' oversea investment behaviors? Evidence from the pilot project of e-CNY. *Finance Research Letters*, *87*, 108877.

For Product Safety Concerns and Information please contact our EU representative GPSR@taylorandfrancis.com
Taylor & Francis Verlag GmbH, Kaufingerstraße 24, 80331 München, Germany

www.ingramcontent.com/pod-product-compliance
Ingram Content Group UK Ltd.
Pitfield, Milton Keynes, MK11 3LW, UK
UKHW021832260926
475702UK00049B/498

* 9 7 8 1 0 4 1 1 0 7 1 0 1 *